DESIGNING
RESEARCH in
EDUCATION

SAGE was founded in 1965 by Sara Miller McCune to support the dissemination of usable knowledge by publishing innovative and high-quality research and teaching content. Today, we publish over 900 journals, including those of more than 400 learned societies, more than 800 new books per year, and a growing range of library products including archives, data, case studies, reports, and video. SAGE remains majority-owned by our founder, and after Sara's lifetime will become owned by a charitable trust that secures our continued independence.

Los Angeles | London | New Delhi | Singapore | Washington DC | Melbourne

DESIGNING RESEARCH in EDUCATION

Concepts and Methodologies

Edited by
JON SWAIN

Los Angeles | London | New Delhi
Singapore | Washington DC | Melbourne

Los Angeles | London | New Delhi
Singapore | Washington DC | Melbourne

SAGE Publications Ltd
1 Oliver's Yard
55 City Road
London EC1Y 1SP

SAGE Publications Inc.
2455 Teller Road
Thousand Oaks, California 91320

SAGE Publications India Pvt Ltd
B 1/I 1 Mohan Cooperative Industrial Area
Mathura Road
New Delhi 110 044

SAGE Publications Asia-Pacific Pte Ltd
3 Church Street
#10-04 Samsung Hub
Singapore 049483

Editor: Jai Seaman
Assistant editor: Alysha Owen
Production editor: Ian Antcliff
Marketing manager: Ben Griffin-Sherwood
Cover design: Shaun Mercier
Typeset by: C&M Digitals (P) Ltd, Chennai, India
Printed in the UK

Library of Congress Control Number: 2016938801

British Library Cataloguing in Publication data

A catalogue record for this book is available from
the British Library

ISBN 978-1-4462-9425-3
ISBN 978-1-4462-9426-0 (pbk)

CONTENTS

THE COMPANION WEBSITE

Designing Research in Education: Concepts and Methodologies is supported by a wealth of online resources to aid study and assist in teaching, which are available at https://study.sagepub.com/swain

STUDENT RESOURCES

Annotated student proposals allow you to see through real examples what leads to a successful course assignment or research grant application – and what does not.

Weblinks direct you to relevant websites, activities, examples and further reading to broaden your understanding of chapter topics and connect you with real world organizations and conversations on education research.

Free **SAGE journal articles** reinforce your learning of key topics and provide an ideal starting point for literature reviews, dissertations, or assignments.

INSTRUCTOR RESOURCES

PowerPoint slides cover the key themes and topics of each chapter.

LIST OF ABBREVIATIONS

ABE: Adult Basic Education

AERA: American Educational Research Association

BERA: British Educational Research Association

BPA: British Psychological Association

BSA: British Sociological Association

CDR: Conceptualising and Designing Research. This is a core research training course at University College London, Institute of Education (UCL/IOE), which this book is based on

CERES: Centre for Education for Racial Equality in Scotland

CRB: Criminal Record Bureau, UK. In 2012, the CRB was replaced by the Disclosure and Barring Service (DBS). These organisations search(ed) to see if a researcher has a criminal record

DBS: Disclosure and Barring Service. See CRB

DHEW: Department of Health Education and Welfare, UK

EdD: Or Doctor in Education. This degree is a professional doctorate that is more structured than a PhD and generally involves some course work and a thesis (usually about 40,000 words). It is aimed at professionals, who frequently carry out their research inside and about the institution in which they work

ESRC: The Economic and Social Research Council is one of the seven Research Councils in the UK. It provides funding and support for research and training work in social and economic issues, such as postgraduate degrees

FE: Further Education

HE: Higher Education

IFS: Institute Focused Study, which is part of some EdD courses, and is a relatively small empirical assignment, usually conducted within the student's own place of work

MRes: A master's degree in Research, which in most cases is designed to prepare students for doctoral research, and as with many master's degrees involves a dissertation

NCRM: National Centre for Research Methods, Southampton, UK

NHMRC: National Health and Medical Research Council, Australia

NOMS: National Offender Management Service, UK

OFSTED: Office for Standards in Education, Children's Services and Skills. It inspects and regulates services that care for children and young people, and services providing education and skills for learners of all ages. It is a non-ministerial department

PhD: Or Doctor of Philosophy. This degree varies considerably according to the country, institution and time period. Usually, a candidate must submit a thesis, normally of about 80,000 words, often consisting of a body of original academic research, which is worthy of publication. In many countries, a candidate must defend this work before a panel of expert examiners appointed by the university

QAA: The Quality Assurance Agency for Higher Education (QAA) is an independent body that monitors, and advises on, standards and quality in UK higher education

RCT: Randomised controlled trial

ABOUT THE AUTHORS

Mano Candappa is a Senior Lecturer in Sociology of Education at University College London, Institute of Education (UCL/IOE), and has more than 20 years of experience in social research, undertaking both primary and secondary analysis. Her research specialisation is in migration, forced migration and issues around social marginalisation, human rights and inclusion, with a particular interest in childhoods and the politics of belonging, which she has researched widely in UK and EU contexts. She is Programme Leader for the Sociology of Education MA and undertakes teaching on a range of courses around the above issues, including bachelor's and master's courses, and was an integral member of the CDR[1] team. She is the sole and co-author of a number of books and academic papers, including *Education, Asylum and the 'Non-Citizen' Child: The Politics of Compassion and Belonging* (2010), with Halleli Pinson and Madeleine Arnot, which won a Society for Educational Studies Prize in 2011.

Olga Cara is a Senior Research Officer at UCL/IOE and has been working in the field of lifelong learning and basic skills since 2005 as both a quantitative and qualitative researcher. She also teaches a variety of methodology courses and supervises undergraduate, master's, PhD and EdD students. Olga gained her PhD in 2013 and has published a number of academic articles. She has been trained as a quantitative sociologist, but has built her expertise in mixed methods research through her master's in Research (MRes) in social anthropology and subsequent mixed methods research projects. Her broad main research interest is in education as a tool for social and economic integration. Olga has expertise in adult basic skills, family learning, intergenerational skills transfer as well as migration and ethnicity in educational contexts. She also specialises in mixed methods research that combines complex statistical designs, such as randomised controlled trials (RCTs), longitudinal data and/ or multilevel modelling with qualitative data.

Will Gibson is a Reader in Social Research at UCL/IOE with a particular interest in 'interactionist' traditions, including Symbolic Interactionism, Ethnomethodology and Conversation Analysis. Much of his teaching and research writing focuses on methodological issues in qualitative methodologies. Will's research involves exploring communicative action and the uses of technology in diverse settings, from healthcare contexts to online discussion forums. He is currently writing a book with Dirk vom Lehn, exploring the contributions that interactionist approaches have made to the study of social institutions.

---

1 CDR stands for Conceptualising and Designing Research. This is a core research training course that I led at my own university, and the contributing authors of this book taught on. There is more information about the CDR course in Chapter 1.

Jane Hurry is Professor of the Psychology of Education at UCL/IOE and is currently Head of the Department of Psychology and Human Development. She has two core areas of research interest: on the cognitive side, literacy development, both typical and atypical; and on the mental health side, adolescent development, particularly focusing on internalising disorders/self-harm and externalising disorders/offending. Jane and her doctoral students have used experimental designs in both these areas. She teaches on a number of master's courses and was a regular contributor to CDR. She has published many academic articles and books.

Rebecca O'Connell is a Senior Research Officer at the Thomas Coram Research Unit, UCL/IOE. Her background is in social anthropology and her principal research interests lie at the intersection of care and work, especially foodwork and childcare, with a particular focus on the home, food practices and the ethics of care. She has taught about ethnography on a number of doctoral courses, including CDR, and led a number of multi-method research projects including, currently, a European Research Council-funded study of Families and Food in Hard Times in three European countries. For more information about the project, see WEBLINK 1. Rebecca's publications include numerous articles in international journals and a book co-authored with Julia Brannen, *Food, Families and Work* (2016).

WEBLINK 1

Families &
food in hard
times

Charlie Owen is a Senior Research Officer at the Thomas Coram Research Unit at UCL/IOE. He also teaches social research methods to doctoral students. He specialises in quantitative methods and has particular expertise in secondary analysis of large datasets and official statistics. His current research interests include early years childcare, including gender in childcare; looked after children; mixed race issues and issues around disability and special education needs. He was an integral member of the CDR course for a number of years, and has published a range of academic books and articles.

Jon Swain currently works at UCL/IOE, where he is Senior Researcher and Lecturer. He carries out mainly qualitative research, which has included a series of numeracy and literacy projects in the post-16 sector. He has also written many articles on boys' masculinities. Between 2008 and 2013, he was programme leader for the MPhil/PhD research training programme and was course leader of CDR. He also has extensive experience in teaching on the EdD programme and he continues to supervise and tutor both PhD and EdD students. His professional career began as a primary school teacher and he took a part-time MA at the Institute of Education in the late 1990s before completing his PhD in 2001.

INTRODUCTION

Jon Swain

BOX 0.1

Overview of chapter

This preliminary chapter includes:

- An introduction on what the book is about and who the main intended audience is.
- A section on how the book is organised and structured, including its pedagogical features.
- A brief summary of each chapter.
- A note on how readers can use the book.

INTRODUCTION

This book is set in the field of education and is primarily about **conceptualising** and designing doctoral research, including how to devise an appropriate **methodology**. It is principally aimed at doctoral students already involved in their research projects (for both PhD and EdD degrees) but it will also be of interest to students considering taking a doctorate, as well as academic tutors, supervisors, lecturers and researchers. This introductory chapter begins by stating what the book is about and who its main intended audience is, and this is followed by a section on how the book is organised and structured, including its pedagogical features. The final section contains a brief summary of each of the 11 chapters and suggests different ways that the book may be used by its readers.

(i) Whom the book is for

The book is about conceptualising and designing **empirical research** in education, and also about constructing a sound methodology. By 'conceptualising', I refer to the process in which underlying concepts are developed and clarified; and by 'empirical', I mean research that is based on direct or indirect experience of observable information, or interaction with, the world (Punch and Oancea, 2014). Although the term 'methodology' is contested in the academic community, I am regarding it as a framework that offers principles of reasoning, which are informed by particular theoretical positions. I also agree with writers such as Crotty (1998), who see methodology as a strategy, or the plan of action, linking the chosen **methods** to particular conceptual assumptions, and showing how a research design is able to offer answers to the particular research questions.

The book does not consider theoretical or philosophical research, or historical research. Neither is the book about how to do research; rather, it is about *how doctoral students conceptualise and design their particular research projects, including devising an appropriate methodology, in order to answer their particular questions and/or to develop and test their ideas*. It also sets out to open up the possibilities of students using different designs for their own ideas. Constructing a research design is not always easy but as the main editor of the book it is my contention that a sound design, and the coherence of the associated **conceptual framework**, will go a long way in determining the satisfaction of a student's examiners.

(ii) The structure and organisation of the book

The book is divided into two parts: Part I, with Chapters 1–5, looks at concepts and philosophical issues that inform research design; and Part II, with Chapters 6–10, looks at the application of these concepts in different research designs. In other words, ideas and concepts that are introduced in the first half of the book are developed and illustrated in the later specific chapters.

Pedagogical features

The book contains a number of features that are designed for readers to consolidate their learning. For each chapter (excluding this preliminary introduction), these include:

- An Overview at the beginning.
- A Summary of the Key Points at the end.
- An end-of-chapter section called Areas for Discussion with some of the issues raised in the chapter to generate discussion/activity.
- Also at the end of each chapter, is an Annotated Bibliography with a list of additional readings, which authors have found particularly influential. In addition, there is a box of Further Reading that authors include either to provide readers with a greater variety of sources or, in some cases, texts that are a little more challenging, and are aimed at readers who want to engage with texts that are more abstruse.
- An annotated Glossary of terms and concepts is provided at the end of the book, together with a full list of References.
- A number of digital links, taking the reader to a companion website, are provided in the majority of the chapters. Some of these provide further, more detailed information, while some links are to other research studies.

Chapters 6–10 contain headings on the definitions of each design, their **epistemological assumptions** (concerning the **theory** and nature of knowledge, and how we understand the world), their key features, including the main methods and methodologies they generally use, their advantages and disadvantages and associated ethical issues. The chapters also contain examples of research carried out by each author as well as digital links (mentioned above) to other research studies using each design.

The organisation of the book

Excluding this preliminary chapter, the book is presented in 11 chapters, which, in turn, are organised under the two umbrella headings mentioned above: Part I: Concepts and philosophical issues informing research designs (Chapters 1–5); and Part II: The application of the research designs (Chapters 6–10). Chapter 11 is a summary and discussion of the main themes explored and outlined in the preceding chapters.

The book ends with a glossary of terms used throughout the chapters (indicated in the text by bold type at first mention), references and the index.

Chapter summaries

- Part I: Concepts and philosophical issues informing research designs

  o Chapter 1 *Jon Swain*: Setting the scene in educational research

  This opening chapter includes a statement of the book's main objectives; a discussion of some of the decisions affecting a research design, including practical and emotional considerations; and an introduction to the author's PhD research, and some of the issues involved in its design.

  o Chapter 2 *Jon Swain*: Designing and managing your research in education in the early stages

  This chapter is about the process of designing and managing a doctoral study, and uses the experiences of eight doctoral students to exemplify a series of themes and issues. It covers guidance on what students might include in their proposal when they first apply to take a PhD or an EdD; a brief section on the research training students can expect and the milestones they need to reach; an introduction to eight doctoral students; the differences between a master's and PhD/EdD; how students manage their time during their early years of study; key figures in the research process, including the supervisor(s); and the influence of research training courses.

  o Chapter 3 *Jon Swain*: Designing your research in education

  The chapter discusses issues around designing your doctoral research project. It looks at definitions of what constitutes a PhD or an EdD doctorate; how students' initial ideas may turn into a doctoral research project; a look at different types of research question and the process of how they may be developed; two major research designs and underlying approaches of deductive and inductive; the idea of positioning students' work in an **empirical and theoretical field**; a discussion of what constitutes a conceptual framework; definitions of the term 'methodology'; the role of theory and theorists in doctoral research; a discussion of the term, **principles of selection**; and some of the challenges students face when they are constructing their research designs.

  o Chapter 4 *Will Gibson*: Constructing knowledge through social research: Debates in **epistemology** and **ontology**

This chapter introduces some of the key debates related to concepts of knowledge (epistemology) in the social sciences, and their relation to social phenomena (ontology). The chapter introduces terminology and debates, including **positivism**, **logical positivism**, **post-postitivism**, **interpretivism**, **constructionism**, **relativism**, neo-relativism and **critical realism**. The chapter will argue that these remain important areas of debate that continue to have real impact on the political environment of social research.

○ Chapter 5 *Jon Swain*: Ethical issues and considerations

The chapter provides a contribution to discussions on the ethics involved in social and educational research, and each of the four main research designs, or approaches, in this book (case studies, ethnography, experiment and surveys) have different sets of ethical principles and priorities. The chapter includes information on writing an ethical review; the role of Research Ethics Committees and the guidance; ethical guides and frameworks; key ethical principles; and research using the Internet.

• Part II: The application of the research designs

Each of the next five chapters (6–10) contain examples of research studies using the specific design presented and carried out by the author as a way of grounding the design in the real world with real life examples.

○ Chapter 6 *Jane Hurry*: Experimental design

Experiment is one of the key research designs, constructed to address causal questions and to test hypotheses. It is therefore of value both for theoretical purposes and to inform evidence based practice about 'What Works'. The chapter covers definitions and epistemological principles underpinning experimental research; the key features of the research design; methods of analysis, interpretation and writing up; ethical issues; advantages and disadvantages of carrying out experimental design; and a list of appropriate research questions that can be use an experimental design.

○ Chapter 7 *Charlie Owen*: Surveys

Surveys involve collecting information from a **sample** of people in order to draw conclusions about the wider **population** which they represent. To achieve this, it is essential that the sample is representative of the population. This chapter discusses the definition of a survey and examines the epistemological principles that underpin surveys, and there are further sections on how surveys are designed; how data are collected and analysed; the advantages and disadvantages of conducting surveys; examples and issues arising from surveys used in research; issues around non-response and other issues of **validity**.

○ Chapter 8 *Rebecca O'Connell*: Ethnography

Situating ethnography within its historical and epistemological context, the chapter begins by tracing its origins to endeavour to understand the world 'from the native's point of view'. The chapter includes: definitions of ethnography; the epistemological principles underpinning ethnographic research; key methods used in ethnographic research and key features of the research design; sections on analysis, interpretation and writing up and practical issues, including roles of the researcher; the advantages and disadvantages of carrying out ethnographic research; and an example of the author's PhD thesis that used an ethnographic approach to examine London childminders' perspectives of professionalisation.

o   Chapter 9 *Mano Candappa*: Case studies

This chapter explores case study research as the study of the particular, and essential features of case study as a research strategy. It includes some of the key debates around and epistemological principles underpinning case study research, a discussion around the concept of **boundedness**, the different types and purposes of case studies, and case selection and design issues. A number of classic and more contemporary examples of case study research are used to illuminate the text, including one carried out by the author.

o   Chapter 10 *Olga Cara*: Mixed methods in education research

Mixed methods design is increasingly popular in the field of social sciences and a growing number of studies make use of this methodological approach, that is, the use of both quantitative and qualitative methods within a single study. The chapter provides students with a working definitions of mixed methods research; the historical context of mixed methods designs; the epistemological issues related to mixing quantitative and qualitative approaches; the advantages and challenges of using mixed methods; some of the most popular mixed methods designs explained; the practicalities of carrying out a mixed methods study; and a series of real life examples of mixed methods research, some of which are conducted by the author.

o   Chapter 11 *Jon Swain*: Summary and conclusions

The final chapter reminds readers of the book's main objectives and discusses some of the main processes and issues that arise when doctoral students construct their conceptual framework, including the research design. It reminds readers that the choice of design is dependent on the aim(s) of the research, the research question(s) and the methodology employed. The final section discusses issues around the doctoral thesis.

(iii) How to use this book

The book can be used in a number of ways. The first five chapters in Part I concern more general issues such as ethical considerations, insights into how to develop a research design, and the theoretical understandings and assumptions that underpin a doctoral project or study. These cover important points and issues that most students will need, or wish, to familiarise themselves with and so it is suggested that most readers will want to read to read them.

Part II introduces the reader to different designs (survey, experimental, ethnography, case study) and also has a chapter on mixed methods. Students begin their doctoral studies with a range of backgrounds, interests and experiences of working in a variety of research traditions. While some have relatively deep understandings of different research approaches and designs (perhaps from research training courses on their master's programmes), others have very little idea of what, for example, the characteristics of ethnography are, or even, perhaps, what the difference is between a method and a methodology. Whilst some students at the beginning of their studies already have their research proposals and designs more or less worked out, the majority will want to read more, discuss and reflect on what they read in this book and/or during their specific research training, and as a result some will begin to develop and change their research designs. Some will modify their original proposals a little, others more fundamentally. Therefore, while some readers may want to target specific chapters to find out more about a particular design, others will want to read about a number of research designs so they can discuss their particular features and principles with their supervisor(s) and other colleagues. This will help them gain a deeper understanding, and find out whether a particular design resonates with their own ideas and values in carrying out their own research study.

 BOX 0.2

A summary of the key points

- The book is set in the field of education and is primarily about conceptualising and designing research for doctoral students and their tutors/lecturers/researchers.
- The book discusses concepts and philosophical issues that inform research design, and looks at the application of these concepts in four classic designs: case study research, ethnography, experimental design and survey design, as well as issues involved in mixed methods research.
- There is a section on how the book is structured and organised, and guidance on how readers can use the book.
- Students begin their doctoral studies with a range of backgrounds, interests and experiences, and have different understandings of different research approaches and designs.
- A summary is provided of the 11 chapters.

PART I

CONCEPTS AND PHILOSOPHICAL ISSUES INFORMING RESEARCH DESIGNS

CHAPTER 1

SETTING THE SCENE IN EDUCATIONAL RESEARCH

Jon Swain

━━ BOX 1.1 ━━

Overview of chapter

This chapter includes:

- A statement of the book's main objectives.
- A discussion of some of the decisions affecting a research design, including practical and emotional considerations.
- An introduction to the author's PhD research and some of the issues involved in its design.

1.1 INTRODUCTION: WHAT THIS BOOK IS ABOUT AND WHOM IT IS FOR

To reaffirm what I wrote in the Introduction, this book is set in the field of education and is about designing and conceptualising doctoral research, including devising an appropriate methodology, which is the theory about the methods and procedures involved, including philosophical insights. It is primarily aimed at doctoral students who have already begun their research projects but it will also be of interest to students thinking about taking a doctorate, as well as tutors, supervisors, lecturers and researchers.

The first section states what the main objectives of the book are and tells readers that many of these are based on a typical core research training course for doctoral students at a particular and prestigious London university, and doctoral students will take similar courses in the vast majority of universities and other institutions throughout the world. The next part considers decisions affecting the research design of a doctoral thesis in general, including the practical and emotional considerations, and the final section discusses the design of my own PhD (Swain, 2001) and some of the processes and issues involved. Many of the themes and decisions concerning my own design will reappear throughout the succeeding chapters (particularly Chapters 2 and 3).

Taking a doctorate can also raise a number of hopes and fears but should be a transformative experience, and the opening three chapters also set out to try and capture this experience of uncertainty that many novice researchers feel.

The research training course

The research training course that I led at my own university, UCL/IOE (University College London, Institute of Education), was called Conceptualising and Designing Research (**CDR**), and is still part of the core research training, albeit in a slightly different format. During my time as course leader, CDR had a number of presenters who were researchers working in their particular specialised field. Typically, each tutor/researcher began their session by introducing and raising issues about the key principles of their particular research design, and then used their own research project(s) as a vehicle to ground it in the real world with real life examples. In this way, students were introduced to different designs and types of research and evaluation, and were able to position research in its wider historical, political and social contexts. The four classic research designs that CDR and this book cover are case study research, ethnography, experimental design and survey design, and the book also considers mixed methods research. This is not to suggest that there are not many other research designs, such as action research, but there was only space on CDR, and in this book, to consider a few major designs. It was also the case that only a few doctoral students at UCL/IOE used these other designs for their research, at least during the years that I was leading CDR.

Main objectives

In addition to focusing on the different research designs, the main objectives of the book are:

- To critically examine a broad range of major research designs.
- To raise awareness about the nature of knowledge and being in research and to introduce some of the key language that underpin these debates.
- To develop students' expertise in formulating researchable questions.
- To increase students' understanding of terms such as 'methodology', 'conceptual framework' and 'principles of selection'.
- To make students aware of the role of theory in doctoral research.
- To highlight a number of ethical considerations that are involved in research.
- To highlight the processes involved for students in constructing a research design and some of the main challenges involved.
- To view research in its social, political and historical contexts.
- To give students an opportunity to reflect on and discuss these broader issues in the context of their own work.

1.2 HOPES AND FEARS AND PRACTICAL AND EMOTIONAL CONSIDERATIONS

As we will see throughout this book there is a wide range of approaches to educational inquiry (Dowling and Brown, 2010; Robson, 2011; Thomas, 2013; O'Leary, 2014; Punch and Oancea, 2014) and, like myself, each student needs to decide what kind of researcher they are, wish to be, or want to become. Perhaps they like to sit at a desk and analyse quantitative statistics, or maybe they like to go out into the world and spend time with people. Of course, research can involve both these activities.

One way to think about research is that it is a method of inquiry that will add knowledge to a field of practice, or activity, that is currently unknown (Dowling and Brown, 2010). Some of the main considerations that you need to think about, and decide upon, and which will be further discussed in Chapters 2 and 3, are listed in Box 1.2.

▬▬ BOX 1.2 ▬▬

Decisions affecting the research design

- What do you want to find out?
- How are you going to find it out?
- Whom (and how many people) are you going to involve?
- Where are you going to do the research?
- When are you going to do the research?
- How long do you think the research will it take?
- How are you going to make sense of, and present, the data?

As well as these choices, which will affect the conceptual design, there are, for most of us, a number of more practical and sometimes more emotional decisions to think about (see Box 1.3).

▬▬ BOX 1.3 ▬▬

Practical and emotional issues and decisions

- Changing the person you are and the way you see the world.
- Doubts and the emotional effects on self and close personnel.
- Time.
- Money.
- Access to the research setting.
- Ethics.

Like all good educational teaching and learning, taking a doctorate can, or should be, a transformative experience and many students will reach the end as changed people, and see the world in a very different way. Thus, many students, including myself, find that taking a PhD or an EdD is a metaphorical journey that affects their personal identity, because you are putting your reputation on the line, and this theme will be explored in more detail in Chapter 2 (Section 2.9). I can remember sitting in the first training course meeting involving the other 100 or so MPhil/PhD students in my cohort, looking around and thinking how clever some of them looked and sounded, and wondering whether I belonged here and whether I was going to be able to 'cut it'. It was a step into the unknown and what would happen if I found out that I was not up to being able to work at doctoral level? I also remember my first tutorial with one of my supervisors to receive feedback on my first piece of work he had asked me to write. As I stood waiting outside the room, my heart was racing in anticipation and I was thinking about the possibility of him saying that he was sorry but this work was not up to a suitable standard.

Studying towards a doctorate needs time and is generally going to take over your life for a few years, and so it is vital that you are passionately interested in your research, otherwise you are going to find it extremely difficult to complete (Phillips and Pugh, 2010; Murray, 2011). A lot of life events can happen over these years and you also need to be prepared for the downs as well as the ups. Studying can sometimes be lonely and you may find that few friends outside the university[1] are interested in your research. It can also be more difficult for partners or close associates, particularly for part-time students, because it is the weekends and holidays that need to be set aside for study, rather than for going out and enjoying yourself. I am not saying that finding the time is impossible, it is just that it is more difficult, and you need to be prepared for it and give a lot of thought to how you are going to organise your time for study.

Gaining funding for a doctorate has gradually become much harder over the last few years and the majority of doctoral students are self-funded, especially those taking part-time doctorates. Some part-time students decide to reduce their professional working hours in order to set aside one or two days a week for study and this has financial implications for themselves and their partners/families.

Another consideration that many students carrying out empirical research need to think about is gaining access to research sites to carry out their fieldwork. I was able to use my professional teaching contacts to gain access to the schools I used for my fieldwork but many students will not have these connections or networks and getting beyond **gatekeepers** can be difficult. Although the student's institution (including their supervisor) will often help, this problem can be exacerbated for international students whom are unlikely to have personal contacts and may also have less understanding of how systems and organisations work.

---

1 I am aware that there are a variety of differently named institutions that run doctoral programmes, including 'colleges' and 'graduate schools'.

Finally, students will need to think very carefully about the ethical implications of their research and, depending on the area and type of research, this can be a long and difficult process. These issues will be discussed in much more detail in Chapter 5.

1.3 MY OWN PHD RESEARCH STUDY

Like many people who decide to study for a PhD, I first took a master's (in Education). At the time (around the early 1990s), I was a deputy head teacher in a junior school and it was difficult to study and carry out my teaching and managerial duties at the same time. Studying was usually confined to weekends and holidays and, as I have mentioned above, this was quite tough on my partner, who was also a school teacher and, quite rightly, was looking forward to spending some of her free time going out together. Having caught the bug of doing research, around two years later I began to explore whether it was possible for me to take a PhD or an EdD[2], which was a new doctoral programme aimed at working professionals researching at their own institutions, that was being set up around this time. By now, I had decided that I did not want to be a head teacher and at first I intended to leave my post as deputy head teacher, work in local schools for two to three days a week, and work on a PhD for the rest of the week. However, after a year of beginning my doctorate, I was fortunate enough to gain funding from the **Economic Social Research Council** (ESRC), which made my life considerably easier and made if possible for me to become a full-time student.

I knew that I wanted my research to be connected to my job and my professional experience, but I was not sure what area or theme to explore. Although my master's research about bullying at school had used mixed methods, I always enjoyed spending more time in environments such as other classrooms, observing and learning about what was going on, and meeting and talking to people of all ages, rather than on my computer crunching statistics. So, at least I knew what kind of researcher I wanted to be, and I knew my research would be mainly qualitative.

At the time of the mid-to-late 1990s, there was a lot of talk in the UK popular press about media and government concerns concerning 'boys' underachievement' (e.g., Bradford, 1997; Bleach, 1998; Epstein et al., 1998), and teaching a mixed gendered class of 10–11-year-olds at the time meant that this was a theme that resonated and began to interest me. Not that I particularly believed in the notion of 'boys' underachievement' because, in my own teaching experience (at that time, of about 15 years), I knew that some boys and some girls worked hard and some did not; some boys and some girls were keenly interested in, say, reading and writing, and some were not. I had never seen gender as a distinguishing variable. Despite these concerns, as I began to read some of the surrounding academic literature, particularly from the teachers' and children's perspectives, this idea formed the basis of my initial proposal.

However, as I read more, I began to realise that a lot of research had already been carried out in this area and that my question of 'What are teachers' and pupils' perspectives on

---

2 Eventually I decided to begin an MPhil/PhD, rather than an EdD, as I saw this as giving me greater flexibility in terms of time.

boys' underachievement?' was too broad and maybe too difficult to come up with a meaningful and worthwhile answer. After a lot of discussion with my two supervisors, I began to narrow down my area of investigation and work on having a sharper focus to my research questions. My study finally ended up with a much smaller piece of research than I initially envisaged, and, as we shall see in Chapters 2 and 3, this is a common theme. What I ended up with was a much smaller study about the boys' world in a junior/primary school. It focused on what they thought it meant to be a boy in a particular school, which was essentially an issue about their masculinity. This was a subject that I knew very little about and I began to read voraciously as many associated academic articles as I could.

At this stage, I was already thinking about another recurring theme, which we will again come across in Chapter 3, namely the principles of selection, which are the choices that all researchers have to make and justify throughout the entire research process. One of the first decisions I made was what kind of literature I should be reading, from which discipline or field. There is a lot of literature about masculinity from psychology, which tends to regard the differences between men (boys) and women (girls) as being more innate or hard-wired into their brains. The book that exemplifies this is *Men are from Mars, Women are from Venus* (1992), written by an American author, John Gray. However, as I had become more interested in the discipline of sociology, these arguments did not make so much sense to me; it was not a question of either discipline being right or wrong, but more of a feeling that certain theories did not fit with my own worldview that I had gained from experience. In addition, there was the fact that my two supervisors were also sociologists, and very influential in my thinking, and this meant that I was able to save a considerable amount of time by jettisoning the psychological literature and concentrating on my readings in sociology, cultural studies and feminist-inspired theories of masculinity.

The next stage of my thinking involved the 'who' and the 'how'. Who was I going to research and what methods should I employ? As I said before, I saw myself as being a qualitative researcher and therefore my main methods were more likely to involve observations of real life contexts (in this case, schools) and talking to people (in this case, the boys and, as it happened, girls as well).

It is important to make clear that none of these decisions were taken lightly; they involved many discussions with supervisors, other academics and peers, and were not always easy. The decision-making was part of the process of designing my study and actually took the best part of a year before I was relatively happy with them.

I will write much more about the principles of selection that I used in my own PhD in Chapter 3 (Section 3.10).

I am a great believer in having the title of a PhD/EdD or a master's or a book or article giving a big clue as to what the content is about. Indeed, see the opening sentence in the preliminary chapter. The final title of my PhD was:

An *ethnographic* study into the *construction* of *masculinity* of *10–11 year old boys* in *three junior schools*

However, this was one of the last things, along with the abstract, that I wrote before my thesis was finished and sent to the binders. Most students will have a 'working title' that will change organically over the course of research.

The key words italicised above suggest that the type of approach was *ethnographic* (see Chapter 8), where the researcher immerses themselves in a particular culture over a long period of time and generally uses the methods of observation, participation, in-depth conversations and interviews. The word *construction* suggests that the study is set in the discipline of sociology or perhaps cultural studies were identities are constructed rather than innate; and the word *masculinity* (or perhaps it should be *masculinities*) connotes that the research is about the qualities associated with boys and/ or men. The sentence concludes by telling the reader the age of the boys (*10–11-year-olds*), the number (*three*) and type of schools (*junior*: for 7–11-year-olds) where the research was set.

As I mentioned above, I like a thesis to make clear what the study is about in the very first sentence. My opening line was as follows:

This thesis is an in-depth empirical investigation into the social world of boys aged 10–11 at school and explores how young boys construct their masculine identities within their own pupil culture. The study considers what it means to be a boy in three different school settings differentiated by the social characteristics of their intake, and it is within this context that I have the following research question:

- How do boys construct their masculinities in a junior school setting?

In order to answer this question it was necessary to investigate two sub-questions:

- o What symbolic resources are available, and which strategies do the boys use to gain status, and to classify and position themselves in relation to each other?
- o In what ways do official school culture and practices contribute to the formation of boys' masculine identities?

Of course, there is nothing obligatory about this; it is just the way I work and it is just one of several approaches. There are many different ways a student can begin a thesis, and they do not have to have one, overarching, research question as I did; they can have a number of discrete research questions, but generally not too many. All of this has to be worked out by the student themselves, in conjunction with their supervisor(s) and many of these decisions will be further discussed in the next two chapters.

▬▬ BOX 1.4 ▬▬▬▬▬▬▬▬▬▬▬▬▬▬▬▬▬▬▬▬▬▬▬▬▬▬▬▬▬▬▬▬▬▬▬▬

A summary of the key points

- The main objectives of the book are based on a typical core research training course and doctoral students take similar courses throughout the world.
- Taking a doctorate should be a transformative experience.
- Conceptualising and designing a doctoral study is often difficult. Taking a doctorate involves many difficult decisions affecting the research design but practical and emotional considerations cannot be ignored.
- In common with many doctoral students, the ideas for my own PhD changed considerably over the first year or so.
- The title of a PhD or an EdD should give readers a strong indication of what the research is about.

AREAS FOR DISCUSSION

- What do you think the definition of 'research' is?
- What are some of the practical considerations that you are thinking about for your own doctorate?
- What do you anticipate some of the main emotional challenges are going to be?
- Introduce your work to the group using *some* of the following headings: What do you want to find out? How are you going to find it out? Who, and how many, people are you going to involve? When are you going to do the research? Where are you going to do the research? How long do you think your research will it take? How are you going to make sense of the data?

ANNOTATED BIBLIOGRAPHY

O'Leary, Z. (2014) *The Essential Guide to Doing Your Research Project*, 2nd edn. London: Sage.

The book offers pragmatic advice with many real world examples, and guides you through every step of your research project, from getting started to analysing data and writing up findings.

Punch, K. and Oancea, A. (2014) *Introduction to Research Methods in Education*. London: Sage.

This book introduces the research process in a range of real life educational contexts and offers practical guidance on every stage of the research process, with chapters on developing research questions, conducting a literature review, collecting data, and analysing and presenting findings. There are, in addition, sections on Internet and mixed methods research (see also the new edition of the book, 2016).

Robson, C. (2011) *Real World Research*, 3rd edn. Oxford: Blackwell.

An accessible and comprehensive introduction to conducting small-scale research. It provides clear, practical advice on a range of methods and has informative chapters on different research designs.

See also:

Robson, C. and McCartan, K. (2016) *Real World Research*, 4th edn. Chichester: John Wiley & Sons.

FURTHER READING

Cohen, L., Manion, L. and Morrison, K. (2011) *Research Methods in Education*, 7th edn. New York: Routledge.

This well-known text incorporates the whole range of methods currently employed by educational research at all stages. It offers practical advice, underpinned by clear theoretical foundations.

Somekh, B. and Lewin, C. (eds) (2011) *Theory and Methods in Social Research*, 2nd edn. London: Sage.

This edited book introduces postgraduate and master's-level student researchers to all the key qualitative and quantitative research methodologies. The chapters explain key concepts and the implications for your research design, and illustrate these with examples from real research studies.

Thomas, G. (2013) *How to Do Your Research Project: A Guide for Students in Education and Applied Social Sciences*. London: Sage.

This highly accessible and informative book is ideal for anyone undertaking a research project in the applied social sciences. It guides you through the complete research process, walking you through every stage, step by step, and using relevant real world examples.

CHAPTER 2

DESIGNING AND MANAGING YOUR RESEARCH IN EDUCATION IN THE EARLY STAGES

Jon Swain

■ BOX 2.1 ■

Overview of chapter

This chapter includes:

- Guidance on what students might include in their proposal when they first apply to take a PhD or an EdD.
- The milestones that doctoral students generally need to reach.
- An introduction to eight doctoral students who are presented as exemplars to consider issues about designing and managing a doctoral research project in the early years of study.
- How students manage their time during their early years of study.
- Key figures in the research process, including the relationship with, and the role of, a student's supervisor(s).
- The influence on research designs from core research training courses.
- The ways that studying for a doctorate can transform a student's identity.

2.1 INTRODUCTION

This chapter begins by looking at what students might want to include in their original research proposal when they first apply to become a doctoral student at a particular institution. I then introduce readers to eight doctoral students who are used as exemplars to consider issues about designing and managing a doctoral research project in the early years of study:

these include the themes of time management; the relationship with key figures, including supervisor(s); the process of constructing the research design; and how doctoral research can be a transformative experience as students begin to see the world in a different way.

2.2 WRITING A PROPOSAL TO GET ACCEPTED ON TO A DOCTORAL COURSE

Writing a research proposal to get accepted on to a doctoral course (PhD or EdD), or an integrated PhD course including a master's in research (MRes), can be a daunting experience and each institution will have its own requirements, criteria and processes of application. However, there are still general headings that most universities will be looking for, which are also often used by academic researchers in proposals when they are applying for monies from external agencies and funding bodies.

Many academics have told me that they rate a lot of the research proposals they receive as being generally poor and they look for the potential in the idea rather than seeing it as the finished article. This is an acknowledgement that designing a doctoral research project is both difficult and is also an organic process that will often change considerably over the course of study. Although, as I mentioned in Chapter 1, some students know exactly what questions they want to ask, which theories and theorist(s) they are going to use and the methodology they are going to employ, many students, particularly those using more inductive approaches (see Section 3.5), are far less sure. Moreover, as we have seen with my own PhD, many of us also start with questions that are too large to answer and often end up with a series of sub-questions of the original idea, particularly, once again, if we are taking an inductive approach. Having said this, it will still be expected that a student will have:

- A clear and reasonably well-defined and original area of interest.
- Be able to provide evidence that they are familiar with some of the literature.
- A set of related questions within the field that they intend to pursue, or a proposition that they wish to argue.
- An idea of research methods they may want to use.

Box 2.2 shows a series of suggested headings that a doctorate student will generally include in a proposal.

━━ BOX 2.2 ━━━

Suggested headings for a doctoral thesis

- Title.
- Area of interest.
- Literature review.

(Continued)

(Continued)

- Research questions.
- Research methods and methodology.
- References.

For EdD students, there is an additional heading of:

- Contribution to professional practice.

2.3 DOCTORAL TRAINING MILESTONES

I recognise that each institution will have its own distinct doctoral research training pro-gramme, and different models vary in different parts of the world, but almost all will have a number of courses or modules, which are compulsory for students to take, commonly within their early years of registration. In the UK, full-time PhD students usually take just over three years to gain their PhD (the viva examination where the thesis is defended is often in Term 10 or at the beginning of Year 4), while part-time PhD and EdD students generally take between five and seven years.

In the UK, almost all PhD students first register on the MPhil programme and then upgrade to PhD level during the first 18 months. Most full-time students, at least in the UK, do this relatively early in their studies, in Term 3[1] or 4, while part-time students usually upgrade in Term 5. The programme is often referred to as the MPhil/PhD.

2.4 AN INTRODUCTION TO EIGHT DOCTORAL STUDENTS

During the research and preparation for the book, I interviewed eight doctoral students, whom I had either taught or supervised, and all completed ethics consent forms. Six of these were taking PhDs, three were part-time and three were full-time, and two out of the six were inter-national students (one from America and one from China). Table 2.1 shows that: three were self-funded; one had full funding from the Chinese government; another had 80 per cent funding from the organisation she worked for; and one student, who was taking an integrated PhD, had funding which began in Year 2, after she had completed her MRes. Jeanette, Rea and Kerry were in their twenties and Kerry, Julia and Hui were in their thirties. I also interviewed two of my own EdD students who I was supervising, Roberta and Rosalind, who were both on the EdD programme. Neither received funding and both were in their thirties, and were, or had been, teachers in specialist schools for children with autism and were extremely busy people.

---

1 In the UK, while some universities divide the academic year into semesters, many divide the years into three terms: thus Term 3 is at the end of the first year, while Terms 4 and 5 are at the beginning and in the middle of the second year.

Table 2.1 Details of the eight students and the working titles of their research projects

Name and working title of their PhD/EdD research	Status	Funded
Kerry: PhD student	PT	Self-funded
Pupil perceptions of progressive education at [name of her school]		
Julia: PhD student	PT	Self-funded but applying for an ESRC grant at time of interview
Isolating predictors of individual variation in KS3* school science to inform and improve teaching and assessment		
Jeanette: PhD student	PT	Funded, 80% from the 'Teach First' organisation
Exploring how peer popularity manifests itself in secondary schools		
Clint: PhD student	FT	Self-funded
An empirical study of student housing/ accommodation in England		
Rea: PhD student	FT	Funded, but not during first year. Gained ESRC funding for 3 years from Y2 (after the MRes)
Social, transformative and sustainable learning: children's communities at Arunachal Pradesh	Took integrated PhD. First year was the MRes	
Hui: PhD student	FT	Funded, 3 years from the Chinese government
A study of the internal governance of private universities in China		
Roberta: EdD student	PT	Self-funded
Family experiences of home educating children with autism*		
Rosalind: EdD student	PT	Self-funded
Understanding, developing and evaluating home–school relationships for children with autism through home school reading[†]		

*KS3 stands for Key Stage 3 and is the first three years of secondary education when students are aged between 11 and 14.

Note: [†] These titles were for their thesis research (about 45,000 words for an EdD) and were not the original ideas from Year 1.

I decided to interview only two EdD students, Roberta and Rosalind, because I am essentially interested in looking at issues that arise during the first year or so, and at UCL/IOE the first year of the EdD programme is taken up with written assignments, marked and examined by module tutors, and many EdD students have relatively little contact with their supervisors until Year 2. However, many of the points that I make about designing and planning research are also pertinent when it comes to EdD students designing the research for their Institute Focused Study (**IFS**)[2], which is part of some EdD courses, and is a relatively small empirical assignment, usually conducted within the student's own place of work.

2 More information about the IFS is provided in Chapter 3.

I use extracts from their interviews as exemplars of points that I want to make, and that are also representative of a wider student community. These extracts also provide a chance to hear the student voice first-hand, and learn about their experiences, views, perceptions, anxieties and concerns during the first three or four terms of doctoral study. For example, with the exception of Kerry, who was more concerned with **sampling** decisions (including the number and type of ex-pupils she wanted to interview), the rest of the PhD students' research proposals had all changed substantially. Although the overall area of study remained the same, by the end of the first year, the methods and methodologies were different and the many of the research questions had begun to become much more crystallised. These changes are clearly captured in the students' comments. For example:

Jon: Right, going back to that original research proposal, how much has it changed from then to now?

Jeanette: Loads, loads. … I think it's become more nuanced, in terms of the content of what I thought I wanted to look at has changed quite a lot as well. I didn't consider social media at all in my proposal, and the more I read the more I, you know, my pilot study has just made me realise it's so integral, you can't kind of ignore it.

Clint: I think it's changed significantly in trying to be, trying to define and hone the research questions to ask better research questions. It went from a very broad sort of what is personal development, what is student housing, and how do you build an understanding of the relationship between those two things, and really the work has been around defining the variables, and defining the question in a way that is a value add [to the field].

I will discuss the process of formulating the research questions further in Chapter 3 (both in Section 3.4), and as part of some of the challenges involved in the students' research designs (Section 3.11).

2.5 THE DIFFERENCE BETWEEN A MASTER'S AND A PHD OR AN EDD

A doctorate is very different from a master's degree. Although some of the differences listed below are not all necessarily mutually exclusive, a doctorate is not only a much larger piece of work with a greater scope, but students need to be able to critically evaluate literature and other research in their particular field, learn about more in-depth, and sometimes more complex, concepts, methodologies and methods of analysis. The research will tend to have a close relationship between theory and data, be underwritten by theory, and as we shall see in Chapter 3, it also needs to make a distinct and new contribution to knowledge. Students also need to be able to justify the decisions they take, whether these are about the methods they use, the form of analysis they have employed, etc., but also about the whole design they have chosen to use. Some of the questioning at the viva may be quite detailed. For instance, if an examiner has a particular interest in methods they may ask why you have chosen to use interviews, rather than questionnaires; why unstructured conversations, rather than structured interviews; what ethical considerations were involved in the interviews and so on, and you need to have well-thought out answers. In addition, I argue that, in general, doctoral students also need to be greater independent thinkers who are more imaginative and creative, and this is what makes carrying out doctoral research so much fun, but also sometimes more challenging:

Clint: I would say a PhD is certainly different [from a master's]. I think that the difficulty is in that part of what makes a PhD researcher to me is not just creating new knowledge, but this idea that we are not just knowledge creators or drivers of this knowledge into creation, but we ask what does it mean to be that kind of a thinker? That's really to me a question that pops into my head, is what does it mean to be a PhD-level thinker? Well that to me signals someone who can go and sit in a variety of perspectives or ideas and begin to make critical judgements about is the argument valid, is the way this has been done valuable or valid? Is it capable? Can you generate your own opinions or your own ideas against the opinions and ideas of other people rather than simply being able to take a point of view on them? Can you challenge them, can you work from them, can you build on them, can you eliminate what's not necessary?

One theme that was picked up in the interviews was how studying for a PhD can be a more lonely experience, especially after students finish taking the core research training courses, and this feeling can be more pronounced for part-time PhD students, who tend to visit the institution on a less regular basis than their full-time colleagues:

Kerry: You are pretty much just doing it on your own. You are doing your own research, you are looking at your own stuff, and the courses are great for getting to meet new people and share ideas and come together, but unless you are on a course you don't really see anyone, because you are just getting your head down, especially if you are part-time, because your focus is on getting to work, and your [professional] job done, coming in when you can. And this, although you try not to put it to one side and you don't want to make it less of a priority it does sometimes become less of a priority, so you don't come into the library as often as you probably could, and things like that, so yeah, I think it can be lonely but I enjoy it.

However, it does not always have to be like this and although both Julia and Jeanette agreed with Kerry that professional work will generally take precedence over academic study, they said that they were so busy at work that they actually looked forward to some solitary time studying. Nevertheless, learning is essentially a social enterprise and students need to try and maintain contact with other students, if only to share ideas and put any difficulties they are encountering in perspective. This is one of the major differences between taking a PhD and an EdD for these latter students tend to meet as a group much more regularly. Having taught and tutored on various EdD modules, and been programme leader for the IFS, it is noticeable how much camaraderie there is, how much the students help each other with ideas (including suggesting books and references), and how much some of them keep in touch and meet socially outside the programme time.

2.6 TIME MANAGEMENT

Table 2.2 gives an indication of the number of hours each of the eight students spent working on their doctoral research each week in their first year of study, excluding time attending research training courses. I also asked each student to estimate the amount of time they spent either reading, writing or in discussing their work with peers or other academics. However, some found it difficult to come up with exact figures during a *typical* week, and the percentages should be taken as a rough guide. It also needs to be pointed out that 'average time per week' is also a little misleading because, when part-time students are working, they tend to have more intense periods of application, during weekends and/or holidays. As Rosalind (one of the EdD students) told me: 'Obviously, there were times when I worked all weekend for several weekends in a row and times when I did very little.'

Unsurprisingly, Table 2.2 shows that the part-time students generally devote much less time working on their doctorates than their full-time colleagues, and with these students this

Table 2.2 Hours each student spent working on their PhD per week, excluding training courses

Name	Hours spent working on doctorate per week during the first year of study, excluding attending training courses
Kerry (PhD)	10 hours
	Reading (50%), writing (50%). Very little time spent discussing work with peers and/or tutors
Julia (PhD)	2-3 hours
	Reading (10%), writing (10%), discussion (80%)
Jeanette (PhD)	8 hours
	Reading (60%), writing (20%), discussion (20%)
Clint (PhD)	30-35 hours
	Reading (65%), writing (15%), discussion (20%)
Rea (PhD)	40 hours
	Equal time spent on reading (45%), writing (45%), discussion (10%)
Hui (PhD)	20-25 hours
	Reading (60%), writing (30%), discussion (10%)
Roberta (EdD)	10 hours
	Reading (45%), writing (45%), discussion (10%)
Rosalind (EdD)	3 hours
	Reading (35%), writing (40%), discussion (25%)

varied from about 10 hours to Julia's 2–3 hours a week, although at the time of the interview Julia was looking after her new baby. The amount of time spent by the full-time students varied between 20–40 hours and many of these students regarded their studies as being akin to working in full-time employment, and therefore expected to treat their studies as a professional job with a full commitment.

Apart from Julia and Rosalind, most of the other students spent the majority of their time reading, although Kerry, Rea and Roberta said that they shared this equally with writing. With the exception of Julia and, to a lesser extent, Jeanette and Clint, the rest of these students did not seem to discuss their work much with peers or academics at the institution, which suggests that PhD research is a relatively solitary experience, particularly when students are not involved in research training courses.

2.7 KEY FIGURES IN THE RESEARCH PROCESS, INCLUDING THE SUPERVISOR
The role of, and the relationship with, the student's supervisor(s)

The relationship between student and supervisor is crucial and the supervisor will often be the most influential person in the process of gaining a doctorate. This was the case with five of the six PhD students whom I interviewed. I have not included the two EdD students in this section because, as I have mentioned above, they do not become fully involved with their supervisor until Year 2.

It is a much more personal relationship than with a tutor on a course module and will last a much longer time. Guidance from the Quality Assurance Agency for Higher Education[3] (QAA) – stipulates that students in the UK should have two supervisors, and this is also the model in the USA, where students also have an advisory panel. In most institutions, students are asked to identify and set up a main or principal supervisor before they apply to take a doctorate, and then a second or subsidiary supervisor will be appointed at a later date. One supervisor will take the lead role and, although this can be 95 per cent of the time, it is more common for supervisors to share the role more equally, perhaps one taking 60 per cent and the other 40 per cent. When there are two supervisors, sometimes the student will see them individually and then together and sometimes always both together – this varies from case to case. Students will generally also have an advisory panel of other academics that will make appropriate arrangements for supervisory cover during periods of absence/study leave/overseas visits, and so on.

Supervisors need to be well matched to their students' interests and tensions can sometimes arise when supervisors come from a different discipline or field. However, it is not always possible to find a perfect match and, particularly when students are investigating areas

3 The Quality Assurance Agency for Higher Education (QAA) is an independent body that monitors, and advises on, standards and quality in UK higher education.

which are relatively under-researched, it is more important that the supervisor understands, and is sympathetic to, the student's conceptual and methodological approach than they have expertise in a particular specialised area.

I see the role of the supervisor being akin to that of a driving instructor: that is, to offer advice and guidance. They will not tell you what to do; the ideas need to come from you. Box 2.3 outlines some of the roles and duties supervisors should have, and some of these are similar to the ones outlined by Thomas (2013: 37).

▬▬ BOX 2.3 ▬▬▬▬▬▬▬▬▬▬▬▬▬▬▬▬▬▬▬▬▬▬▬▬▬▬▬▬▬▬▬▬

The role of your supervisor

- Talk ideas through with you.
- Offer advice about setting up and conducting your fieldwork.
- Read and make critical comments on drafts of your work.
- Guide you to areas of reading you need to engage with in your field, including possible theories and theorist you can explore.
- Offer you guidance about training courses.
- Offer you suggestions to gaining access to research contexts for fieldwork, where appropriate.
- Discuss the overall research design.
- Discuss methods and methodologies, and ways of analysing data.
- Discuss how you can organise and structure your work, including when it comes to writing up and presenting findings.

Some of these themes are picked up by Kerry in the extract below:

Jon: What about the role of your supervisor in your research, and how influential and helpful has he been in this?

Kerry: Really influential in terms of pointing me in the right direction, what to read and where to start navigating this whole issue around education, and it being historical, then he's always very helpful. If I have a problem I'll just email him and he gets straight back to me, so that's great, but he's also willing to take a step back and let me come to my own conclusions about stuff; he is happy to hear my ideas, so he doesn't force me down a particular route, he just guides me.

You can see how the supervisor is encouraging her to be independent and creative, and come up with her own ideas, and this is also echoed in the following quotation from Julia where her supervisor helps her to shape her thoughts by providing suggestions on how to develop them:

Julia: He's incredibly helpful and very influential; … I generally turn up to meetings with these six or seven different ideas of what I want to do and he is very good at listening properly to them, giving me feedback, giving me a sense of OK, I think that would work quite well, you know, maybe that needs this or that, and also thinking about who maybe I might contact to discuss it further, where I should look for more information about that and sending me papers that were relevant to our discussion.

We can also see that Julia tends to set the agenda for her supervisory meetings, or the schedule is negotiated between both parties, and Table 2.3 shows that this was the most common model for the majority of the six students. Before the meeting it is often a good idea for students to draw up a list of queries they want to discuss.

The number of meetings is likely to be highly variable and specific to individual institutions and in the UK QAA guidance only stipulates that meetings should occur on 'a regular basis'; however, most full-time students can expect to meet with their supervisor around once a month. During my time as programme leader of the MPhil/PhD the guidance was that students were expected to see their supervisor between 9 and 15 times a year if they were full-time, and between 6 and 9 times if they were part-time. Of course, the number of supervisions may average out across the duration of the student's registration on the degree programme because some periods of the research process are more intense than at others.

Table 2.3 Number of meetings and hours spent in supervision over one academic year

Name	No. of meetings with their supervisor per year and who generally set the agenda
Kerry	ONE supervisor
	10 meetings around an hour each: about 10 hours a year
	Kerry mainly set the agenda
Julia	ONE supervisor
	6-7 meetings, around 1.5 hours each: about 10 hours a year
	The agenda was negotiated between student and supervisor but Julia often took the lead and made suggestions
Jeanette	TWO supervisors
	About 6 meetings, around 1.5 hours each: about 9 hours a year
	Supervisors mainly set the agenda
Clint	ONE supervisor
	11 meetings, around 1 hour each: about 11 hours a year
	The agenda was negotiated between student and supervisor
Rea	TWO supervisors
	About 9 meetings, around 1 hour each: about 1.5 hours each, but also meetings by SKYPE: about 20-25 hours per year in total
	Rea mainly set the agenda
Hui	ONE supervisor
	About 15 meetings a year, around 1 hour each: about 15 hours a year in total
	The agenda was negotiated between student and supervisor

Table 2.3 shows the number of meetings and the total number of hours of supervision that each of the six PhD students experienced in their first year of study, although the number of meetings do not seem to differ much between those studying full-time and part-time. The table also indicates who generally set the agenda for these supervisions. EdD students are not included in the table as we need to remember that at UCL/IOE, they do not begin to fully engage with their supervisors until Year 2.

It is noticeable that only two out of these six PhD students had two supervisors and this is because the new regulations at UCL/IOE requiring students to have two supervisors only came into force in 2015.

Other influential figures

During the interviews, I asked the students if they had any heroes or role models who they identified themselves with, perhaps as a model for the type of researcher they wanted to be, or as a writer or theorist? My hero was Raewyn Connell and I drew on her theories of masculinity and carried one of her books around with me that I used like a bible, but I also based my style of writing on other feminist-inspired scholars. Four of the PhD students said that their supervisor (or supervisors) was/were the main influence on their research, including the design, the questions they were asking and the methodology they were using. However, Rea also cited several academic writers and some key teachers/lecturers from her research training, and Clint also mentioned teachers and fellow students whom he discussed his work with on a regular basis.

2.8 THE INFLUENCE OF RESEARCH TRAINING COURSES

PhD students view the core research training programmes differently. While many want to find out about how different researchers work in general, and are happy to learn about a range of different research designs and approaches, others take a more instrumental approach and are only essentially interested in hearing about their own approach, whether it be, for example, case study research or survey design. This also depends on their previous knowledge and experience and the type of learner they see themselves as being. For instance, Julia told me that:

> I'm quite an independent learner, so I think having jumped through a hell of a lot of courses and done two master's degrees and the postgraduate certificate here before I did the master's here. I felt quite ready to just sort of be left to go, well actually if I want to learn about how to do a questionnaire I will go and find out how to do a questionnaire and read it, but I am much, much, more a reading person than I am a lectures person, so for me lectures have never been a very great way to learn.

I always say that it is worth keeping an open mind and finding out about how different designs work in general: firstly, because during, and perhaps beyond, their doctoral research students need to be able to critically appraise a range of research; and secondly, many students' designs will change, particularly during their first year or so. I have heard many say that, for instance, 'I was interested in conducting a survey but have now become much more interested in spending time in the local setting and carrying out ethnographic research.' It was just the case that they did not know what ethnography was or how an ethnographic researcher worked.

During the first year, the EdD programme is different and will often have a greater emphasis on the professional context, on writing a research proposal, and on designing, conducting and analysing a small piece of research, generally within their own professional context.

Sometimes, certain 'breakthrough' or 'lightbulb' moments will occur during a student's research, either perhaps during fieldwork or reading or perhaps someone such as a supervisor may suggest a particular theorist or concept which the student has never thought about before and which resonates with them and seems to make perfect sense. This happened to Kerry during a research training course at a time when she was still worrying about which theories, or which methodological approach to use:

Kerry: We've always been told about theories and they say that we should be using theories, but I've never known what theories to use or whatever, so I was always of the thought that I would try and just use grounded theory, if I could, to formulate my own theory … And then Catharine [a course tutor on a qualitative analysis module] did her talk on constructed grounded theory and I thought yes, that actually fits with what I want to do and that makes sense to me, yeah, that was it.

One of the most beneficial parts of attending courses with their peers for all doctoral students is that they get the chance to introduce and talk about their work. In the quotation below, Hui recalls how the feedback she received from other more experienced students made her realise that her idea was too large for a PhD project, and that she needed to reduce its scope and find a sharper focus. In the first few months, she was thinking about looking at the quality of teaching in private universities in different parts of the world but gradually began to think about focusing only on these institutions in her home country of China:

Hui: I still remember when I introduced my own original draft, original proposal, it was the very beginning, and everybody said, 'Wow, wow, so many things you want to do, how will you do that? It's impossible.' But at that time I had no idea about this and I didn't recognise my wrong direction, [it was] just kind of like a big map, with a mess, a massive thing that I wanted to do, and everybody told me about this. … Most of them [the students] were in the second or third year or even fourth year, so if everybody said this about my work, that you should really think about that, it made me really think about it.

In some courses (like CDR), students get the chance to introduce their work to their peers, and listen to others, in a non-threatening, informal atmosphere in small groups. These groups are sometimes facilitated by more experienced students. As the extract below illustrates, this not only makes students justify their principles of selection, but they also learn the skills of critically appraising other designs and offering formative advice:

Jeanette: I think the groups were useful for two reasons. Like firstly it's just nice to, I mean maybe because I'm more isolated, but it was nice to actually practice speaking about your research, in a safe space, which I think that's probably what I value the most out of it, and then I also enjoyed the process of being a kind of critical friend to other people as well.

Jon: Yes, so kind of learning what questions to ask, and what should you ask, and what's important, and how did they justify their sample and things, and that helps you think about well how am I justifying mine.

Jeanette: Yeah, exactly, seeing how other people do things is so fascinating.

Talking about your work is all part of the process of presenting your work in a public arena, whether it is at a poster conference, an academic conference or as a written paper. As we speak about our work and respond to questions about it, we begin to realise that we are more confident about particular aspects than others. I remember thinking when I used to talk about my own work that, yes, I know that I am talking about when it comes to justifying my methods but I need to do more thinking about certain aspects of the sample, for example why I was not interviewing parents as well as children? We all need to have our work evaluated and appraised by the academic community for this is how we learn and move on. All of our work will be criticised or critiqued to some extent and it is how we learn from and react to these comments that is important. If a student's work remains private and hidden, there is less chance for the thinking to develop and move on, and you certainly do not want the first chance to present your study to be the viva itself. Headings that students may want to use when they introduce their work to other students can be seen on WEBLINK 1.

WEBLINK 1

Suggestions for group tasks to talk about your project

2.9 SEEING THE WORLD IN A DIFFERENT WAY AND CHANGING STUDENTS IDENTITIES

As I stated in Chapter 1, like all good teaching and learning, taking a doctorate should be a transformative experience and many students begin to see the world through a different series of lenses and therefore in a different way. For EdD students, in particular, this helps with their professional vision and development but, of course, is also true for PhD students like Kerry, who was a teacher:

Jon: Do you feel in a way you are seeing the world in a different way?

Kerry: Yes, yeah, especially about education, yeah, so much, and realising that there's so much about education that you don't know, and so much that's been written that you don't get access to on your teacher training … And unless you do a master's or a PhD, or anything like that, you don't actually get introduced to anything, you go your whole teaching career and not know about them.

For other students, the research will change who they think they are and who they think they are on the way to becoming. In other words, it can have a profound affect on their identity and at the end of the research they will have become different people. Clint exemplifies this feeling below, and in the exchange below we can see how personal, and how much his doctorate means to him:

Clint: I came here and I would say that as much the fact that I am self-funded, I'm spending my own life savings to do the thing that I told my mother when I was 12-years-old would be the ultimate dream accomplishment of my life. I came to be a research student because I told myself before I died I wanted to be able to do that thing, to be that, because I love to learn, I've always loved to learn. And for me I swim in these things, and I swim in them, not just because I'm paying for them but I swim in them because as much as I try to maximise the experience I just feel like the more you test yourself, the more you try, the more you become aware of what it is that's out there and what interests you.

         …

         I mean education has taken me from a place of poverty as a child to being able to operate in the spaces I'm able to operate in to contribute to them. I think this is very powerful means of social justice. I don't know, to me that's the whole point.

Jon: It's very much connected with your personal identity isn't it?

Clint: It's absolutely your personal identity, I think there's so much of me that gets up every morning and goes how cool is it that I am able to do this, and therefore I just go into it as if it was an act of joy. That's very idealistic but that's also very honest.

▬ BOX 2.4 ▬▬

A summary of the key points

- Many initial student research proposals are underdeveloped and supervisors are often more interested in their potential to produce a doctoral thesis.
- Almost all universities run core research training programmes, although these will vary in the content and stipulated number of hours. Almost all PhD students first register on the MPhil programme and then upgrade to PhD level during the first 18 months; EdD students often need to have their proposal for their dissertation approved before they can progress.
- One of the main differences between a master's and doctoral degree is that the latter are more likely to be underwritten by theory and needs to make a distinct contribution to knowledge. Doctoral students also often need to be more independent and creative thinkers.
- The relationship with the students' supervisor(s) is crucial and their role is akin to that of a driving instructor who is able offer expert advice and guidance.
- One of the most beneficial parts of research training courses is the chance for students to present their ideas in a non-threatening environment, and be able to learn how to critically evaluate other research.
- By the end of their studies, many students begin to see the world in a different way.

AREAS FOR DISCUSSION

- What headings does a student need to consider when they are constructing their research design?
- What are some of the key roles that a supervisor needs to play?
- What are some of the main challenges and/or difficulties that you have found so far in your doctoral research?
- How useful or beneficial have you found the core research training courses and how could they be improved?
- How does a doctorate differ from a master's degree?
- What or who have been some of the main influences on your doctoral research?

ANNOTATED BIBLIOGRAPHY

Bryman, A. (2012) *Social Research Methods*, **4th edn. Oxford: Oxford University Press.**

The author presents students with a comprehensive guide to the principle qualitative and quantitative methods and methodologies used in the field of social research, including advice on how to effectively collect, analyse and interpret data and disseminate those findings to others. There are also sections on the 'supervisory experience' and on Internet research.

Murray, R. (2011) *How to Write a Thesis*, **3rd edn. Maidenhead: Open University Press.**

The book provides a highly accessible guide and practical tips to help students construct their PhD and EdD theses. It covers all aspects of the research, writing and editing involved in the process of completing a successful thesis.

Phillips, E. and Pugh, D. (2010) *How to Get a PhD: A Handbook for Students and their Supervisors*, **5th edn. Maidenhead: Open University Press.**

An accessible introduction to what is needed to gain a PhD or an EdD that gives clear and practical advice. The book has useful chapters on the characteristics of a good doctorate, the research process and different research designs (see also the new edition, 2016).

FURTHER READING

Williams, K., Bethell, E., Lawton, J., Parfitt-Brown, C., Richardson, M. and Rowe, V. (2010) *Planning Your PhD*, **Pocket Study Skills. Basingstoke: Macmillan.**

This short readable book offers students practical guidance about the key processes and major challenges involved in undertaking a PhD, including how to develop initial ideas.

Williams, K., Bethell, E., Lawton, J., Parfitt-Brown, C., Richardson, M. and Rowe, V. (2011) *Completing Your PhD*, **Pocket Study Skills. Basingstoke: Macmillan.**

This is a helpful guide aimed at PhD students seeking to successfully complete their thesis. Based on students' direct experiences, topics include managing your time, developing your argument(s) and the viva, including what examiners will be looking for.

CHAPTER 3

DESIGNING YOUR RESEARCH IN EDUCATION

Jon Swain

BOX 3.1

Overview of chapter

This chapter includes:

- Definitions of what constitutes a PhD or EdD doctorate.
- How initial ideas may turn into a doctoral research project.
- A consideration of different types of research questions and the process of how they may be developed.
- A look at two major research designs and underlying approaches – deductive and inductive.
- The idea of positioning students' work in an empirical and theoretical field.
- A discussion of what constitutes a conceptual framework.
- Definitions of the term 'methodology'.
- The role of theory and theorists in doctoral research.
- A discussion of the term, 'principles of selection'.
- The processes involved for students in constructing a research design and some of the main challenges involved.

3.1 INTRODUCTION

This chapter discusses issues around designing your doctoral research project. The first five sections examine what a doctorate is and how initial ideas often start large and gradually get narrowed down to something much smaller and more manageable. They look at the process of developing research questions and consider fundamentally different designs and approaches such as deductive, inductive or complementary. The next two sections introduce the idea positioning your work in an empirical and theoretical field, and how over the research process you need to think about developing a conceptual framework. The final four sections look at the meaning of the term 'methodology', the place of theory in doctoral research, a discussion of the term 'principles of selection', which run throughout the whole development of the design, and some the processes and challenges involved for students in constructing a research design.

3.2 WHAT IS A DOCTORATE?

A PhD degree varies considerably according to the country, institution and time period, and in the last few years the traditional PhD (Doctor in Philosophy) model has begun to be challenged. There are now a number of different types of doctoral degree (Murray, 2011; Maslen, 2013). Apart from a Professional Doctorate, or Doctor in Education (EdD), which has been running now for about 20 years (Doncaster and Thorne, 2000), these include PhD by publication (of academic work such as papers, books, book chapters that have been subjected to external reviews, and much of it published before enrolment), and a PhD in the Arts and Humanities where candidates can be assessed on a portfolio of original artistic or technological work, which may take the form of objects, images, films, performances, musical compositions, web pages, software, and so on. These last two degrees must be accompanied by an analytical commentary and, like all doctorates, demonstrate a contribution to knowledge (see below).

The main difference between an EdD and a PhD is that a greater proportion of the former follows a more structured programme, including course work and a thesis; it is only available for part-time study; and, whereas the PhD can be used as an induction into an academic career, the EdD places that emphasises on students' professional practice and development within a particular professional context.

Both the EdD and PhD in education and social sciences are usually assessed by a bound thesis supplemented by oral examination, or viva voce. The maximum length of a PhD thesis is usually about 80,000 words, although this can vary between countries and, for example, in some institutions candidates may be able apply for an extension of up to 20,000 words if they have a good reason. My own thesis was about 100,000 words and my justification was that it contained a series of extensive quotations from my fieldwork, which were used to exemplify the arguments I was making. An EdD thesis is usually about 40,000–45,000 words and the other 35,000–40,000 words are made up either by a series of assignments from taught courses and/or perhaps by the inclusion a smaller empirical study. At some universities, there is an Institute Focused Study (IFS) of 20,000 words, which is positioned between the early taught courses and the thesis. The IFS enables a student to study an educational institution or organisation with which they are generally professionally connected to, and is often the first time that they begin to integrate theory and data.

A PhD and an EdD thesis must be the candidate's own account and the greater proportion of the investigation needs to be undertaken during the period of registration under supervision for the degree. At its core, the thesis must be an integrated set of ideas that present a coherent argument that is maintained throughout and is able to be defended at the viva.

An empirical PhD or EdD must be correct and precise, and demonstrate that the student is fluent in the appropriate techniques of designing the study, setting the research up by gaining access to the field, constructing a set of research questions, deciding on and using appropriate theories, methods and methodology (see Section 3.8), carrying out the analysis and presenting the findings and conclusions.

Importantly, a PhD or EdD thesis must form a distinct contribution to the knowledge of the field of study. That is, it needs to afford evidence of originality by the discovery of new facts and/or the exercise of independent critical powers that develops the discipline or field in which the research is set (see Section 3.6). Whatever questions are asked at your viva, you can be almost certain that you will be asked what you consider your original or distinct input to be. A lot of students get exercised about this but you may not be able to articulate this input until you begin to carry out your analysis. What you do need to ascertain before you begin your doctoral research, though, is that there is a 'space' in the empirical and the-oretical field(s) (see Section 3.6) for your idea, and that the questions have not been investigated before, at least using the same research context(s) and/or methodology.

Few of us are going to discover anything life-changing (like discovering DNA), or produce a brand new theory that is going to change our view of the world. For most of us, our claim to originality is going to be much more modest, although it still needs to be made clear and explicit. The list in Box 3.2 is based loosely on definitions from Phillips and Pugh (2006: 63–4) and Murray (2006: 59), although they are only intended as a guide.

▬▬ BOX 3.2 ▬▬▬▬▬▬▬▬▬▬▬▬▬▬▬▬▬▬▬▬▬▬▬▬▬▬▬▬▬▬▬▬▬▬▬

Ways of claiming originality

- You say something that has not been said before.
- You carry out empirical work that has not been done before.
- You interpret someone else's findings in a new way.
- You test existing knowledge in an original way.
- You add to knowledge in a way that has not been done before.
- You work across disciplines, using different methodologies.
- You use new methodologies in new ways.

As can be seen from the above, you do not have to find something completely original or say something unique. Many students will generally be carrying out research in relatively under-researched areas or in more familiar contexts from a new angle, while others can make an original methodological contribution that has not been, or rarely, used before. What I would be a little concerned about if I were a supervisor is if the research idea seems too orig-inal or innovative, or even a little too 'zany'. As we will see below, to some extent, gaining a doctorate is about learning to play a game and this game has certain defined codes and rules. Anything too out of the ordinary can make it difficult to understand and define the problem that is going to be researched, and I have known a number of students who have got into difficulties and have had to change their first ideas into a more orthodox study.

Even if your research appears to be quite similar to what has been done before, the chances are that it will still be suitably different. Say, for example, that you are interested in how people learn to read using digital technologies like computers and smartphones. Perhaps this has been done with adults and older children but not with young children and, even if it has, the context will almost certainly be different and you will also be asking different questions, and perhaps be generating data from different methods.

Examples from some of my own students whom I have supervised can be seen in Box 3.3, which outlines how they made an original input.

━━━ BOX 3.3 ▰▰▰▰▰▰▰▰▰▰▰▰▰▰▰▰▰▰▰▰▰▰▰▰▰▰▰▰▰▰▰▰▰▰▰▰▰▰▰

Examples of students' research making an original contribution to the field

Roberta's EdD research explored a relatively under-researched area of home schooling. This had been done before, but the more original aspects was that the children in her research were autistic and that she carried out home visits and observations and interviewed both the parents and the children.

In contrast, Rosalind's EdD research explored a highly researched area, that of reading. However, like Rachel's research, the aspect that gave it greater originality was that the children were again autistic, and she also used a more innovative methodological technique of asking families to film shared family reading practices at home using their smartphones.

Delia's PhD research also investigated a commonly researched area, that of teachers working in secondary school. She used narrative interviews with teachers in her own school, which, again, have been used many times before. However, her claims to originality came from her main idea, which was to assess the impact that teacher representations in the media have on their daily practice and teacher-student relationships.

Clint's PhD research was about student housing/accommodation in England. He used interviews and observations of students and staff in two student residences. His claims to originality came from his focus on postgraduate students, and his application of spatial syntax theory to explore and compare the interface of physical buildings on social relationships of students and staff.

Depending on the area and type of research, a thesis can make a (usually small) contribution to the development of theory itself. In my own PhD research (see Section 1.3), I proposed a new form of masculinity, which I called 'personalised'. This was different from the accepted forms of masculinity at the time of my research such as 'dominant' and 'subordinated', and this is elaborated on further in Section 3.9.

You will also need to position your research in a particular empirical and theoretical field and make a contribution to them, and I will explain this in more detail in Section 3.6.

Briefly, and in terms of the theoretical field, you and your supervisor will need to identify academics working in your particular field who have the knowledge and expertise to be able to make a judgment on the quality of your own work, and hopefully conclude that it presents a coherent argument and does, indeed, make an impact to this particular field. By the end of your doctoral research, you should be on the way to becoming an expert (even *the* expert) in your specialised area within the particular field in which you have positioned your research.

One of the most challenging things for many students, is learning to write in an academic genre with all of its associated rules and conventions. I have met many students, often taking an EdD degree, who are highly skilled professionals and who are highly accomplished at writing readable, clear and succinct professional reports, but who find it difficult to adjust to academic writing. Some take longer than others and the only way I can think of suggesting how to go about it is to read, read and read as many academic publications as you can, making careful observations of the language, syntax, style, etc. It's like learning to write poetry: if you want to become a poet, you will usually need to read a lot of poetry, noting the rules and conventions carefully.

Some students worry about which style to adopt in their academic writing but this is associated with what type of researcher you want to be and in which field you are going to position your work. For instance, in my own research, I was using feminist-inspired theories of masculinity and, so, I was always going to have to use the first person in my writing, rather than the third person that researchers coming from a more positivist position tend to use. I remember one of my supervisors telling me that 'it's like joining a club', which has its own strict codes and rules. If I wanted to publish my work in the particular journals that were most relevant to my own work and kept on appearing in my reading, I had to play the game and perform by their rules. It is as simple as this: you may not agree with all the rules and (sometimes) rather idiosyncratic conventions, but if you do not abide by them, you will not be admitted. For example, if I had written, '*The researcher* asked *the females* what they thought,' rather than, '*I* asked *the women* what they thought,' my papers would have been rejected by the journals I was aiming to publish in.

I also recommend that students read some theses early on in their doctoral careers. In this way, you can observe the structure, organisation and writing style, and see roughly how many words have been allocated to chapters such as the literature review (if there is one), the methodology and findings, etc. The main part of your thesis should be the findings, which as a rough guide based on my own experience, I think should be about 35 to 40 per cent of the word count (e.g., 30,000–35,000 of a PhD thesis and 15,000–20,000 of an EdD thesis; see Figure 3.1). You can also see what the author's claim is for their contribution to knowledge.

My supervisor, in addition, gave me the sound advice of treating my writing as a *pedagogic text*; that is, it needs to teach the reader, in this case the examiners (who are your first and main audience), the process of how you did it. You need to metaphorically take them by the hand and walk them through, stage by stage: the process of constructing the design, the choice of methods and analysis all need to be made visible and transparent so that a

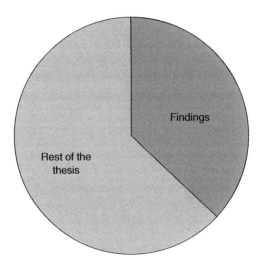

Figure 3.1 Sections devoted to research findings as a proportion of the whole thesis

judgement can be made of how you reached your conclusions. You will need to use sign-posting to make it readable by reminding the reader what they have just read and what they are going to read next. You also need to make sure that your main arguments, points and/or findings 'ring out' and are made as clear as possible. On some occasions you might consider using bullet points (e.g., about your contribution to knowledge).

One of the qualities that I also look for when I am examining a thesis is how much of the work is suitable for, or worthy of, academic publication in a peer-reviewed journal or an edited book. I always encourage students to identify areas or themes that they consider will be suitable for an article or paper. This will show a further development to the discipline and/or field post-thesis but it is also a good idea if you can publish papers in academic journals during your period of registration, usually, but not always, towards the end of your research. Although it can be hard to find time to do this, I would encourage you to try and publish at least one paper, if not two. I managed to have one paper published (Swain, 2000) and I had one accepted for publication (Swain, 2002) before my viva, and the fact that my academic peers had validated my work gave me a lot of confidence for my impending examination.

The ideas for a paper do not necessarily have to be about findings; it is also possible to write a paper around a theme that emerges from the background literature, or perhaps, as I have already mentioned, about a new and innovative methodological approach or method of analysis. You can also publish co-authored papers, sometimes with your supervisor, but it is preferable if you are the first named author. If you do publish work in a journal during your period of registration, you can still use it in your thesis, although you will generally have to get copyright permission from the journal.

Different countries have different traditions and, for example, in the USA, students are encouraged to publish their work much earlier, often in the first year during their period of research (generally Year 4 of a typical five-to-six-year PhD programme). However, the advice to publish work during your doctoral studies generally applies to many doctoral pro-grammes in countries throughout the world.

Publishing your work is also important if you want to remain in academia after your post-graduate course has finished, and I managed to publish nine papers based on my doctoral research in the immediate years after I was awarded my PhD in 2001.

3.3 FIRST IDEAS FOR A DOCTORAL PROJECT

Most doctoral (and master's) research stems from a student's personal interests and, so, is essentially autobiographical: the question(s) usually comes from something you are interested in, although sometimes you will know a lot about it and sometimes you will not. As I've already said, you will need to have a deep and continuing interest in your area/topic as much of your time over the coming years will be devoted to your research and your commitment cannot be in any way half-hearted. I have already made the point that while some doctoral students know exactly what questions they are going to ask, and have a good idea of the strategy or methodology they are going to use to try to find the answers, for many students the initial ideas will tend to be more nebulous and take time to develop before they are able to articulate a clear and compelling rationale for their research and construct a design that has conceptual clarity. Thus, for many, the research process often begins with vagueness and hes-itation and moves towards greater precision and coherence (Dowling and Brown, 2010).

Carrying out research, particularly doctoral research, involves, amongst other things, learn-ing a set of skills and techniques, a set of rules, understanding a series of (sometimes quite difficult) concepts and acquiring a specialised language. As I wrote in Chapter 1, research is a method of inquiry that will add knowledge to a field of practice, or activity, that is currently unknown (ibid.). Dowling and Brown view research as a *mode of interrogation* and the produc-tion of a systematic and coherent set of statements, which are located within explicitly stated theoretical and empirical contexts (ibid.).

Punch and Oancea (2014) maintain that, at its most basic level, research needs to be built around three key concerns: what are the questions the research is trying to answer; how will it answer them; and are the answers meaningful and worthwhile. In addition, the researcher will often also want to think about: whom they are going to involve; when and where they are going to do the research; how long it will take; and how they are going to make sense of it all (see Section 1.2).

Conducting research can be frustrating: almost invariably the research process seldom goes exactly to plan, and it is rare for it to run smoothly from beginning to end, even if the design is sound and known at the beginning. The traditional or conventional idea follows, what looks like, a linear or top-down plan, and has similarities to how a thesis might be organised. The simplest version for the organisation or structure of a PhD thesis would be the research question(s), literature review, theoretical outline, methodology/methods/sample, analysis, findings and discussion (see Figure 3.2).

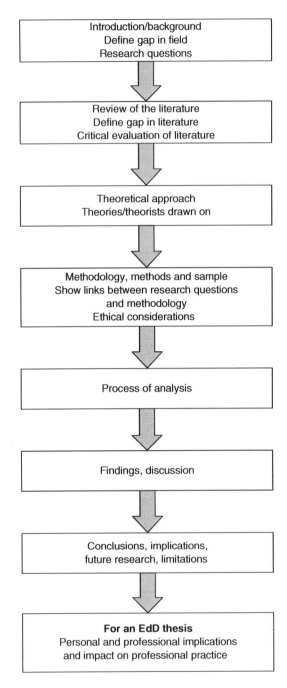

Figure 3.2 A classic research design

Of course, this is only a rough guide, which corresponds to seven or eight chapter headings. You will notice that for an EdD thesis there is an extra chapter. This usually comes at the end and is about the implications of the research, both personally and professionally, for the researcher and for the profession in general.

Moreover, and more typically, the process is, as in real life, far messier and more recursive (Thomas, 2013), which has several stages informing each other. Often, your reading for a literature review, or perhaps your attendance of a core research course, will help to inform your question(s) and maybe redefine it/them. It may also change your mind about what methods and methodologies you are going to use and which theories/theorists you are going to draw on. The analysis may also throw up new questions that need to be explored or investigate, and this in turn will require a further review of the literature. Maybe you won't have a discrete chapter called 'The Literature Review', but, like myself, decide to integrate references into the surrounding literature as you present your findings. The point is that research questions, the relevant literature, theories and methodologies, methods of data collection and analysis can all change and, depending on the approach (see Section 3.5), the research for a doctoral thesis can often be carried out in any order; the only part that you cannot begin with is the findings.

3.4 RESEARCH QUESTIONS

Research questions act as a frame of reference and will set the agenda for your inquiry; they will also help keep you focused by setting boundaries that help prevent you go wandering off to investigate irrelevant areas/issues (Robson, 2011; Punch and Oancea, 2014). During my PhD, I used to have my research questions pinned up on the wall in front of my desk at home to continually remind me about the questions that I was exploring and help me not to stray off-course and lose focus. O'Leary (2014) writes that these questions will direct you to the literature you will need to search, the theories that you may use and the strategies and methods by which you will gather or generate the data in order to answer them. They will define your topic, and the nature of the inquiry (whether is be to describe, explain, explore, discover, or compare); define variables such as gender, ethnicity, age, income, sexual orientation, etc., and whether you see a relationship between them, or perhaps a correlation or cause (ibid.). They will also define the type of researcher you want to be, perhaps going out, interacting with people and interpreting what they do and say, or spending a greater proportion of time working at your desk analysing statistical and/or secondary data. Finally, they will define the success of the doctoral research by focusing on whether the results of the research have found credible answers (Robson, 2011) when you return to say how you have answered them towards the end of your thesis.

Although there are many different kinds of questions, and each kind will lead you to different types of inquiry that employ different approaches, they tend to fall into the two categories of *descriptive* or *explanatory*, the latter of which will generally be more complex as they seek to try and explain an issue or problem. Often, a student's research questions will contain a mixture of both:

Typical descriptive questions focus around *what's going on?* (e.g., What are the most common reading schemes that schools use in the London Borough of Tower Hamlets?).

Explanatory questions may include: *what happens when?* (e.g., What happens when schools allow children to have a free choice in the books they take home to read with their parents?), or *what is the relationship between?* (e.g., what is the relationship between gender and attainment in primary schools?).

Also see Thomas (2013: 7–20) for a more detailed discussion of different types of questions.

Research questions are one of the hardest parts of the design; they need a lot of thought and must be very precise and, as every word needs to count, I regard them as akin to writing a line in a poem. Depending on the type of research being done, I tell my students (who are usually involved in **inductive**, rather than **deductive**, designs – see Section 3.5) that they should regard their research questions as a set of 'working questions' that are tentative, or provisional, and likely to change. It is often only toward the end of the research process that the questions become much more focused and stable. Most research questions from the inductive tradition change throughout the research. Thomas (2013) makes the point that they begin as *prima facie questions* (meaning, on their first appearance), and are therefore speculative and expected to develop and change as new thoughts, theories and possibilities emerge. Of course, and as we shall see later, for those researchers using a more deductive paradigm, some questions are fixed from the beginning of the research and will remain unchanged throughout the research process.

In my experience, research questions for doctoral theses often start large and end up being much smaller (see my own original questions and ideas in Section 1.3). Students generally need to realise that once space had been taken up with possible introductions, a literature review, sections on theories, methodologies, analysis and conclusions, the findings in a doctoral thesis constitute a relatively small individual research study (albeit of about 30,000 words), and that their questions need to be disentangled, focused or narrowed down so that they are more achievable and manageable. Often, students will find that the research questions they end up with are a series of sub-questions of their original question.

3.5 TWO MAIN RESEARCH DESIGNS: DEDUCTIVE AND INDUCTIVE

Many researchers often refer to two broad and contrasting methods of reasoning as being **deductive** and inductive (mentioned in the previous section), and this involves two fundamentally different philosophical and research approaches. Each has its associated epistemological assumptions about the theory and nature of knowledge (see Chapter 4) and uses its own distinctive language but, although the relationship between theory and research differs for each approach, they can also be complementary.

Deductive approach:[1] Creating a hypothesis from theory and then testing it out by collecting data to see if it is confirmed or not.

---

1 This section is based on: This is 'Inductive or deductive? Two different approaches', section 2.3 from the book *Sociological Inquiry Principles: Qualitative and Quantitative Methods* (v. 1.0) by Amy Blackstone.

This research is top-down where the move is from a more general level to a more specific one. The researcher studies what others have done, reads existing theories of whatever phenomenon he or she is studying, creates a hypothesis and then proposes a series of questions to test it out. The main difference between a question and hypothesis is that the latter is expected to be testable and have a conclusion of 'Yes, this is the case,' or 'No, this is not the case.' Researchers therefore need to know the literature that details the issues involved. Epistemologically, a deductive approach to research is the one that people typically associate with a scientific, positivist, design, which again we will find out more about in Chapter 4. In a similar way to researchers working in the physical or hard sciences, the idea is to set up an experiment (see Chapter 6): the researcher(s) decide on the sample, isolate particular variables, and then collect the data. The analysis either confirms or refutes the hypothesis and if it is the former, the researcher(s) will typically be able to make generalisations to the wider community (see Figure 3.3). An example may be a research study that is aimed at

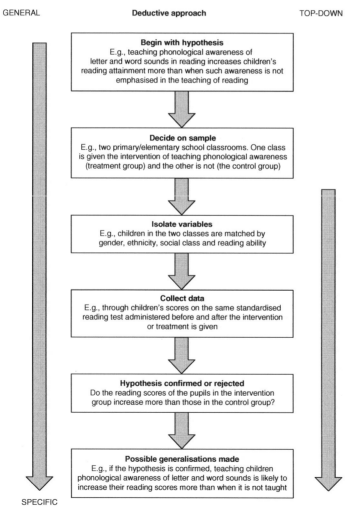

Figure 3.3   The deductive design

seeing whether teaching phonological awareness of letter and word sounds in reading increases children's reading attainment more than when such awareness is not used in the teaching of reading (see Chapter 6).

Researchers using this approach use words like 'test' or 'verify'. Typical research designs are the experiment (Chapter 6) but also the survey (Chapter 7).

Inductive approach: Generating initial data leading to the development of new but tentative theories/hypotheses, which are then tested out with new data.

Researchers taking an inductive approach take the steps described above for deductive research and reverse their order (see Figure 3.6). In an inductive approach, researchers may not have a set of fully formed research questions and may not always know very much about the question they are exploring. They will identify an initial sample and begin by entering the field and generating data that is relevant to their topic of interest. The reason why I am using the word 'generating' rather than 'collecting' data is that researchers using an inductive approach are likely to be working with a more **interpretivist framework** where meanings are created or constructed by people, and are therefore subjective, rather than 'found' from a pre-existing and objective source. Thus, data that is generated tends to be new whereas data that is collected is thought to already exist and needs to be captured. This notion will be further discussed in Chapter 4.

Once an extensive amount of data have been produced, the researcher(s) will then step back from the data and begin some early analysis, looking for patterns (or regularities) and relationships in the data, and working to develop some tentative or provisional theories that might explain these patterns. In this way, the theories are emerging from the data. So, inductive research is bottom-up: researchers begin with a set of observations and then they move from those particular experiences to a more general set of propositions about those experiences. In other words, they move from data to theory, or from the specific to the general (see Figure 3.4). An example of a study using this approach may be where a researcher wants to explore how children make decisions about choosing the books they read at school and at home.

Researchers tend to use words like 'explore' or 'investigate'. Typical research designs using this approach are ethnography (Chapter 8), case studies (Chapter 9) and action research, although in my experience this last design tends not to be used very much in doctoral research.

These two methods of reasoning have a very different 'feel' to them. Deductive reasoning is more focused, while inductive reasoning, by its very nature, is more open-ended and exploratory, especially at the beginning of the process. For a fuller explanation of these two approaches, see the Social Research Methods Knowledge Base see WEBLINK 1.

WEBLINK 1

Research methods knowledge base

Robson (2011) calls these two major types of research design 'fixed' (for deductive) and 'flexible' (for inductive). Although fixed designs almost always depend on the collection of quantitative data, and flexible designs are generally more associated with qualitative data and seem quite different, both designs can actually be complementary and often use mixed methods (Chapter 10), which Robson (2011) refers to as *multi-strategy designs*.

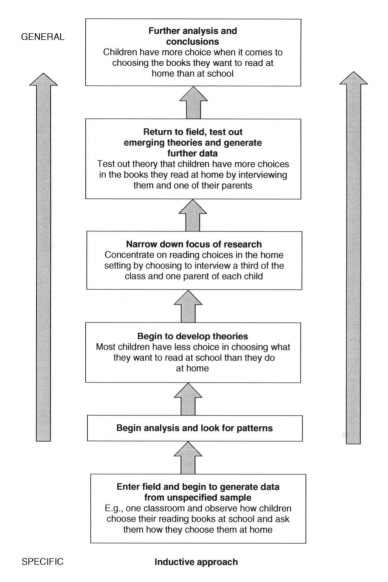

GENERAL

Further analysis and conclusions
Children have more choice when it comes to choosing the books they want to read at home than at school

Return to field, test out emerging theories and generate further data
Test out theory that children have more choices in the books they read at home by interviewing them and one of their parents

Narrow down focus of research
Concentrate on reading choices in the home setting by choosing to interview a third of the class and one parent of each child

Begin to develop theories
Most children have less choice in choosing what they want to read at school than they do at home

Begin analysis and look for patterns

Enter field and begin to generate data from unspecified sample
E.g., one classroom and observe how children choose their reading books at school and ask them how they choose them at home

SPECIFIC   Inductive approach

Figure 3.4 An inductive approach

Complementary approaches

As we shall see in Chapter 10, in some cases, researchers will plan for their research to include both deductive and inductive components, perhaps using a more quantitative survey followed up with qualitative interviews. In other cases, a researcher might begin a study with the plan only to conduct either inductive or deductive research, but then he or she discovers that the other approach is needed to help illuminate the findings. Perhaps the responses from the survey questionnaire are too narrow and a better way of exploring the reasons behind something (or answering a research question) can best come from talking to the participants directly.

For example, I might want to find out what students' motivations are for taking a doctorate at my own institution. I have read a lot of associated literature; I think I know most of
the answers and I want to test out my hypothesis by sending out questionnaires to the
first year doctoral students (100 of them). However, as with all questionnaires, I have a
dilemma that if I ask for too much in-depth information, including for some views
expressed in open text replies, I won't get enough returns – my aim is to receive response
from at least half of the cohort – but, if I make the questions too simplistic or too closed,
I won't get enough data that begins to uncover the students' real views. I decide to administer the questionnaire by email; however, although I receive a sufficient number of replies,
I do not feel that the data uncovers all of their reasons. Moreover, I now begin to realise
that students' motivations are much more complicated and frequently overlap. After analysing the questionnaire data, I therefore decide a few weeks later to take a more inductive
approach and interview a **purposive sample** of 20 students (20 per cent of the cohort)
selected by variables such as their gender, whether they are international or home students, part-time or full-time, and whether they have attended previous research training,
perhaps as part of their master's course. The interviews are unstructured and exploratory
and I try to keep an open mind about what the students are going to tell me. This is a
sequential explanatory design, which will be further explained in Chapter 10, and consists
of two distinct phases of data collection and analysis (Ivankova et al., 2006). First, you
collect and analyse one type of data, and then a second phase complements the first one,
meaning that the two types of data and the findings are integrated (see Figure 3.5). No
data source has any greater **weight** than the other; both are seen as being of equal status
in trying to answer my research question.

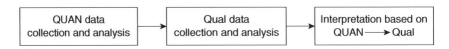

Figure 3.5 A sequential explanatory design in mixed methods research

3.6 THEORETICAL AND EMPIRICAL FIELDS

Dowling and Brown (2010; also see Brown and Dowling, 1998) introduce us to two arenas
within which the research process occurs as it is narrowed down from the general to focus
on the particular: these are the *empirical field* and the *theoretical field* (see Figure 3.6, adapted
from Dowling and Brown, 2010). This process is connected to the principles of selection,
which operate at all stages of the research project, and which not only refer to the empirical
sample of participants. I have already introduced readers to this term in Chapter 1 and the
concept is further elaborated on below (see Section 3.11).

The *empirical field* consists of a broad range of practices, experiences and locations. It may
begin with, for example, the schooling sector, but in order to be manageable it needs to
undergo a process of localising towards a narrower focus, which may be particular sector, such

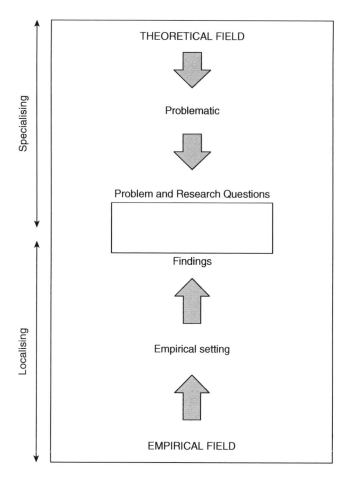

Figure 3.6 Positioning work in the theoretical and empirical fields
Source: Adapted from Dowling and Brown (2010)

as primary or elementary, schools, and then an individual school or group of schools, and then a particular or group of classroom(s), which is referred to as the *empirical setting*. Of course, the planned empirical setting may be different from the setting that is finally achieved.

The *theoretical field* refers to the theories, debates and other empirical findings and this includes the community of academics/researchers, professionals and/or practitioners who comprise the authorities on the particular area you are researching. This is where you find the books, journal articles, professional reports, etc., some of which are connected to the academic disciplinary knowledge with its own canon of knowledge (e.g., sociology, psychology), but also possibly the professional disciplinary knowledge (e.g., assessment, the curriculum). The *theoretical field* also contains the potential readers of the researcher's own writing and these will also need to be identified for the viva examination.

It will be generally necessary to locate or position your work in a particular theoretical field or perhaps fields, and often these will overlap. For instance, within a general theoretical field of educational theory, you might then have two different theoretical fields of (1) Reading and (2) Assessment, which at some points will intersect and merge.

Because this notional theoretical community is, like the *empirical field*, going to be unavoidably broad, the process needs to begin to specialise to find a narrower range of key works and debates that Dowling and Brown (2010) call the *problematic*, within which the research is situated or positioned. Although the *problematic* might be one that is already established and has a body of associated work, sometimes the researcher will need to organise a space for themselves, although they should generally still be able to cite some work that relates to the area of study (e.g., home tutoring with autistic children). There will be work from a number of different genres (e.g., professional publications, government reports, journal articles) but you need to mark out the research that is in the academic genre. Dowling and Brown (2010) point out that this is not because it is in some way superior but because this is the genre you are working in when you are writing a doctorate.

Towards the middle of the diagram we can see where the research process has become sufficiently crystallised to allow the researcher to define the specific *problem* they are exploring (or comparing, evaluating, describing, explaining, etc.) and perhaps construct a series of research questions. It is important to note that different parts of this figure can be completed at different stages and that some areas will overlap. As we have seen, some researchers know what their research questions are at a very early stage, while others will know what theories they are going to use. Some researchers will have one major theory or theorist, while others will draw on many. The only space in the diagram that needs to be completed last is the box showing the findings. If you know what these are before the research commences, it is not possible to call your study or project 'research'.

Two examples using the Dowling and Brown Framework

Example 1: Research investigating home schooling with children with autism

In this first case, the research example was for an EdD (home tutoring with autistic children, see Section 3.2), and the research was situated in two main *theoretical fields*: home tutoring (or home schooling) and children with autism (including more general theories of children with special educational needs).

The *empirical field* began opportunistically with family households, which became eight families in one town – *the empirical setting* – as the student needed to localise.

In the *theoretical field* and *problematic* the student (Roberta, whom we read about in Chapter 2) actually had many theories that she drew on; these included theories on special educational needs, theories of autism, theories of schooling and pedagogical theories of child-centred or progressive education, which began to emerge during the fieldwork. She also had epistemological theories of interpretivism (see Chapter 4), and as she became particularly interested in social relations and practices she set her study within the discipline of sociology of education.

Defining the *problematic* also helped her define her literature search. In my experience, it is often useful to think of the fields of the problematic as an overlapping Venn diagram (see Figure 3.7). Reviewing the literature has two primary functions as it not only enables you to learn what other people have written about your topic of inquiry, but it also shows you how the topic or issue has been investigated (including the number in the sample and the methods and methodologies used), which you can critically analyse and borrow from. Although the student found a number of relevant works (including articles and reports) on home tutoring, and about children with SEN, she could only find a few key studies about the problem she had decided to explore: autistic children being tutored at home. Through this process, she was able to confirm that there was a space in the research literature for her own particular study (see Figure 3.7).

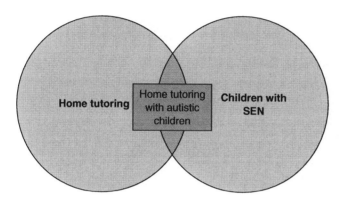

Figure 3.7   Overlapping fields in a literature search

Example 2: Research exploring the construction of masculinities at junior school

A second example comes from my own PhD research that I introduced readers to in Chapter 1 (see Section 1.3). I began with the *empirical field*, which was the school sector, and which then became the junior school (for 7–11-year-olds), and for the specific *empirical setting* I chose three junior schools differentiated by the social characteristics (or the social class) of their intake.

The *theoretical field* began as a broad sociological approach to the effect of gender in education, before specialising in the area of feminist cultural studies of masculinity. After identifying a series of key works and positions – the *problematic* – I was eventually able to formulate my research question(s), or *problem*. Thus, after much effort, a set of personally interesting but vague ideas and proposals were transformed and refined into a considered, coherent and explicit design.

I personally found it very helpful to locate or position my work in a particular *theoretical field*, which involved the disciplines of sociology and cultural studies. As I mentioned in Section 1.3, this meant that in my literature search I could reject all the texts from the discipline of psychology, which effectively removed hundred of articles and books at one stroke. This was not because psychology is somehow inferior to sociology, but is just that I needed to think about and focus on my main areas of interest, which were the observed children's social practices and relationships, and I was not concerned with the role of the unconscious and deeper motives. Once more, this was not because they are not important, but if I had positioned my work in the discipline of psychology it would have been a different study, with different research questions. As we will see, these decisions are connected to the concept of the principles of selection.

3.7 A CONCEPTUAL FRAMEWORK

A well-thought-out research design is often a constituent part of a conceptual framework, which is a systematic way of articulating what you are doing, or what you have done, and the reasons behind the decisions you are making or have made (Robson, 2011). You know that you finally have a conceptual framework when you have come up with the following (see Box 3.4).

═══ BOX 3.4 ═══════════════════════════════════════

Features that suggest that you have a conceptual framework

- You have a good idea and know what topic or issue you are going to research.
- You can provide an explicit rationale for why your research is important.
- You can say where you are going to situate your research.
- You can say how your theories and theoretical ideas are able to help to understand what is going on.
- You can say how you plan to gather or generate information about it.
- You can say how you are going to analyse this information and what you will do with your findings.

As with the research design, it is obvious that not all these stages happen at once or in any particular sequence.

Miles and Huberman (1994, 2013) emphasise that conceptual frameworks are organic, malleable and ongoing, which evolve over time as connections and relationships become more apparent. In other words, they will change and develop over the lifetime of the project, often because the information you gather from reading, attending research training courses, talking to people, and collecting empirical data will lead you to new ideas and understandings. Thus, Ravitch and Riggan (2012: 9) see conceptual frameworks as 'a guide and ballast in research', they are works in progress and are 'simply the current version of the researchers' map of the territory being investigated (Miles and Huberman, 1994: 9).

While some academics use the terms 'conceptual' and 'theoretical' frameworks interchangeably and treat them as essentially the same thing (e.g., Ravitch and Riggan, 2012), my view is that the conceptual framework is a construction that is more encompassing and links and helps to organise all the elements of the research process from beginning to end, and also includes the empirical and theoretical fields (including the literature) in which the research is situated or positioned. As we will see below, I argue that a conceptual framework is more closely connected to the methodology than a theoretical framework. The conceptual framework can be shown as a visual representation with an accompanying narrative but it needs to show the reader (and examiner) that the research project has a clear framework and structure, and has a systematic and coherent rationale for the choices that are going to be, or have been, made.

3.8 METHODOLOGY

I am conscious that in this discussion of conceptual frameworks I have not mentioned the word 'methodology', which has a number of different meanings in the literature. For Punch and Oancea, a methodology is a type of 'theory about the design, methods, and procedures, and involves philosophical tools and insights' (2014: 34). O'Leary develops this idea and writes that methodologies are:

> overarching, macro-level, frameworks that offer principles of reasoning associated with particular paradigmatic assumptions that legitimate various schools of research ... [they] provide both the strategies and grounding for the conduct of a study. (2014: 10)

These appear to be closely connected with the conceptual frameworks discussed above in Section 3.7. In other words, a methodology can be said to be a system of principles that guides the research, which are based on the researcher's understanding of the world, their theories and their beliefs (Robson, 2011).

For Crotty, a methodology is also a strategy or 'plan of action' (1998: 7) that is integral to the design and (as O'Leary and Punch and Oancea maintain above) provides a rationale for the choice of particular methods and forms of analysis. Once again, he makes the point expressed above that behind any methodology lies our theoretical perspective, which is based on a number of personal and philosophical assumptions and 'our view of the human world and social life within that world' (Crotty, 1998: 7). What is obvious is that the methodology that you use is 'neither objective nor value-neutral' (Ravitch and Riggan, 2012: 7).

Reminding ourselves that a thesis needs to present a coherent argument, a study will be undermined if a researcher does not make connections between its design and its associated methodology: for instance, an ethnography (Chapter 8) usually involves researchers immersing themselves in a particular context to try and understand the participants' point of view and is therefore unlikely to use structured questionnaires as its main method of data generation. So, ethnography can be characterised as a methodology, a consistent approach that underpins the research project, based on particular epistemological and ontological assumptions (see Chapter 4), using certain theories and associated methods such as **participant observation** and, perhaps, a series of in-depth interviews or more informal conversations.

It used to annoy me when I was carrying out research for various UK government departments that, when it came to writing the report, I would be told that the section on methodology should be kept short, often not much more than a page or so, and sometimes the methodology was even removed from the main body of text to appear in the appendices. Methodology can make a crucial difference to the findings and needs to have integrity and be transparent. I find it frustrating when reading about research in the media that the genre of (particularly popular) journalism also seems to be uninterested in how the research was carried out and, for example, how the questions were asked.

The importance of methodology was brought home to me by the experiences of a colleague some years ago. She had carried out some research into attitudes to reading amongst a group of adolescent 16-year-olds and she used two different methods and methodologies. She first held a focus group of boys and asked them open questions about their reading behaviours, attitudes and practices. From this group, she concluded that the boys did not like reading very much, certainly not as much as the girls; they did not read books very often and found the Shakespeare plays they were studying for GCSE to be 'boring' and 'irrelevant' and so on. I am sure that you get the picture, which you can imagine being typically painted by many newspapers with headlines like:

TEENAGE BOYS HATE READING

TEENAGE BOYS ARE TURNED OFF BY SHAKESPEARE

However, she then decided to interview the teenagers again, but this time as individuals. Although she asked the same questions, she got very different answers: many of the boys read far more than they were prepared to admit in front of their peers, including books, and many of them actually enjoyed reading and studying Shakespeare. This is a stark reminder that the context of an interview, and how the questions that are asked, are vital. Methodology matters and as it will have a considerable effect on the findings it needs to be given deep thought and carefully justified.

3.9 THE ROLE OF THEORY AND THEORISTS

Theories come in many forms and have many purposes, and help us piece the world together. Many writers (e.g., Robson, 2011) point out that the word 'theory' in social research can mean different things to different people, and as we have seen above, some researchers see it as being inextricably linked to methodology (e.g., O'Leary, 2014; and Punch and Oancea, 2014). Thomas (2013) maintains that one of the great debates in social science is about whether theory should be the aim of the research that enables us to explain and predict particular outcomes, or whether it should be used as a device (or tool), which helps us explain something that we are researching, possibly by the generation of new theories. This will of course depend on what kind of researcher you are or want to be: namely, whether you are using a more deductive or inductive approach, and, of course, these two positions do not have to be mutually exclusive within one particular project.

Carrying out mainly inductive research, I see theories as being analytical frameworks, which act as a lens to see through, providing insights that help us explain what is going on by providing 'a link between the very specific and particular and the more abstract and general' (Plummer, 2001: 159). Punch and Oancea (2014) call these 'substantive theories': they are content-based and move the research beyond description and by abstracting ideas from the data they move towards deeper explanations about some phenomenon or issue of concern. However, theories can also range from small, informal, personal hunches, as well as being these more formal large-scale systems developed within academic disciplines and paradigms (Robson, 2011). And, of course, there are not only *theories* (e.g., human capital theories, post-structuralist theories, feminist theories, personal construct theories, etc.), but also *theorists* (e.g., Foucault, Rousseau, Piaget, Vygotsky, Bourdieu, etc.).

Some academics advocate the abandonment of all theory because they see it as having a stifling effect on practice (Robson, 2011) and they suggest using a 'pragmatic' approach of 'What Works'. There is a lot of debate in the academic community about how much a doctoral thesis needs to be underwritten by theory. I used to be of the firm opinion that one of the factors that distinguished doctoral work (D-level) from master's level (M-level) was that the former was theory-informed. However, since then, I have come across successful theses that contain very little theory. Obviously, the amount of theory a thesis contains will depend on the questions that are being addressed and, in my experience, EdD theses tend to place a little less emphasis on theory than PhD research, although there are many exceptions to this. Some doctoral work is non-empirical and purely theoretical (e.g., in philosophy), while other students are much more interested in theory than others. For instance, how do the theories of Vygotsky help us to understand how children learn? In this case, the student will know from the beginning both the theory and theorist they are going to draw on and the research questions they are gong to ask. For others, the search to find appropriate theories and theorists is an ongoing process and is often a struggle – a theme that we will pick up in Section 3.11. While some students use one or two theories and theorists, others are more like magpies and draw on many. There is no right or wrong way. In my own research, I drew on feminist theories of gender and masculinity to help explain how identities are constructed but also on theories of symbolic interactionism to help explain children's social interactions. I also had theories of identity but also theories of space and how children are disciplined and controlled. Although my principal theorist was Raewyn Connell, I also drew on a whole range of thinkers to help me explain various aspects of school life.

Depending on the area and type of research, the quality of a thesis can be raised if you can make a (usually small) contribution to the development of theory itself. Of course, this is not always possible, necessary or desirable.

In my own PhD research, I proposed a new form of masculinity, which I called 'personalised'. This was different from the accepted forms of masculinity from the 1990s such as hegemonic, dominant and subordinated. The generally accepted theories of masculinity at the time, at least in the fields of sociology and socio-cultural studies (in which I had positioned my work in), came from Connell, who proposed that were a number of different forms of masculinity that could be found in any one setting, such as a school. Rather crudely paraphrasing his highly influential work, these included hegemonic or dominant forms, which many of the boys in my schools aspired to and tried to emulate, and the accepted wisdom was that there would also be subordinate forms of masculinity that were derogated by the boys representing the hegemonic type. Again, in crude terms, in some schools the active, sporty boys represented the hegemonic form and the passive, non-sporty boys symbolised the subordinate form and may have been bullied because of their seeming lack of sporting prowess. However, I found many boys did not fit into either category: they did not wish to be sporty, could not be sporty and did not try to be sporty. They had their own interests and were largely left alone and not subordinated by the hegemonic group, and I conceptualised these as 'personalised masculinities' (see Swain, 2006).

3.10 THE PRINCIPLES OF SELECTION

I want to return to a theme that I introduced in Chapter 1 by looking at the choices that all researchers have to make. These are the 'principles of selection',[2] and they are an integral part of the research process, which run from the beginning to the end. They start with the choices you make about the area you are going to research: who, where, when, how? For example, for my own PhD, I settled on the idea of exploring boys' identities or masculinities at school. As I have written, one of the first decisions I made concerning the empirical context was to concentrate on the school, rather than including other arenas or fields of identity construction such as families, sport, the media and so on.

I then had to make the choice of which age group to focus on. I could have carried out my research with very young children or with adolescents, but there had already been some other studies involving these groups and, besides, I was a junior school teacher (7–11-year-olds), and this was the age group I knew best.

I always liked the idea of being able to have at least two groups so that I could look for similarities and differences that allowed me to compare and contrast. Of course, I did not have to limit myself to the junior school sector. I could have researched boys in schools in junior and secondary schools, or in infant (5–7-year-olds) and secondary schools (12–18-year-olds).

Once I had decided to focus on boys in junior school, I had to make more choices: should I focus on one age group or compare masculine identities between, say, 7- and 11-year-olds? My pilot study began doing just this but I soon realised that I my research would lack the in-depth investigation that I wanted and so I made the decision to concentrate on just 11-year-olds in their last year of junior/primary school before they transfer to secondary school.

The principles of selection were not finished. Should I carry out my research in just one school or many schools? Why not in 10 schools? Again, I thought that if I had a relatively large number I would be spreading myself too thinly, and on a more practical level, it would take a lot of time and effort contacting schools and getting them on board. I decided on three. Two might have been OK but I was worried what would happen if one dropped out at the last minute, perhaps because of an unannounced external inspection. So, having decided

---

2 I do not wish to claim that this phrase is my own, it is one that was used by one of my PhD supervisors, Andrew Brown: this is the same person as the A. Brown cited in the references in this book.

on three, what were the principles that I was going to use to select them? Having decided against using the school sector, or age, as a key variable I decided to choose social class. I could have chosen ethnicity or both social class and ethnicity but, using my contacts from my days as a primary school teacher, I finally selected three schools 'differentiated by the social characteristics of their intake'. See WEBLINK 2 to find out more information about the three schools, the theories I drew on, the sample and the methods employed.

WEBLINK 2

Information about schools & methods used in Jon's PhD research

There were many other decisions regarding the sample: once inside the school, which classes should I concentrate on? – one or more – and once I had decided on observation and interview as my main methods of data collection, whom should I observe and interview: where, when and again how?

All of these decisions were taking place in parallel with me working out which theoretical field to position myself in and which theories to draw on. As I have written above, I knew from an early stage that I was going to use the discipline of sociology and the associated field of cultural studies but should I draw on post-structuralist theories or theories connected to social constructionism? I will stop here but I hope that the reader is able to see how the choices and principles of selection are an ever-present feature of the research process and all the choices have to have been thought through carefully and fully justified. I remember at my viva being asked questions such as: 'Why did you choose three schools?' and 'Why did you not use ethnicity as one of your key variables in the construction of masculinity?'

3.11 THE PROCESS OF CONSTRUCTING A DESIGN AND SOME OF THE MAIN CHALLENGES INVOLVED

This final section returns to the six PhD students whom I introduced readers to in Chapter 2, and looks more closely at the process of constructing a coherent research design, within an appropriate conceptual framework, and some of the problems that they faced in the first few terms of study. As I have already written, this is far from straightforward and is often an organic process, particularly for those using an inductive approach. It goes without saying that all decisions relating to the design are carried out in conjunction between student and their supervisor(s), although, as we have seen in Chapter 2, there will be many influences on the final blueprint.

All six of the PhD students regarded their designs as being a work in progress and most were not satisfied that they were approaching a final design, or a design that they and their supervisor(s) were happy with, until well into their second year of study. Having said this, it needs to be acknowledged that all six were using inductive approaches. Some of the main challenges involved themes already discussed in earlier sections: namely, finding a sharper focus for their initial idea, formulating research questions, making decisions regarding the principles of selection, and finding a suitable theory or theories to underpin the study.

The first challenge mentioned is one we have come across already in Chapter 1: i.e., the realisation for the need to narrow the research area down, including the empirical and theoretical fields and finding a sharper focus. Rea exemplifies this point below:

I was happy before starting the [research training] classes, so before like engaging with the classes and like getting to know how research works better, I was happy, but then I realised that I wasn't because I felt it was still too broad, and when I would get feedback from people, like my course mates and professors, they would always be like yeah, but what is it that you are trying to find out? Oh, it's not clear yet. I wasn't happy with that. I struggled a lot, I remember telling my supervisors that it felt lost and didn't have a focus.

Rea also talked about matching the literature and theoretical framework and developing meaningful research questions.

Other students, like Jeanette, spoke about the principles of selection and exploring the philosophical conceptual understandings that she was going to draw on:

Jon: OK, tell me about the different challenges.

Jeanette: I think the design is just … I find it difficult at the moment because I'm at a crossroads; I am finding it kind of tricky, which way do I want to go, do I want to go into one school and do in-depth work, or do I want to go into a broad amount of schools? That's fundamentally what I've got, initially and with the research design. It's also kind of the epistemological kind of understanding and the philosophies behind that underpin research design, that was a challenge: I had to do a lot of work on that when I first started in the first kind of term, because it just felt like a minefield.

Clint, below, reveals how important these kinds of decisions regarding selections can be, and the amount of anxiety they can cause because of the pressure to get them right:

What I'm just trying to do is find the best way to start, the best place to start, in order to write the lifetime of work I want to do, but you have to set it somewhere then, and that selection is tough because it's your life, it's your life's work.

As he says later in the interview, 'It's tough. I have to commit!'

In Section 3.9, I wrote that many students worry about finding the right theory, or theories, to use and while some may settle on one or a few, other researchers will draw on many where they feel they add to the understanding and explanation of a particular area, theme and/or concept. It is important that, if you are using a number of different theories, that they form a coherent match. As Rea told me:

The hard part for me was the fact that I drew from different areas, different fields, so connecting those together was the hard part, but recently I had a discussion with my colleague, and considered like new theories that had nothing to do with my current theoretical framework, so yes, that's the hard part.

Clint also mentioned the challenge of how students need to learn to articulate their, sometimes complex, ideas in an appropriate academic language, which he termed 'the language of description'. He stressed that this was not something that could be developed overnight but came from regular reading and continual writing practice and redrafting.

Other challenges that these and other students on the CDR courses mentioned were around how to deal with abstruse concepts through readings, from courses, or during conversations. I was always conscious that after the first few sessions of the course many students had only a partial understanding of concepts such as epistemology and ontology, and this was particularly so for many international students whose English was still developing. There is so much to learn and many of us are unlikely to grasp complex ideas at the first go. I see the process as being rather like a jigsaw: at first there are several individual pieces of various sizes scattered all over the place but they gradually begin to join up and fit together once you become aware of the relationships and interconnections.

━━ BOX 3.5 ━━━

A summary of the key points

- A doctoral thesis needs to contribute new knowledge to the field.
- It is a good idea to think of the thesis as a pedagogic text.
- Research questions often begin large and end up being much smaller. They can be one of the hardest parts to get right of the research project.
- Two major and very different approaches to carrying out research are deductive and inductive. Sometimes they are referred to as fixed and flexible designs. Some research studies use both approaches, which complement each other.
- It is useful to think about positioning your work in theoretical and empirical fields.
- A sound research design is part of a coherent conceptual framework, which should provide your work with a systematic way of articulating what you are doing, or what you have done, and the reasons behind the decisions you are making or have made.
- The methodology is a valued system of principles and strategies that are used to guide the research.
- A doctoral thesis is generally underpinned by theory.
- The principles of selection are important. They run through the whole research process and need to be justified.
- The process of constructing a research design is an ongoing process that often has many challenges.

AREAS FOR DISCUSSION

- Are your research questions more descriptive or explanatory, or a mixture of both?
- What are the key characteristics that an examiner would look for in a 'good' thesis?
- What are the principles of selection that you will need to think about in your own research?

- Which theoretical and empirical domains or fields will you position your research in?
- Think about how you could approach a study of the relationship between gender (or age) and watching horror films (or buying trainer shoes). How could you learn about this relationship using an inductive approach? What would a study of the same relationship look like if examined using a deductive approach? Try the same thing with any topic of your choice.

ANNOTATED BIBLIOGRAPHY

Creswell, J. (2013) *Qualitative Inquiry and Research Design: Choosing among Five Approaches*, 3rd edn. London: Sage.

A very readable and informative text for qualitative researchers. Explore philosophical underpinnings and key characteristics of five qualitative designs including ethnography and case studies.

Crotty, M. (2009) *The Foundations of Social Research*. St Leonards, Australia: Allen & Unwin.

This book links methodology and theory and explains philosophical concepts such as epistemology and ontology. It also helps you to decide whether your chosen methodology is appropriate, and whether your methods are consistent with the theoretical perspective you take.

Dowling, P. and Brown, A. (2010) *Doing Research/Reading Research*. London: Routledge.

Both authors are, or have recently been, active researchers and experienced supervisors. Andrew Brown was one of my supervisors. The book shows how to organise, plan and implement small-scale research projects and includes guidance on how to develop research questions and situate research in theoretical and empirical fields.

Ravitch, S. and Riggan, M. (2012) *Reason & Rigor: How Conceptual Frameworks Guide Research*. London: Sage.

This book sees conceptual frameworks as organic works in progress, which are a method for aligning the literature review, research design and methodology. The authors view conceptual framework both a process and a guide, which help researchers through the process of constructing a sound design.

Williams, M. (2003) *Making Sense of Social Research*. London: Sage.

This book is aimed at undergraduates and postgraduates engaged in quantitative and qualitative research. It is particularly useful for constructing research questions and their relationship with an appropriate methodology.

FURTHER READING

Blaikie, N. (2010) *Designing Social Research*, 2nd edn. Cambridge: Polity.

In this accessible text, there is a particular emphasis on the formulation of research questions and the selection of appropriate research strategies to answer them. There are very useful sections on research proposals and major research designs, and also an expanded discussion of the relationship between theory and research.

Clark, A., Flewitt, R., Hammersley, M. and Robb, M. (2013) *Understanding Research with Children and Young People.* **London: Sage.**

This book helps you to understand how research is designed and carried out to explore questions about the lives of children and young people. It tackles the methodological, practical and ethical challenges involved, and features examples of actual research.

Denzin, N.K. and Lincoln, Y.S. (eds) (2011) *The Sage Handbook of Qualitative Research,* **4th edn. Thousand Oaks, CA: Sage.**

An essential reference for students interested in the practice of qualitative research, this book presents a collection of papers covering a wide range of approaches that cover both the theory and practice of qualitative inquiry. The book also includes sections on methods of data collection and modes of analysis.

Hammersley, M. (2002) *Educational Research, Policymaking and Practice.* **London: Paul Chapman.**

Aimed at postgraduate and doctoral students in research methodology, education, and social science disciplines, the author interrogates the demands being made on educational research against the complexities of the relationship between research and practice.

CHAPTER 4

CONSTRUCTING KNOWLEDGE THROUGH SOCIAL RESEARCH

Debates in epistemology and ontology

Will Gibson

BOX 4.1

Overview of chapter

This chapter includes introductions to:

- The concept of epistemology as it applies to social researchers.
- The relationship between debates in epistemology and the work of social researchers.
- The perspectives of positivism, logical positivism and post-positivism.
- The perspectives of constructionism and realism.
- The concept of ontology and its relevance for social research.
- The perspectives of realism, neo-realism and relativism.

4.1 INTRODUCTION

The aim of social research is, in the end, to produce some knowledge and understanding of the world. For many researchers, there is also a desire to use that knowledge to make the world better somehow; i.e., not just to create some abstract academic understanding, but to do so in a way that has impact outside of academia. Producing knowledge through research is of course not unique to academia. Journalists, for example, also engage in research, analyse social contexts and contribute to people's understandings of the world. Novelists, with their invented stories and characters, quite often base their work on detailed research into communities and forms of life. Both journalists and novelists also change the world, in some cases generating a significant readership and having an impact on societal discourse that is more far reaching than many social researchers based in academia, think tanks or other research organisations generally achieve.

From this comparison, a quite important question emerges: what is the difference between the kinds of research work undertaken by social researchers based or trained in academic circles (i.e., the kinds of people who would be likely to read this textbook) and the research work undertaken in other contexts? Are we 'academic researchers' (if you forgive the looseness of the term) just another kind of storyteller/social commentator like novelists and journalists or is there something special about what we do?

For many social researchers, the answer is likely to be a firm 'yes'. The answer has to do with taking great care with the methods through which knowledge is produced; having an awareness of the strengths and limitations of the various tools that might be used to collect data; understanding the nuances of the different kinds of research designs that may be employed; sensitivity to the role of the researcher as an interpretive being in the process of constructing knowledge, and how all of this leads to particular kinds of understandings of the world. In short, it has to do with the *craft* of research, and our sensitivity to the role we play in this craft (all of which, incidentally, is precisely the topic of this book). So, we can answer the question 'What is so special about 'academic' social research?' in very practical ways – by showing the care that we take to make our knowledge reliable and valid.

So far, so good. But notice the words I have just used: 'reliable' and 'valid'. These words do not just describe research 'practices' – they invoke ideas about the nature of knowledge itself (ideas about 'epistemology' see Box 4.2). Of course, these terms *can* be described in technical and practical ways: 'reliable' knowledge is knowledge that can be produced again and again, so that when a researcher says 'this is a reliable finding' they mean something like 'you can go and follow my methods and test my procedures and you will get the same results'. When they say that their knowledge is 'valid', they mean that it is really about the thing they claim it is about. So, if I ask someone their opinions about immigration, their answers are *really* about immigration and they are *really* their opinions, and not just any old response to keep me happy.

▬ BOX 4.2 ▬▬▬▬▬▬▬▬▬▬▬▬▬▬▬▬▬▬▬▬▬▬▬▬▬▬▬▬▬▬▬▬▬▬▬

A definition of the term 'epistemology'

'Epistemology' refers to theories about knowledge and debates regarding how and what we can know about the world. The term also describes a branch of philosophy that is concerned with these issues. In social research, epistemological questions emerge when we start asking about the nature of the knowledge produced through our investigations.

However, not all researchers agree that these are the best terms to describe what they are trying to do. Many qualitative researchers prefer terms like 'trustworthiness' or 'credibility'. To understand why we need to think about some important questions that relate to issues of epistemology – such as: why would someone want to repeat a study, and why would it matter if the answers they get were different? – you might say, 'Of course it matters. If the story changes every time, it is not much of a finding is it?' But, why not? Why insist that the only good finding is one you can repeatedly demonstrate? As *social* researchers we are dealing with people, and people have the peculiar habit of changing (their mind, their circumstances, their perspectives), so why would you expect things to be the same? Also, people are not all the same, so why would you expect research with a variety of people to produce 'regular' findings? And, anyway, can you ever really be sure that you understand people perfectly, or that they can understand you for that matter? Try as we might, in our lives we quite regularly make mistakes and misinterpretations, so why think that social researchers could ever be exempt from such things? 'Ah,' you may say, 'but surely we have to *try*. The point of social researchers is to be as rigorous as possible to avoid confusions and misunderstandings and to be as certain as we can be'. And continuing with this invented argument, I might say, 'Is it? Is that the point? Who says that social research has to be like that?' and then perhaps you make the fatal move and say, 'Well, that is what science is all about.'

'Science' is a word that describes a set of assumptions about what research ought to be like and how it ought to operate. The problem is that those assumptions have been of considerable debate, to the extent that there is a great deal of discussion as to whether or not we want to use the word 'science' in describing social research at all. Embedded in all of this are competing ideas about the kinds of knowledge that we want to produce through research. I said before that we can answer the question of 'What is so special about academic social research?' with reference to the craft of social enquiry. That is true, but then a next logical question is, 'What should that craft look like?' and this is a topic that has preoccupied researchers for the last 150 years, since the beginning of the social 'science' disciplines. The aim of this chapter is to introduce some of the key language and ideas that underpin these debates. The history of these debates is very well documented and there is nothing new in what I am about to describe. In the discussion here, I will deliberately avoid some of the nuances of these issues, as my intention is not to offer a thorough guide through this terrain (see the Annotated Bibliography for some texts that do provide this) but to provide a foundation for further reading.

Actually, as I will show at the end this chapter, there is most certainly no particular requirement that social researchers are experts in these kinds of historical and philosophical issues. However, some very general familiarity with terminology and the basic arguments is useful simply because of the frequency with which these kinds of issues are brought up in debates about research. The discussion that follows is divided into three sections: I will start by reviewing different models of knowledge production in the social 'sciences'; and then move on to think about some of the underlying assumptions about the nature of knowledge within these different models; the final conclusions will show why these debates remain relevant to practicing social researchers.

4.2 EPISTEMOLOGY AND MODELS OF KNOWLEDGE PRODUCTION IN THE NATURAL AND THE SOCIAL SCIENCES
Positivism, truth and knowing

The term 'positivism' is often the start point in the story of how social research developed as an area of practice. As we will see in the final section of this chapter, many people still argue that the principles of positivism should be the basis of how social research operates. The term 'positivism' came to prominence in the eighteenth century as a way of describing the basic principles on which scientific work should be based. A central principle of positivist philosophy was to distinguish *belief* from *knowledge*, i.e. to privilege things that we can 'positively verify' as being factually true as against those that we can't. When people refer to positivism, they tend also to mean that scientific enquiry should be directed towards establishing facts and law-like generalisations (i.e., statements that apply across different contexts and are not specific to particular contexts), and that this should be undertaken through a scientific method, which involves observing the world objectively and free from **bias**. One of the core aspects of the notion of scientific enquiry is that of **empiricism** – i.e., that we can come to understand the world by looking at it through our senses. A final tenet in most forms of positivism is the idea that such knowledge should be useful, and it should have a role in the betterment of society (see Box 4.3 for an outline of these general ideas). All of these principles have been the basis of the notion of how the hard sciences should operate pretty much since their inception.

▬ BOX 4.3 ▬▬▬▬▬▬▬▬▬▬▬▬▬▬▬▬▬▬▬▬▬▬▬▬▬▬

The key features of 'classic' positivism

The basic tenet of 'classic' positivism is usually described as involving the following features:

- The basis for understanding the world should come through our experiences of it (empiricism).
- Knowledge should be *positively* verifiable – i.e., we should be able to prove any claims to knowledge.
- We can prove or verify knowledge through the scientific method.
- The scientific method involves observing the world objectively and without bias.
- Through this method we can (and should) create generalisations about what the world is like.
- Our knowledge should be of practical value and lead to an improvement of the world.

Towards the end of the nineteenth century, when the social sciences such as sociology and psychology were emerging, these same positivistic ideas were a key part of how these new disciplines justified themselves as legitimate areas of study. Auguste Comte (1798–1857) played a key role in developing positivistic ideas. Of central importance to Comte was the idea that, as with the hard sciences, the methods of the social sciences should also be based on the scientific method and its empiricist principles. As we have seen, empiricism refers to the idea that it is through our experiences that we derive our knowledge of the world. By looking at the contents of the world (the *facts* of the world), we can build up our under-standing of it. So, empiricism is the commitment to neutrally observing objectively knowable *facts*. Through this empirical method, we can create the 'law-like generalisations' referred to above – the *regularities* that are seen to exist within the phenomena we are observing. It is this search for laws and generalisations based on experience that, for Comte, marks out truly scientific enquiry. Integral to this idea is the notion that the objects of the world (be they social or natural objects) can be understood objectively, independently of an individual's subjective interpretation of them.

For example, if a researcher wants to understand the relationship between gender and higher education achievement in a particular country, they can do so by gathering data on the success rates of men and women, looking at the numbers and percentages of female and male graduates, differences in the grades they achieve, and how those differences vary across different subjects, institutions, geographical areas, and so on. The analysis should not be a matter of a researchers' 'opinions', but observable and demonstrable in the data that is available.

At the end of the nineteenth century, Émile Durkheim (1858–1917) took forward Comte's ideas in developing the discipline of sociology; here, we see the application of these positiv-istic principles and the creation of a clear model of how society can be examined empirically. For instance, Durkheim's studies of suicide looked at the regularities of patterns of suicide across European countries, and examined the statistical relationship between these rates and other social phenomena such as forms of religious participation, or levels of marriage or unemployment rates. Through these studies, Durkheim aimed to show that social phenom-ena (or social 'facts', as he called them) could be explored and established in exactly the same way that facts were studied in the natural world. A very similar development happened at around the same time in psychology, with German psychologist William Wundt estab-lishing the first laboratories for studying the subjective experiences of people's minds and consciousness.

Positivism gave a clear model of how knowledge should work. It put the social sciences on a level pegging with the hard sciences, and showed that people were a legitimate area of study. The enthusiasm for positivist principles was part of a general modernist attitude of progress, improvement, betterment, a march to freedom and the liberation of humanity through knowledge. However, in contemporary social research communities, the 'magic' of positivism has, for many, disappeared. Hammersley notes that, 'No one today, or hardly anyone, refers to themselves or their own work as positivist. Instead, references to positivism are primarily used as a device for promoting other positions' (1995: 1). Bryant makes a very similar point when he says that, 'In the last two decades in sociology, "positivist" and "neo-positivist" have become so much pejorative terms that self-avowed positivists are hard to come by' (1985: 1). In my view, these claims are overstatements, and, as we shall see at the end of this chapter, there are still communities of scholars in sociology, psychology, social work and many other areas that are perfectly happy with the ideas of positivism. However, there are certainly many examples of researchers who entirely reject positivist principles, and if Hammersley and Bryant are right that this is a very common tendency, we might quite legitimately ask, 'Why?' What went wrong with positivism and its ideals of scientific enquiry? A part of the answer comes in how positivism itself developed as a conceptual vision of scientific work, and we will look at this in the next section.

Logical positivism and theoretical concepts

Logical positivism emerged at the beginning of the nineteenth century and offered some refinements to the general model of science embedded in 'classic' positivism. This area of philosophy, which was particularly associated with the work of Ludwig Wittgenstein, Ernst Mach and A.J. Ayer, involved a continuation of the faith in science and in the positivist model, but, at the same time, it paved the way for some critiques that would undermine many of its ideals.

One of the tenets of this 'classic' positivism that I described above was the idea that scientists can neutrally observe the facts of the world. However, logical positivism shows that in producing scientific theories there is more than mere 'observation' involved, and that scientific theories include not just 'neutrally observed phenomena', as empiricism claimed, but also non-observable theoretical ideas that can only be inferred from data, not observed within it. Theoretical concepts are the resources through which observations are turned into abstractions that are used to make generalisations. So, for example, the concept of the 'Big Bang' cannot be 'seen' – it is a theory that puts data into a form of explanation. Many parts of scientific theory cannot be observed, but can only be inferred from the things that can be observed. So, returning to Durkheim's (1897) theory, in addition to describing the different patterns of suicide across societies, he argued that we can identify different types of suicide that correspond to different social conditions. For example, 'anomic suicide' occurs when there is a lack of social cohesion, where people are unsure of how they relate to a social system, and there is a lack of solidarity or shared goals and low economic success in the society. In contrast, 'altruistic suicide' occurs in contexts where there are high levels of social cohesion, where individuals are regarded as less important than society. These concepts are not 'observable' as such: they are theoretical descriptors used to give empirical or observational data some sense and shape.

One way of thinking about logical positivism is in helping science to understand where its theoretical ideas move beyond the empiricist criteria of 'observable facts' and become abstract theoretical and non-observable concepts. There are various solutions in the works of logical positivists as to how the problem of going beyond empirical statements may be resolved – the main point to note for our purposes though is the quite simple observation that non-empirical theoretical components are in fact an integral aspect of scientific work.

Although the logical positivists where keen to defend the role of empirical enquiry and scientific research as conceived within positivism, their observation about the non-empirical content of scientific theories does open up an important issue: namely, that scientific work is actually not *just* about observing the world, and not *simply* a matter of finding 'facts' – it is also a matter of *constructing* an understanding of the things being studied and of using concepts to *interpret* data through theory. Theory is not a neutral description of *facts*, but a way of presenting them. This is a useful lead-in to a set of developments in the positivist doctrine that criticised many of the central tenets of classic positivism.

Post-positivism and the humble scientist

Karl Popper and Thomas Kuhn are two of the figures that are most commonly associated with the post-positivist critiques. In different ways, they both argued strongly that classic positivism was illusionary and that it traded on ideals of practice that scientists do not and cannot live up to. Writing in the early to mid-twentieth century, Karl Popper took particular issue with the model of theory production held by positivism. Popper (2002/1934) argued that the classic empiricist notion that 'data drives the production of knowledge' actually gets things backwards: it is not *data* that starts the process of scientific enquiry, he argued, but *questions, problems, theories,* and *ideas*.

Popper's contribution to the philosophy of science was extensive, but his most well-known and often cited critique concerns the notion of 'verification' that had been at the heart of positivism and, more substantially, the ideas of certainty and of generalised laws that underpinned the entire exercise of science. As we saw, positivism claimed to use its observations of the facts of the world as the basis for its enquiry, with the repeated observation of these facts used to make generalised claims. Popper pointed to a logical problem with this view, which is this: you can observe the same phenomena as many times as you like without actually proving it as a *fact*. His famous example was that a theory that 'all swans are white' is not *proven* by the observation of 10, 50, 1,000 or even 10,000 swans, because there always exists the possibility that a swan of a different colour does exist but just hasn't been seen yet. With this simple analogy, Popper showed that there can never be absolute certainty in science, and that the much exalted notion of 'truth' in science is really a myth. At best, science can make statements along the lines of: 'as far as we know …' or 'according to what we have seen so far …' but never 'it is a fact that …' or even 'it has been proved that …'

In place of this model of 'verifying' the word by looking at it, Popper suggested that a better model of how science operates involves 'falsifying' (or disproving) theories rather than proving them. So, instead of trying to prove a theory by looking for cases that support it, scientists should search for cases that contradict their claims. For Popper, a proper scientific theory is one that can't be rejected, rather than one that can be 'proved' with reference to data. As Crotty playfully puts it, in Popper's schema, 'An advance in science is not a matter of scientists making a discovery and then proving it to be right. It is a matter of scientists making a guess and then finding themselves unable to prove the guess wrong, despite strenuous efforts to do so' (1998: 31). This is close to the mantra of the post-positivist that Popper was so instrumental in developing. In this 'post-positivist' movement, there remains a faith in science as an activity of knowledge production, but the model of how science works was wholly reworked to encompass this new vision of partial, even humble knowledge. Very importantly, in Popper's view, it is not *data* that drives the production of knowledge, but theoretical ideas or questions in the form of hypotheses.

Thomas Kuhn (1962) was another philosopher of science working in a similar period to Popper and he offered some further critiques of positivism, this time focusing on two different but central components of classic positivism: those of 'objectivity' and of 'progress'. The idea that science should work in a way that is 'free from bias' and that is entirely distinct to 'mere opinion' is perhaps the most important tenet of positivism, but Kuhn showed that the matter of bias is by no means straightforward. In positivist research, to be biased means to be prejudiced towards a particular worldview rather than allowing the data to 'speak for itself' in the production of accurate objective knowledge. Kuhn agreed with Popper that science doesn't work like this, and that the basis for scientific enquiry is theory. However, Kuhn argued that Popper's idea that scientists try to reject their theories through research was also wrong. Actually, most of the time, Kuhn argued, scientists don't try to reject their theories because doing so would leave them with nothing to work with. Instead, the theories are the basis for all their work and are the resources through which problems are raised and research questions are posed. In what Kuhn called periods of 'normal science', a research community generally agrees on a set of theories and uses them to frame every aspect of their work. Far from trying to reject them, they are the very material of the science at that time. To put the matter in rather alarmist terms, science is *necessarily* 'biased' because it *needs* a particular perspective in order to work.

As if that wasn't problematic enough, Kuhn also showed that the development of knowledge in science is not a matter of 'progressing' by accumulating evidence; rather, new ideas develop because the old ones do not work anymore; because some set of problems became insurmountable within the current framework; because there is sufficient disagreement in a community to mean that some new theory is needed. In short, *change* in scientific perspective or theory (or 'paradigm', to use Kuhn's word), is the result not of the progressive accumulation of evidence, but of the failures of existing theory. The new theories create an entirely different (and often an *incommensurate*) view of the world that is an alternative to the previous vision, but it is hard to say that the new theories are necessarily *better*. The reason that we can't make this judgement of whether one theory is 'better' or 'worse' than another is because the very criteria for making a judgement belongs to the theory, and two different theories make two different sets of judgements. It is analogous to the difference in perspective between two different religions: in the end, it comes down to a matter of faith and perspective. I will come back to this point in more detail below.

While all of this might sound inescapably damming, Kuhn did not intend his criticisms to undermine science or to argue against its importance. His point was not that science *doesn't* progress – after all, can we really say that we do not live in a more scientifically advanced society than we did 100, 50, 20, even 10 years ago? Rather, his argument was that science does not progress in the way that positivists had claimed it does.

So far, we have seen how the model of science has changed through the critiques that logical and **post-positivism** offer to 'classic' positivism. Further descriptions of the ideas of positivism and post-positivism can be seen on an online methods course run by William Trochim at Cornell University (see WEBLINK 1) but what does all of this mean for the social 'sciences'? Neither Popper nor Kuhn were particularly interested in the social sciences and their commentaries were directed largely to the natural science subjects. However, the critique of the ideas of science of course has implications for any subject discipline orientating to it as a model. As the model changed, so did the ideal of its appropriateness for social studies. One of the strongest alternative visions for what social research ought to look like came through a set of theoretical debates in the social sciences. In the final part of this first section I will turn to look at these debates.

WEBLINK 1

Positivism &
post-positivism
descriptions
from Cornell
University

Constructionism, interpretivism and the turn to 'meaning'

The terms 'constructionism' and 'interpretivism' are in some ways more difficult to define that positivism because they do not refer to a particular philosophical position but to a set of implications from quite diverse disciplinary areas including sociology, anthropology, philosophy and psychology. Further, in the methodological literature, you can see quite varied articulations of the terms. Crotty (1998), for example, makes a firm distinction between constructionism and interpretivism, characterising the first with a particular set of epistemological ideas (see Figure 4.2) and the latter with more specific theoretical accounts in sociology and the like. Other authors are less clear on this and sometimes treat the terms almost interchangeably.

As a working definition we can think of constructionism (or sometimes 'constructivisim' – these terms are often used interchangeably, although the latter actually does have a more specific meaning, so I prefer the former term) as the idea that people *construct* their understandings of the world rather than encountering those meanings passively, as 'classic' positivist theory had suggested. In this alternative view, the things of the world do not have inherent meaning: instead, the meaning is constructed through culture and language. See WEBLINK 2 for a podcast that explores ideas of social construction with the philosopher Jesse Prinz. 'Interpretivism' (or 'intepretism') describes a range of theoretical perspectives that are interested in the processes of human interpretation and how people make and give sense to their experiences. Just from these definitions we can immediately see why the terms can be hard to keep distinctly from each other, as, clearly, in any process of constructing meaning there is a process of interpretation and vice versa.

WEBLINK 2

Social
construction
podcast with
Jesse Prinz

For the purpose of this discussion, it is not necessary to maintain a particularly firm distinction between the two: the important point is to notice the particular conceptual implications of these ideas, the main tenets of which can be described as shown in Box 4.4.

BOX 4.4

Central tenets of interpretivist/constructionist theory

The basic points about interpretivist/constructionist theory can be summarised with the following ideas:

1 Language and culture are the perspectives through which all meaning is situated.
2 People interpret the world through the perspectives of their own lives, languages, cultures as well as their own biographies ...
3 ... and they produce/negotiate meaning with other people in particular social contexts of activity.

Therefore:

4 Meaning is not static but changing, multiplicitous, and dependent on context.
5 Facts are not independent of our perspectives on the world, but are always interpreted through our own frames of reference.
6 Social researchers need to try to understand culture from the insider's point of view, not from the point of view of their own culture.

An important point to note straight away is that nearly all of the ideas shown in Box 4.4 are readily conceded by post-positivists: so, points 1, 2, 4 and 5 are certainly readable in the Popperian and Kuhnian critique of naive empiricism and the idea that knowledge is constructed through the passive observation of data. The main significant points of departure between interpretivism/constructionism and post-positivism are perhaps found most clearly in the implications of point 3.

The emphasis on the contextual nature of meaning has significant implications for the methodological frameworks used to study social phenomena. If meaning is contextual (to biography, to specific setting, to language, to culture) then we need to use methods that enable us to understand in detail the working of those 'contexts'. That is, we need to be able to gain knowledge of people's biographies; the 'local practices' of particular contexts; the ways that language works (both globally as a linguistic system and locally in terms of specific linguistic communities) in constructing people's experiences and understandings; and the cultural norms and rules that frame all of the above. The aim for many social researchers is to get as close to the meaning of the people being researching as possible and to understand the 'insider's' point of view. In ethnography, for example, the complexity of cultural meaning in any research setting means that a researcher needs to gain significant expertise in and knowledge of a culture before they can hope to achieve anything close to an insider's view of it. This involves significant periods of fieldwork where the researcher immerses themselves in the practices and activities of those being researched. However, in ethnography and the various qualitative methods that it can involve (like interviews, participant observation, or document analysis), researchers do not typically assume that meaning 'exists' as a set of social facts, or that the researcher can unproblematically step out of their role to understand the lives of those being researched. Rather, the interest is typically on the mutual construction of knowledge and in gaining a deep **reflexive** awareness of how the researcher contributes to the knowledge being produced. It is through these types of ideas and their articulation in various theoretical perspectives that we see a radical departure from post-positivist ideas. Figure 4.1 gives a very partial conceptual map of some of the perspectives that can be thought of as broadly 'constructionist' in their outlook.

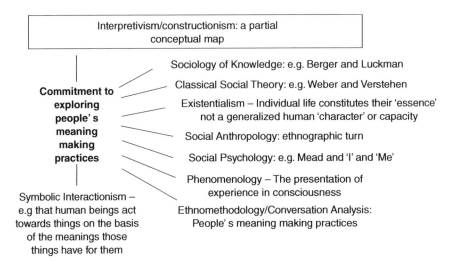

Figure 4.1 A partial map of interpretivist theoretical positions

Within interpretivist/constructionist views, knowledge itself is a construct, an interpretation and a methodological creation. This implies a wholesale change in the language, or vocabulary, for thinking about research: not 'research subjects' but 'research *participants*'; not 'data collection' but 'data *construction/generation*'; not 'research instruments' but 'research *processes*'. It also entails the use of research methods that can help realise the goals of gaining nuanced understandings of complex social processes: from an interpretivist point of view, to understand the world is to be *in* it, and any methodology that fails to recognise that researchers do not 'collect' meanings but *produce* them is naïve and ineffective. A good methodology for *social* researchers is one that facilitates reflection on the construction of meaning. The scientific method, even in its post-positivist articulation is not equipped to do that because it still insists on the creation of generalised knowledge and on causal explanation, both of which are anathema to these aims.

To return to the point I raised at the beginning of this chapter, we can describe the *craft* of social research in terms of methods and techniques for dealing with data. But, to do so is to orientate to a lot of taken-for-granted assumptions about *why* you might use one method over another; why an ethnographic researcher might reject the use of a predefined questionnaire as against a semi-structured interview; why a researcher might regard a sample of ten interviewees as opposed to 100 an appropriate strategy for their research. These assumptions involve going beyond the methods themselves require us to think about the epistemological underpinnings of social life.

In the next section of this chapter, I will introduce another set of terminology that cross-cuts the positivism–constructionism/interpretivism debate, and which relates to a set of issues about what is *in* the world (ontology), rather than simply how we come to know about the world (epistemology).

4.3 THE ONTOLOGY OF THE SOCIAL WORLD

▬▬ BOX 4.5 ▬▬▬▬▬▬▬▬▬▬▬▬▬▬▬▬▬▬▬▬▬▬▬▬▬▬▬

A definition of the term 'ontology'

'Ontology' refers to a set of philosophical debates related to discussing the nature of being and the contents of the world. In the social sciences, classic ontological debates concern the nature of 'being' or of 'existence', such as what the difference is between 'human' and 'animal' or between humans and machines, the physical architecture of people such as the existence of 'minds' or, in Chinese and other alternative medicine, the existence of energy like Chi.

Relativism and the difficulties of knowing 'the world'

One of the core debates in the methodology of the social sciences relates to conceptions of the structures of social reality and the implications of these structures for social researchers. As we saw, in classic positivist philosophy there is an empiricist assumption that we can understand the world by looking at it. Implicit in this idea is the notion that we humans have a direct and unmediated access to the world. We can see the 'facts' of life, be they the physical facts of the natural world, or the social facts that Durkheim was interested in examining. These facts impress themselves upon us and, through the empirical methods of science, we can analyse them. As we also saw, interpretivism and constructionism involve a rejection of these empiricist notions.

However, this raises an important set of questions. Are we to say that there is no 'reality' and that everything is 'just a matter of perspective'? That social life (and indeed science) is just *constructions* and, therefore, that science is no more useful or important than any other view of the world? As we have seen, within science there are many different positions and theories and each gives a different perspective on the world. In Kuhn's view, these theories cannot be evaluated against each other in objective terms because the very categories of evaluation belong to the theories themselves. The relativist debate involves thinking about how to address the types of questions I raised at the beginning of this paragraph.

A useful way to approach these ideas is through a famous and lively historical debate between two anthropologists, Edward Evans-Pritchard (whom we will come across again in Chapter 8 on ethnography, by Rebecca O'Connell) and Peter Winch. The debate concerned the analysis of practices of witchcraft in the Zande tribes of North-West Africa. Both Winch and Evans-Pritchard had undertaken fieldwork with this group, attempting to explain the structures of belief within Zande culture. However, Winch took Evans-Pritchard to task for trying not only to describe the belief systems but also to actually evaluate them. Winch offers the following as a parody of Evans-Pritchard's general position:

> We know that Zande beliefs in the influence of witchcraft ... are mistaken. Scientific methods of investigation have shown conclusively that there are no relations of cause and effect such as are implied by those beliefs and practices. All we can do then is to show how such a system of mistaken beliefs and inefficacious practices can maintain itself in the face of objections that seem to us so obvious. (1964: 307)

The problem that Winch sees with this idea is that, for Evans-Pritchard, the proper (and only) check for rationality is in reference to an external reality. Nevertheless, Winch suggests that while this idea of 'checking' against reality is not exclusive to science, it is one that is particularly strongly emphasised in it (as we saw in our discussion of empiricism). Winch argues, however, that we can only interpret a system of beliefs in relation to a particular people's own 'way of life', and that it is sufficient to note simply that the Zande have a different conception of reality: a conception that is constituted in their language and belief system, just as the scientific notion of reality is contained within its own belief and language system. To try to use a system of rationality to judge the other is to make a mistake, as it implies that it is possible to find a conceptual scheme outside of a worldview to evaluate two different frameworks. As far as Winch is concerned, it is not.

This example is a particularly useful one as many people might well want to agree with Evans-Pritchard that science is more rational than a belief system that involves making important life choices on the basis of witchcraft and oracle consultations. Winch's point is that any criteria you have for making that kind of evaluation (the morbidity and mortality rates in society; the levels of technological advancement/literacy/civic infrastructure, or whatever) are *all* relative to and situated within a particular form of life. There is no standpoint outside of a form of life from which an evaluation can be made of two systems. More importantly, the 'rationality' of one system is not defined by whether or not it accords with a different system, but can only be defined by its own concepts and frameworks.

Let's now return to the idea of 'relativism'. Winch's position can be thought of as a form of 'descriptive relativism' – i.e., one that holds that there are different ways of understanding the world, or different **epistemes**, to use a more formal word, that are relative to particular forms of life. In this form of relativism, there is also a view that people operate within frameworks of meaning: so, the Zande operate within a cultural framework, just as 'we' scientifically ('bewitched') Westerners do. One of the areas where this form of relativism has found some of its most controversial expression is in studies of language. One of the most famous examples of what is known as 'linguistic relativism' comes from linguist Benjamin Whorf. Following a number of in-depth studies of various Native American languages, Whorf (1956) argued that the language people speak shapes the way that they think about the world. One of his famous examples was of the Hopi Indians, whose language, he argued, does not have the same ways of describing past, present and future as most Latin languages do for example, and, therefore, he argued, the Hopi do not think about time in the same way. The language *conditions* the ways they see and think about the world.

There are numerous controversial aspects to Whorf's claims: while there may be a general link between language and thought in the sense that our concepts enable us to visualise the world, the claim that we are somehow imprisoned by language, unable to step outside of it to see the world differently has been strongly criticised (see McWhorter, 2014). It is on this point that we see the dividing line between the radical Whorfian idea of linguistic relativism, and Winch's cultural relativism. For Winch, the point is not so much about what is 'thinkable', but about the structure within which thinking occurs. So, for Winch, the Zande are perfectly capable of seeing the logic of science, they just don't because it is not in their cultural framework. For Whorf, in contrast, Hopi *cannot* see time in the same way through their language – for them to be able to do so would require a modification of their language. Winch, on the other hand, would view the possibility of translating one cultural framework into another as perfectly plausible.

Neither Winch nor Whorf go as far as to say that we can't understand other cultures, as both of them think we can: for Whorf, understanding a different world would involve learning a new language; for Winch it would entail an adequate ethnographic description of the cultural practices. The main questions that their work raises are: (a) how easily can people step outside of their own systems of understanding to see from different perspectives; and (b) can we comparatively evaluate different systems and from what position would we do so?

However, more extreme forms of relativism can be found in in postmodernist social theory. **Postmodernism**, which began as an influential movement in social theory in the second half of the twentieth century, is usefully thought of as a rejection of the 'certainties' offered by science or any fixed interpretation of the world. If, as we have seen, truth is relative to perspective, then rather than trying to 'fix' meaning into particular perspectives, we (researchers) should embrace ambiguity and difference, and we should accept the fact that meaning is always contingent on context, and that it is changing, ambiguous and negotiable. Meaning is dependent on language and culture, and therefore there is no objective world, no 'real', no 'true', no 'false' – there is just language. The implications of all of this, for postmodernism, is that the role of research and theory should not be to try to 'establish' meaning, but, in a sense, to *destabilise* it – to show all its contradictions and mess. Anything else is, essentially, disingenuous as it implies a stability where there is none. Jacques Derrida's approach to deconstruction is a good example of this tendency towards destabilisation. Derrida (1978) argues that language creates meaning, and that our role as researchers should be to show the limits of that meaning, to show the ambiguities in it. All language, all written or spoken text can be analysed and deconstructed in this way, including Derrida's own work of course.

Realism and the return to 'reality'

For many researchers the implications of radical relativism go against the aims of social research. If we accept the postmodernist view that we can't know anything for certain, that there is no world of shared experience, no truth or reality, just the construction of language, then the aims of trying to understand different communities and social conditions becomes impossible. It is for this kind of reason that many researchers wholly reject such a radical perspective and wish to return to a notion of an independent reality that is 'knowable' by us (i.e., **realism**). A particularly prominent example of realism in the social sciences is that of critical realism, which aims to tread a line between the ideas of empiricism (where the objective character of the world is available for study, but where the social character of knowledge is not recognised), and extreme relativism (where the social character knowledge is recognised but where a conception of the objective character of the objects in the world are lost; see Benton and Craib, 2001, for more discussion on this distinction).

BOX 4.6

A definition of the term 'realism'

'Realism' refers to the idea that the things of the world exist independently of our understanding of them. Both in the social and the hard sciences, realism is used to identify as objectively real the objects under scientific study, and to separate this reality out from any theoretical ideas used to describe them.

Realism refers to a general commitment to the idea of an independent 'world out there'. For natural scientists, a 'world out there' refers to the phenomena described through physics, biology, chemistry, and so on that constitute the world we live in and the organisms we are. Post-positivism represents a recognition that we only understand this physical world through concepts and theories, but that, nonetheless, these things are real and actual, and not inventions of language, even if our understandings of them are constituted in language. In the social sciences, the idea is similar: sociological terms like social class, gender, ethnicity, or psychological descriptions of addiction, memory, or 'disease' states like Alzheimer's or depression are linguistic and cultural forms, but they are also *real*. Class *is* related to one's possibilities of educational attainment; depression *is* a real phenomenon that does impact on peoples' sense of selves and quality of life.

The commitment to the exploration of this objective world is nicely illustrated in the following quote:

> an account is valid or true if it represents accurately those features of the phenomena that it is intended to describe, explain or theorise ... I recognise that we can never know with certainty whether (or the extent to which) an account is true; for the obvious reason that we have no independent, immediate and utterly reliable access to reality. Given that this is the situation, we must judge the validity of claims on the basis of the adequacy of the evidence offered in support of them. (Hammersley, 1992: 69)

The general idea is that just because language is partial and perspectival, we do not have to decide that gaining knowledge of people's social realities is impossible – instead, we should return to the spirit of empiricism and use evidence (as gained through careful methodological processes) to judge the 'fitness for purpose' of our claims. There is something very pragmatic about this argument, as the idea is essentially that we should not get too muddled by the theoretical ideas we have been discussing, and should not lose sight of our aims as researchers (i.e., to understand and, often, to *improve* the world). Rather, we should be as careful as possible to be systematic and methodologically rigorous in our research. In other words, our preoccupation should not be with abstract epistemology or ontology, but with *methodology*. That is why, as I stated, many people that the sorts of debates being discussed in this chapter are irrelevant to social scientists – because our role is to think about methodology (the topic of most chapters in this text) rather than philosophy.

In its general shape, this view has much in common with post-positivist ideas and the commitment to gaining knowledge and understanding through research. The ideas of critical realism (which began in the early 1970s) refer to a very specific set of perspectives that agree with this general idea, but which form quite detailed and varied theoretical ideas about the character of knowledge and its relation to the processes of scientific activity. As this chapter is merely an introduction to these ideas, I will not discuss them here (but see the Annotated Bibliography for some suggestions on further reading in this area).

By way of concluding this section, it might be useful to think about the relationship between epistemology and the ontological positions that I have been introducing. Figure 4.2 gives an indication of some basic linkages between 'classic' positivism and realism, and between interpretivism/constructionism and relativism. For example, it suggests that we might draw a link between 'classic' positivism and realism, or between constructionist/interpretivist ideas and relativism. As we have seen, though, just because a person adopts an interpretivist stance does not necessarily mean that they will adopt a relativistic position, too. As you explore these positions in more detail, it is interesting

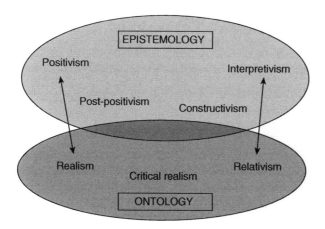

Figure 4.2 Linking epistemology and ontology

to reflect on how you may link up different positions with one another, on the ontological implications of particular epistemic views and vice versa.

4.4 EPISTEMOLOGY, ONTOLOGY AND CONTEMPORARY SOCIAL RESEARCH

At the beginning of this chapter, I argued that the questions, 'What is the difference between social research and other areas of knowledge production?' could be answered with reference to the practices of social research, and with no need to resort to the more abstract ideas that most of the discussion here has dealt with. It is most certainly the case that researchers engaged in empirical enquiry don't typically need to discuss epistemology when engaged in research. As Dowling and Brown put it:

> it is no more necessary to resolve your epistemology or ontology in your empirical research than it is to incorporate a declaration of your religious affiliation, though some would consider one or more of these essential. Unfortunately, however, the tendency to make a pass at metatheoretical discussion is commonly presented in lieu of adequate theoretical development. (2010: 143)

The point being made here is that to analyse a particular research problem and to produce findings in research does not require you to resolve an epistemological stance. However, while this is indeed the case, issues of epistemology and ontology are common areas of discussion in social research. This tends to occur when people ask the kinds of questions that I raised earlier on: 'What is research for?' 'What is the aim of research?' 'What is the difference between the knowledge produced in *this* kind of research and *that* kind of research?'

As a means of concluding this chapter, I would like to give a small concrete illustration of how these kinds of issues can occur in discussions about social research. The 'evidence-based practice' movement in the UK is a good example of how these kinds of discussions come to be invoked. The basic idea comes from an argument that professional practice (in health-care, education, social work, for example) should be based on evidence of the effectiveness of that practice. Instead of doing 'any old thing', professionals should orientate towards what we *know* is effective. The movement to evidence-based practice created heated debate in a number of disciplinary areas, but for simplicity's sake I will focus on the context of education.

David Hargreaves (1997) argued forcibly that if educational research was to be effective, it must adopt a model of enquiry that could contribute properly to the formation of clear 'evidence-based' standards and procedures. Essentially, this evidence would show the causal relationship between two phenomena and, as such, he privileged methods such as experiments (particularly randomised controlled trials) and systematic reviews that could produce such causal findings. Other commentators, such as Tooley and Darby (1998), also openly criticised qualitative enquiry for its failure to lead to changes in, as they put it, the 'quality' of educational practice. These positions are clear examples of positivistic notions of research because: (a) they preference methods of enquiry for the study of social phenomena that are derived from the hard sciences (notably, experiments and systematic reviews of literature); and (b) they aim to build generalisations across social contexts in the form of recognised patterns of cause and effect.

In his strong rejoinder to Hargreaves' position, Hammersley (2000) pointed to the epistemological assumptions underlying Hargreaves argument, particularly what Hammersley regarded as the failure to recognise the distinctive forms of knowledge that qualitative research produces. Hammersley took to task the idea that knowledge could be used in the kinds of instrumental ways that the evidence-based practice movement wanted (i.e., in determining the causal relations between phenomena). His critique pointed to exactly the kinds of issues that we have been discussing here, particularly the difficult of generating universal social laws that are adequate to explain people's lived contexts. This critical point raises complex questions about the nature of 'scientific' procedures in social research, the role of interpretation in the production of knowledge, and the nature of 'certainty' in the creation of findings. Elliot (2001) suggests that, in the light of these critiques, Hargreaves subsequently softened his approach somewhat, although he still maintained a preference for generalised findings and conclusions and did not depart radically from the general positivist positions outlined above.

4.5 CONCLUSION

In this chapter, I tried to show that the kinds of methodological decisions that researchers make have behind them a complex history of ideas relating to *how* we can know the world and *what* is knowable within it. These ideas are not the things that we typically use to design research projects, but they are, nonetheless, implicit in almost everything we do as researchers. Dealing with epistemology is, indeed, a different kind of activity to 'doing research', but the debates that they relate to are almost inescapable. They are, I hope you will agree, also extremely interesting, and reading the great works of authors such as Popper, Kuhn, Winch and company is, I have found, an inspirational way to immerse yourself in these ideas. It is my strong hope that you may pick up some of the works that I list below and find something of value within them for yourself.

▬ BOX 4.7 ▬▬▬▬▬▬▬▬▬▬▬▬▬▬▬▬▬▬▬▬▬▬▬▬▬▬▬▬▬▬

A summary of the key points

- Epistemology and ontology are areas of debate that social researchers frequently encounter.
- These debates are hard to escape entirely and it is useful to have a sense of the general arguments.

(Continued)

(Continued)

- The debates are still very much live issues in the social 'sciences', and they are likely to remain so; there is no universally agreed upon solution to the problems these issues raise.
- While researchers do, I think, need to have a good awareness of these ideas, the problems raised by the debates should not get in the way of producing knowledge through research.

AREAS FOR DISCUSSION

- Why was there a reaction again positivism in the social sciences?
- Should social researchers call themselves 'social scientists'?
- If researchers adopt an interpretivist position, should they continue to use terms like 'objective', 'reliable' and 'valid' to describe their research?
- It is ever possible to entirely understand the lives of people from cultures other than our own?
- Is there any point in carrying out research if we cannot be objective and we are just left with subjective views and opinions?
- Are one researcher's interpretation as good as another's?

ANNOTATED BIBLIOGRAPHY

Benton, T. and Craib, I. (2001) *Philosophy of Social Science: The Philosophical Foundations of Social Thought*. Basingstoke: Palgrave.

This book offers a thorough overview of theoretical positions and ideas in the social sciences, which makes the case for the importance of 'philosophical' thinking in social research. The authors cover all of the points that I have raised here, and in much more detail.

Crotty, M. (1998/2013) *The Foundations of Social Research*. London: Sage.

This text is very popular with graduate students wanting an introduction to social theory, and with good reason. It gives a clear overview of a wide range of important but complex theoretical ideas.

Kuhn, T.S. (1962) *The Structure of Scientific Revolutions*. Chicago, IL: University of Chicago Press.

Kuhn's work is a classic and very readable thesis on the nature of scientific knowledge. Anyone with an interest in the study of models of scientific activity really should read this at some point.

McWhorter, J.H. (2014) *The Language Hoax: Why the World Looks the Same in any Language*. New York: Oxford University Press.

This text deals with the very specific issue of relativism and language. Its accessible language make it a useful starting point for exploring some of these fascinating debates.

Popper, K. (2002/1934) *The Logic of Scientific Discovery*, 2nd edn. London: Routledge.

The depth of Popper's analysis makes his work challenging, but the carefulness of his thought and writing are invaluable in thinking through post-positivist ideas.

Winch, P. (1958) *The Idea of a Social Science and its Relation to Philosophy*. London: Routledge.

This is Winch's classic thesis on the relationship between how we understand the world and our forms of life (a much more elaborate and detailed version of the text I quoted in this chapter). This, too, is a complex text in some ways, but the nature of the prose as well as the arguments themselves are interesting, indeed, invaluable.

FURTHER READING

Bhaskar, R. (1998) 'Philosophy and scientific realism', in M. Archer and R. Bhaskar (eds), *Critical Realism: Essential Readings*. London: Routledge.

Popper, K. (2002/1934) *The Logic of Scientific Discovery*, 2nd edn. London: Routledge.

Searle, J. (1995) *The Construction of Social Reality*. London: Penguin.

CHAPTER 5

ETHICAL ISSUES AND CONSIDERATIONS

Jon Swain

▬▬ BOX 5.1 ▬▬▬▬▬▬▬▬▬▬▬▬▬▬▬▬▬▬▬▬▬▬▬▬▬▬▬▬▬▬

Overview of chapter

This chapter includes information on:

- Writing an ethical review.
- The role of Research Ethics Committees.
- Ethical guides/frameworks.
- Key ethical principles.
- Research using the Internet.

5.1 INTRODUCTION

The chapter provides a contribution to discussions on the ethics involved in social and educational research. Each of the four main research designs, or approaches, in this book have different sets of ethical principles and priorities but, in general, qualitative researchers face more challenging issues that those using more quantitative approaches (which are characteristic of positivist epistemologies), and some of these are concerned with the ability to respond to contingent events within localised contexts. Therefore, ethical issues are more likely to occur and arise in ethnographic or case study research, which have flexible, fluent, designs than in experimental designs or surveys.

The term 'ethics' usually refers to the moral principles or rules of conduct, which are held by a group or profession that guide the conduct of the research, whether it be sociologists, psychologists, medical doctors or others. Ethical issues are not always clear-cut but are often complex and sometimes a researcher needs to balance a whole range of conflicting issues. Decisions about ethical matters will also involve the researcher's own worldview, in other words their ontology, epistemology, values, and so on, as well as their disciplinary assumptions and methodological position.

Over the last decade or so, there has been an ever-increasing interest in, and attention paid to, the ethics of educational and social science research, and the responsibilities that researchers have to their participants, fellow members of the research community, and to the institution where they work in and/or study have been made increasingly clear. This follows a number of controversial ethical cases in social research and in medicine, and more details of these appear in a number of textbooks (e.g., Robson, 2011; Thomas, 2013; and on WEBLINK 1). A number of key principles have evolved that have become expectations of what constitutes professional, ethical, behaviour and practice and these are discussed further in Section 5.5.

WEBLINK 1

Controversial
cases in ethics

There has been a general move away from the authority and status of the researcher, and where previously they were seen more as an expert who was able to make judgements, and sometimes in-the-moment decisions as they emerged in the field, some researchers have voiced concerns that ethical issues have moved toward becoming a predefined, fixed set of principles that can be regulated and assessed by fellow professionals working in their particular field. Thus, the focus of research ethics has gradually but inexorably become sanitised as it has moved away from the individual knowledge and expertise of the researcher towards the authority of the institution.

Many researchers think this has led to a greater stability in research ethics, and have welcomed the fact that they can turn to a set of generalisable principles, aspirations and aims that can be used to unite their fellow researchers within a professional, academic, community. As educational and social research involves people, there is a potential for them to suffer anxiety, stress and even physical harm, and, as Robson (2011) points out, few people would seriously argue that these judgements and decisions should be left solely to the discretion of the researcher – and, yet, until around the 1980s, this was the norm. Few researches are trained in law or have access to free legal advice and there is always the fear of litigation if a participant considers her/himself to have been harmed or perhaps libelled. So, following a code of practice provides at least some kind of safeguard both for the individual researcher and their institution.

However, there are others who regard the increasing bureaucratisation of research in the social sciences as having a more negative effect on the field. They see debates being 'closed down' and reduced to discussions around a series of, what are becoming, familiar themes (e.g., **covert** research, anonymity, past ethical indiscretions) or 'a priori methodological certainties' (Markham and Baym, 2009: 9), with researchers ticking off a list of key ethical principles or expectations that they are going to cover. Some seem to know what constitutes sound or good ethical behaviour and practice even before the fieldwork commences, and this has the danger of reducing debates about more contemporary and everyday issues.

There are other commentators, and this includes myself, who recognise the need for a balance between instruction and general guidance. While counselling about a system that is so loose that it becomes a free-for-all, May warns that too rigid a set of ethical rules might result in researchers concluding that the 'only safe way to avoid violating principles of professional ethics is to refrain from doing research altogether' (2001: 61), and so research activity will be stifled and reduced.

One question is about the researchers' **agency** (their capacity, or competence, to understand, to make choices and act). How far should researchers remain agents of their practice when it comes to research ethics, as they are in decisions about methodological and practical issues regarding research design, choice of questions, research context, and so on?

How the world has changed: my own PhD

I generally welcome the growing recognition from institutions and individuals of the importance of ethical issues. In 1999, when I began the fieldwork for my own PhD research, which took place in three primary schools, the situation was much more lax than it is today. I gained access to the schools through professional contacts I had made as a teacher and the head teachers were regarded as acting in *loco parentis*. No letters were sent to parents about interviewing children and, although most were conducted in pairs, on occasions I was left alone with a child for up to an hour. Because I was a teacher, it seemed to afford me a degree of trust but no one mentioned anything about the need to have a document from the Criminal Record Bureau (CRB)[1] as it did not come into existence until 2002 . How the world has changed in 15 years!

In one of the schools, I also interviewed children during curriculum time and, although I felt this could be justified, not least because it developed their speaking and listening skills, I would not usually be permitted to do this today. Finding the time to conduct in-depth interviews with children can now be difficult, as there is generally not enough time during breaks and lunchtimes to conduct the interview in one go. After school is also more problematic and so interviews may have to be conducted over more than one session, which can break the flow of the conservation and mean that additional time might be needed to build up trust and a conducive atmosphere.

5.2 WRITING AN ETHICAL REVIEW[2]

As in every institution, all students (and professional researchers) at UCL/IOE require ethical approval before entering the field of research. There are some students whom I have come across who see getting ethical approval as a rather tiresome bureaucratic exercise to be overcome before they begin their study, and they can regard ethical approval as a 'bolt-on' to the writing, or as part of a list to be ticked off and 'put away' and forgotten about. However,

---

1 In 2012, the CRB was replaced by the DBS (Disclosure and Barring Service (DBS)). These organisations searched to see if a researcher has a criminal record.
2 This phrase may be called something different in other countries. For example, in Australia, it is called an 'ethics approval application' or 'ethics clearance application'.

ethical issues should be regarded as an integral and reflexive, where the researcher reflects on the research (including their interpretations), and is aware of the effect of their presence on the setting and process from beginning to end.

Dowling and Brown argue that writing the 'review of a research project in ethical terms' (2010: 36) is a research activity in itself (2010), and Brooks et al. argue that 'poorly designed research is by definition unethical since it is likely to waste participants' time' (2014: 60). Ethical concerns should be at the forefront of any research project including the design, but they will also frequently surface throughout the fieldwork and analysis, data curation and storage, and should continue through to the dissemination stages, publication and beyond, such as data disposal. Indeed, ethical issues often begin to arise at the very start of any project when you are selecting a topic to research and will depend on the kind of researcher you want to be (e.g., whether you like meeting and talking to people, or whether you prefer working in front of a computer) and the design you are going to use. For instance, your research will bound to involve more ethical issues if it involves you interviewing young children, or if you are researching your own community, or perhaps a particularly vulnerable group such as people with disabilities, than if you are carrying out secondary research. Whiteman (2012) argues that the ethical position that the researcher comes to adopt will come from their engagement with theories and be informed by the debates around the particular ethical issues likely to be found in their own field(s) of research through their interrogation of the literature, as well as the contingencies of the local empirical context.

Ethical concerns are particularly similar to the methodology in that they not only need to be regarded as being an integral part of the whole research process but, just like your methodology and other principles of selection (e.g., how you draw the sample), you will need to make, and then be able to defend, the various ethical decisions from an informed position in articles that you may write, at conferences, and of course, at your viva.

In many institutions, students who wish to collect data from human participants have to undertake a full ethics approval application. At UCL/IOE, students carrying out empirical research have to complete a relatively short ethical document, which has a number of helpful headings, and covers the key ethical principles (see Section 5.5). See WEBLINK 2 to view students' ethics forms for research applications. Depending on the area and methodology adopted, students may take two or three iterations before their supervisor is satisfied. The form is then cleared by your supervisor(s) and one member of their Advisory Panel[3]. Sometimes, research designs and methodologies change, and where these are judged by you and your supervisor(s) to be substantive (e.g., introducing interviews rather than, or in addition to, questionnaires), a further ethics application will be necessary. There is a lot of guidance available and a valuable source of information is *The Research Ethics Guidebook* (see WEBLINK 3).

WEBLINK 2

Student ethics application forms & ethics guidelines

WEBLINK 3

The ethics guidebook

---

3 Each doctoral student at UCL/IOE has an advisory panel of about 5–6 other members of academic staff. These people are can be drawn on for advice on subject like ethical clearance and may also be used for upgrades from MPhil to PhD, or, perhaps, as internal examiners.

Doctoral and master's students need to engage with the research ethics community (see Bridges, 2009) and get in the habit of discussing the ethical issues involved in their research with their peers, as well as with their supervisor. At UCL/IOE, forums are held twice a year, on an informal basis, where students have the opportunity to present and discuss ethical issues that have arisen during their research with other students and a senior member of staff. In this way, students not only learn more about the conventions and rules but they also learn the associated language used to discuss them.

5.3 RESEARCH ETHICAL COMMITTEES (RECS)

A key development in the increasing ethics surveillance was the publication of the Economic Social and Research Council's (ESRC) research ethics framework in 2006 (updated in 2012 and 2015) and the subsequent introduction of Research Ethics Committees (RECs) throughout HE institutions.

UCL/IOE's own REC was created in 2005, and I have been a member since 2011. Others have existed in a number of British universities for some time, which have comparisons to the established use of Institutional Review Boards in the USA higher education system, which were introduced after the National Research Act 1974.

According to the ESRC guidelines:

> A Research Ethics Committee (REC) is defined as a multidisciplinary, independent body charged with reviewing research involving human participants to ensure that their dignity, rights and welfare are protected. The independence of a REC is founded on its membership, on strict rules regarding conflict of interests, and on regular monitoring of and accountability for its decisions. (2015: 44)

The referral of a student's work to the REC is comparatively rare and there are only a small handful submitted to the REC from the PhD or EdD cohorts each year. However, as a part of quality control, the REC samples and considers ethics reviews of a number of students each year, in order to ensure that they are of a high standard (approximately 1 per cent at master's level and below and 5 per cent at doctoral level), and confirm that the approval decision was correct.

The remit of research committees is to ensure that researchers do not engage in unethical behaviour (Hammersley, 2006), but they are also there to protect the institution and, when there are any, the funders from legal action brought by a participant(s) who feel that they have been unfairly treated and have a grievance.

One of the most vocal critics of RECs is the ethnographer Martin Hammersley (ibid.). He argues that ethics is a highly complex, and often contested, area and that the literature shows that there are often major disagreements amongst social scientists about key ethical issues. He maintains that ethics is a field where there is often not only no agreed answer, there is not generally a single right answer. He points out that some decisions require weighing up a range of ethical and methodological considerations against each other and this often requires detailed knowledge of the research context, which is always situated (Simons and Usher, 2000; Brooks et al., 2014) or contextualised in each unique research setting. He also questions whether RECs have the expertise to tell researchers how they should conduct their research, and argues that research committees do not have the detailed knowledge of the research context to be able to make decisions, and that they rely heavily on medical and psychological models where informed consent is particularly crucial (see Schrag, 2011). He also makes the point that, unlike in medical research, the risk and level of likely harm to participants is comparatively low. See WEBLINK 4 for my own experiences of being on the ULC/IOE REC. Although I feel that Hammersley makes a convincing case about how all research is context specific I still believe that doctoral students benefit from at least some guidance based around a series of principles from a Code of Conduct.

WEBLINK 4

Jon's experience of Research Ethics Committees

5.4 ETHICAL GUIDES/FRAMEWORKS

Apart from the ESRC's research ethics framework there are also a number of other frameworks and guidelines that researchers are able to draw on, and you need to familiarise yourself with the code or codes most relevant to your particular theoretical and empirical field. The most common of these in the UK are the British Educational Research Association (BERA, 2011), the British Psychological Association (BPA, 2009) and the British Sociological Association (BSA, 2002, updated 2004). See WEBLINK 5 for URL addresses for these frameworks. Dowling and Brown refer to these various codes or frameworks as the theoretical ethical field (2010: 36), and each of them have their own particular merits and omissions. Robson (2011) points out that many websites from these organisations contain earlier versions so that is possible to see how ethical ideas have developed and changed over time.

WEBLINK 5

Links to ethical associations for social research

Over the last decade or so, ethical principles and expectations from these frameworks have become normalised and, although useful as a guide, still need to be subjected to interrogation, contestation and debate. To view the six key ethical principles from the ESRC framework as an example, see WEBLINK 6.

Brooks et al. (2014) point out that these frameworks are largely based on the three main principles enshrined in the Belmont Report[4] (DHEW, 1979), which is widely recognised as creating the first set of formalised guidelines for research involving people. These are: (i) respect for persons; (ii) doing good and avoiding harm (beneficence and maleficence); and (iii) justice. Brooks et al. (2014) also trace the philosophical links back to the movements of utilitarianism (choosing an action on the basis that it maximises good and minimises harm) and deontology (where certain ideas are seen as intrinsically right or wrong and where some rules have a universal application). Research codes are particularly strong in the English-speaking countries such as the USA (American Educational Research Association's *Code of Ethics*, 2011), and Australia *(Australian Code for the Responsible Conduct of Research*, AG, NHMRC and ARC, 2007).

WEBLINK 6

The 6 key ethical principles from the ESRC

---

4 The report was prompted by problems arising from the infamous Tuskegee Syphilis Study (1932–1972) outlined in WEBLINK 1.

The frameworks recognise that many questions do not have simplistic answers and the impossibility of producing a straightforward list of rules and directives that can guarantee that the research will be ethically conducted. They attempt to provide a balance between the interests of the researcher, the interests of research participants, the academy and the institution where the researcher is based. One of the difficulties with these guidelines, or protocols, is that they need to cover a whole variety of situations and behaviours and are therefore often, by definition, nebulous and vague. Whiteman calls them 'broad placeholders for a range of ideas/values' (2012: 139), and for some types and areas of research some of these codes raise more questions that they seek to answer (Dowling and Brown, 2010). Moreover, as we have seen, many social researchers argue that ethical issues and dilemmas are often highly context-specific and it therefore need to be left up to individual researchers to interpret the meanings and how to fit them into their particular project. As Robson maintains, researchers need to adopt a 'situational relativist' approach (2011: 197), which means that researchers have to be flexible and able to respond to localised events (see Whiteman, 2012). This viewpoint will be developed further in later sections.

5.5 KEY ETHICAL PRINCIPLES

In this section, I want to draw out some underlying themes and signal the main points which, I hope, will generate a number of issues leading to further thought and discussion. Although I am aware that these key principles can come across as another tick list, similar to those I have been critiquing, I am arguing that the great majority of researchers working in the social sciences and education would agree that, although ethics can be intrinsic to, or immanent in, the research process, there are also a number of extrinsic, universal principles. Although there is no single set of catch-all rules, you still need to be aware of, and understand, the ethical issues, even if you are going to reject them.

I wish to argue that there are six key ethical areas that I always check to see if they have been covered in the research proposal that I am asked to review, whether it be for students or professional researchers (see Box 5.2).

▬ BOX 5.2 ▬▬▬▬▬▬▬▬▬▬▬▬▬▬▬▬▬▬▬▬▬▬▬▬▬▬▬▬▬▬▬▬▬

Six key ethical areas

1   Explanations about the research.
2   Informed consent.
3   Voluntary participation.
4   Right to privacy.
5   Avoidance of harm.
6   Data stewardship and security.

I will now expand on each of these six key areas, although I will have much more to say about some than others, namely about the particularly contentious areas of consent and the right to privacy.

(i) Explanations about the research

Telling participants what the research is about is a fundamental principle, although of course you may not always know all the details yourself, and have only a vague idea of how the research might end up looking like, particularly if you are conducting ethnographic research. Nevertheless, the research will have aims and you will probably have a research question or questions, however vague they are at the beginning, and however much they might actually change as the fieldwork develops. You will have to make a judgement as to how much information you tell participants – most people, in my experience, only want brief details, and some are not interested at all. I have prepared information sheets to be distributed and many a time I have subsequently found out from participants that these have remained unread. Nevertheless, this is still good practice and they are can always be taken away and read later. It may also depend on the age and capacity of the participant to understand, and the time you are planning to spend with them. In my own PhD, I told the children (10–11-years-old) that I was interested to find out what it was like to be a boy or girl in their school and that I was planning to turn it into a book; I obviously gave the head teachers and the class teachers a little more details of my intentions. Similarly, if I am carrying out market research using a short, structured, questionnaire with people in the street, I am inclined to provide them with less information than if I am going to spend time interviewing someone.

Examples of information sheets that I have used can be viewed on WEBLINK 7 but I try and keep information down to one side of A4. I usually have a brief paragraph about what the research is about; the participants' role in the research (e.g., a 30-minute interview); what will happen to data collected; and my own contact details (an email address and telephone number). The information sheet will also emphasise that their participation is voluntary and that all names of people and places will be changed. Some researchers use the back of the information sheet for a consent form but I will write more about this in the section below.

WEBLINK 7

Examples of information sheets

Of course, telling participants about what is involved in the research project assumes that you are not carrying out covert research and that you are being as overt, or upfront, as possible. The theme of covert research is discussed later in this section.

Sometimes, issues arise during the research process that could not have been anticipated beforehand and you have to make a judgement about how much to tell your participants. A recent example of this came from one of my colleagues at UCL/IOE, who was running a project that involved screening children for stereoscopic vision, which is where people have difficulty in seeing objects in depth or in 3-D, although they can often compensate this by other means. She discovered that two of the children had this condition and was unsure whether or not to tell the parents, particularly as the condition is often hereditary. In the end, she did tell them but told me that she regretted it as it caused them unnecessary anxiety.

This example shows the difficult balance that a researcher might have between withholding certain pieces of information against the rights of participants to know everything that is being discovered.

(ii) Informed consent

The concept of informed consent is linked to the ethical principle of ensuring respect for the autonomy of the participants, and also highlights worries concerning how power relations are articulated during research relationships (Brooks et al., 2014). However, although some research designs are more straightforward than others, issues around informed consent are often slippery, complex and generally characterised by disagreement. We need to adopt a highly sceptical stance towards the whole concept of informed consent and whether it is possible for people to sign up to a research study with the full knowledge of what it is about.

The notion of informed consent is in inherited from the field of biomedics, and many researchers working in education and the social sciences have questioned the whole concept of 'informed consent' (Wiles et al., 2004, 2007). They have examined the many tensions and dilemmas that are likely to arise, particularly for those of us engaging in qualitative methodologies (see, e.g., Thorne, 1980; Burgess, 1989; and Malone, 2003), and conclude that will always be an element of the research that remains hidden, both from the researcher as well as from the participants. As Eisner argues, 'the notion of informed consent implies that researchers are able to anticipate the events that will emerge in the field about which those to be observed are to be informed' (1991: 215), while Malone writes that 'truly informed consent is impossible in qualitative research studies seems to be a given' (2003: 812).

Asking participants for their consent to take part in the research should not only happen at the beginning of the study and, particularly for longer periods of fieldwork where people may be interviewed more than once, consent should be reviewed on an ongoing basis.

Opting in and opting out (implied consent)

An important distinction needs to be made between two forms of consent – opting-in and opting-out. When opting-in, participants are asked to make an active choice of whether they, or perhaps their child, want to take part in the research. Box 5.3 gives an example of what a typical opt-in question on a consent form might look like.

▬ BOX 5.3 ▬▬▬▬▬▬▬▬▬▬▬▬▬▬▬▬▬▬▬▬▬▬▬▬▬▬▬▬▬▬▬▬▬▬▬▬▬▬▬

A typical opt-in consent form

A researcher, Jon Swain, from University College London/Institute of Education, will be attending your child's class next Wednesday to observe their science lesson. The main focus of the research is to evaluate children's understanding of the concept of gravity. He will only be observing the lesson and will not be talking to any of the children in the class. If you are happy for him to visit the class on this day, please sign the form below and return it through your child to their teacher, Mrs Glass.

Jon Swain has had a full Disclosure and Barring Service (DBS) certificate.

I give my permission for Jon Swain to observe my child's science lesson on xx November 2016.

Print full name: ....

Signed: ....

Date: ....

The opt-out form has implied consent and you tell participant what you intend to do and assume that they give their consent unless you hears something to the contrary. This kind of consent form would look something like the one shown in Box 5.4.

■■■ BOX 5.4 ■■■■■■■■■■■■■■■■■■■■■■■■■■■■■■■■

A typical opt-out consent form

A researcher, Jon Swain, from the Institute of Education, will be attending your child's class next Wednesday to observe their science lesson. The main focus of the research is to evaluate children's understanding of the concept of gravity. He will only be observing the lesson and will not be talking to any of the children in the class. If you are **not** happy for him to observe your child in the class on this day, please sign the form below and return it through your child to their teacher, Mrs Glass.

Jon Swain has had a full Disclosure and Barring Service (DBS) certificate.

I do not want my child to be observed in his/her science lesson by Jon Swain on xx November 2016.

Print full name: ....

Signed: ....

Date: ....

Other examples of consent forms can be seen in WEBLINK 8. Of course, there are a number of potential problems with both of these consent forms. The first is that, if the form of communication is a child's book bag[5] you cannot be sure if the parent has received the

WEBLINK 8
Consent forms

---

5 A receptacle such as a satchel or rucksack that children use to carry things between home and school such as books and school notes, etc.

form. Second, it is not clear what would happen if a parent decides to opt her/his child out of your observation. Does the child have to go somewhere else? Do you make sure you don't include this particular child in your fieldnotes? Much may depend on the nature of the observation: will be it be passive, with you observing from the back of the class, or will your visit also involve you actively going round the class and asking children what they are doing or thinking?

It is a lot more straightforward with interviews where my view is that parents should always have to opt-in, whatever the subject of the research is.

Written or verbal consent?

This question usually provides a subject of rich discussion during the CDR session: once again, there are no easy answers, and much of it is context dependent. Some people insist that researchers should always be required to have written consent from participants as a safeguard in case anything goes wrong and, say, the participant says they were forced to take part. I have never known or heard of this happening. However, it is interesting to speculate on the legal status of a consent form: are they legal documents and what would be their status in a court of law if it were ever tested? In my experience, many participants regard consent forms as a burden and while they seem happy to sign the form, many do not bother to read what is says. Once again, while I always obtain written consent from parents if I am interviewing their child, I am less likely to ask for this from adults. Recently, I arranged for some mentors working in Further Education (FE) colleges to attend a focus group at UCL/IOE. Some people think that I should have begun the interview by asking them to sign a consent form but my argument is that they were willing autonomous human beings and would not have turned up to meet me if they had felt coerced in anyway. In other words, their attendance was their consent. Sometimes, I have to interview people by telephone. They have previously been sent a questionnaire, and at the end there is a section asking them if they are willing to be interviewed by me by telephone. If they are, then they supply their telephone number (and sometimes their email address) and indicate the time of day that is most convenient for them. When I ring them up a few weeks later, I make it plain that their participation is voluntary but I take it that their consent has been given by: (a) saying so on the questionnaire; and (b) picking up the phone and not hanging up. Besides, the practicalities of sending them a consent form by post, or even by email, seems to me to be an unnecessary burden, not least on the potential interviewees.

One question that you might want to consider is the participants' capacity of competency to consent to take part, which leads us into the next heading.

Research with children

WEBLINK 9

Carrying out research with children

Ethical decisions are particularly complicated, and often conflict, when the research involves children. For more information on children's capacity of competency to consent to take part in research, see WEBLINK 9. Decisions that often emerge include how a researcher might weigh parent's rights to whether their child should take part in a study against the rights of the child, particularly when their own opinions may be at odds with the views of their parents? Of course, this also depends on the area of research: for example, a study into the strategies children use for long multiplication, against children's views on taking drugs or matters concerning their sexuality. If I was interviewing 16-year-olds about controversial matters, I might want to ask for the parents' permission but the young people might be more unlikely to give truthful responses if they knew that their parents were aware – they would certainly be very interested in what was going to happen to the data and it would be vital to stress confidentiality.

The age of the child is also important and there is obviously a big difference between a 4-year-old and a 16-year-old. Debates in the literature around whether or not you need to seek parental permission to interview adolescents, say between the ages of 16 and 18, are messy. Although, in some countries, the 18-year-old rule is fixed, this is not the case in the UK – however, in practice, most RECs tend to use the biological age (rather than, say, evaluating the young person's maturity) as the main determinate of whether parental consent needs to be obtained (Brooks et al., 2014). I interviewed young army recruits aged 16 and did not seek parental consent, but in a way the army acted as an organisation similar to *loco parentis*. Although the majority of the questions were about the basic skills provision they were undertaking (all had been chosen because they had relatively poor basic skills), some of the interview questions were about potentially sensitive issues such as early family life and perhaps getting into trouble during their early adolescent life. Even so, it would have seemed strange, even perverse, to seek their parent's permission.

Sometimes, young people need protecting for their own good as on average they have less idea of the repercussions of what they say and do than an adult and this is recognised in law. Sometimes, in the social-media-obsessed world, a young person might make a comment that they later come to regret and the problem is that, although this may have been a transient view, it becomes fixed and permanent and one day somebody might try and search for it to check out a person's history.

Some of the most important people when researching children are the gatekeepers, who control access to the research, whether they be parents, head teachers or other professionals in mainstream services. The general guidance is to ask the parents' consent to approach children and then ask for the children's consent. Interviews with children (almost) always require parents' permission. Observations often don't but it depends on the nature of the activity involved. As a rule, if a researcher wants to observe behaviour and practices in the playground, he/she needs the permission of the head teacher; if they want to observe a class, they need the permission of the head teacher and the class teacher; if they want to observe a group of children for any sustained length of time (of more than a few minutes), they need the permission of the head teacher, the class teacher and the parents.

Covert research and deception

As we have seen, many ethical decisions are complex and not straightforward. Sometimes research can be, and needs to be, covert, which involves deceiving people. Most codes of ethical practice allow for covert research as long as it can be soundly defended and the end justifies the means, and Hammersley (2006) questions whether some degree of deception is unavoidable if we want to carry our research on powerful groups or politically sensitive topics. Thus, there is a utilitarian argument for justifying deception in that if there is an overall benefit and it tells us something useful it is for the greater good. One example may be if a researcher wants to evaluate public reaction to a stranger having a cardiac arrest in a public place and see who, if anyone, comes to assist. They stage the incident with an actor in, say, a park, and then observe. Does the researcher need consent from the watching public – but if they sought it this would ruin the experiment. It also raises other ethical issues, of course: what if a watching member of the public becomes distressed and is therefore caused harm? See WEBLINK 10 for further information about two studies involving covert research from Humphreys (in the 1960s) and Fielding (in the 1970s).

WEBLINK 10

Two examples of covert research & further readings

For students, obtaining ethical permission from the REC is obviously going to be harder when some element of deception is involved. In my experience, this is comparatively rare for doctoral research but I remember one doctoral student who wanted to investigate the extent to which schools used institutionally racist practices. She told the school that she was looking at assessment procedures and, although this was not the main focus of her research, she could hardly tell the school what her real purpose of the data collection was. Her application was passed by the REC: she used the justification that her research was a means to an end, that her design required her to act in the way she did, and without some degree of deception or even subterfuge it would have been impossible to collect or generate the necessary data. In Section 5.6 on Internet research, we will come across another doctoral student, Natasha Whiteman, who also had to engage with issues of deception when she carried out observational online research on two Internet-based fan groups.

(iii) Voluntary participation

Participants must take part in the research on a voluntary basis and be told that they can freely withdraw at any time. One question that students sometimes ask is whether people can say they are withdrawing from the research after the research project is finished? Well it depends on what you mean finished? If the research findings have been published, or are in the form of a bound thesis, then the answer is 'no'; however, until this point has been reached they can say that they wish to withdraw their data from the research. Although I have never had this happen to me, a colleague of mine was frustrated when one of her interviewees told her that she wanted to withdraw from the research and requested that her data was not used. This was exasperating for my friend as the interview had been a particularly good one and had produced rich data. The participant's concern was that she believed that she had mentioned certain colleagues in an unfavourable light and, although my colleague offered to show her the transcript and remove any contentions passages, the participant could not be persuaded and the data was lost.

Some people get worried if researchers offer any gifts or incentives as they can possible contaminate the research by only attracting a particular type of person and by undermining the principle of free choice, on which informed consent is based (Farrugia, 2013). It depends on what the circumstances are, and what the nature and value of the gift. For example, when I held the evening focus group for FE lecturers working as mentors (whom I mentioned above regarding obtaining their consent), I felt it was only courteous to provide them to provide refreshments in recognition of them giving up their time for me after a hard day's work. Moreover, the halls of residence around UCL/IOE are full of adverts for psychology students to be paid a few pounds to give up their time to take part in various experiments.

Coercion is a more difficult area. Whilst people should never be asked to take part in your research when you judge it to be against their will, other people might take part in, say, an interview as a personal favour. There have been times when I have felt a little uneasy when working in schools. I have asked the head teacher to nominate a class that I can use for my research and I have been conscious that, although the head teacher will normally choose a teacher who is competent, confident and obliging, it may also be the case that the teacher concerned may not have any real choice, and will feel awkward if they refuse to accommodate me.

There can also a problem when people are being observed. For instance, during my PhD research, I observed some of the Year 6 (11-year-old) boys playing football in the playground and I was also interested in other playground interactions. This meant that I was also observing hundreds of other children whose consent I did not have, either from them or their parents. Of course, it is a matter of degree and I could argue that no one was going to be named, nor likely to come to any harm. Nevertheless, it raises the issue about the rights that people have about being or not being observed as part of a research project. How can they withdraw from the research? During my fieldwork, I also wrote down a countless number of overheard conversations from both children and adults in my field diary, and it was simply not practicable to have asked individuals to give their permission every time. In many ways, it is about what is researchable and who can be researched? Too many restrictions will make research impossible and I feel that there are always going to be decisions that ultimately are made in-the-moment, and come down to the researcher's own judgement in situ.

(iv) Right to privacy

Measures should be taken to ensure participants' privacy and these include the *attempt* to guarantee confidentiality and anonymity. I say 'attempt' because this is not always possible, particularly for researchers carrying out a study in or about their own institution, and where it is possible to Google the name of the student and identify where he/she works. This, then, is a particularly pertinent matter for EdD students, many of whom are, in effect, insider researchers, but it also applies to any doctoral student conducting research inside, or about, their own workplace.

The difference for me between confidentiality and anonymity is that if someone tells me something they regard as private, I will hold it in confidence and not tell anyone else, unless it is about something that breaks the law, while anonymity is the guarantee that I will change names of all people and places, and they will not be able to be identified. An interesting story

WEBLINK 11

Consequences
of revealing
names of
people &
places

about the consequences that can result when a researcher behaves without integrity and reveals the names of people and places can be seen on WEBLINK 11.

Protecting participants' privacy is particularly apposite when it comes to children. Some of these issues have already been discussed under the section 'Informed Consent' and come within the area of child protection. The term currently used in the UK is 'safeguarding', which is broader than 'child protection': this takes priority over other considerations and relates to the action taken to promote the welfare of children and protect them from harm.

Revelations

Glesne reminds us that: 'when others trust you, you invariably receive the privilege and burden of learning things that are problematic at best and dangerous at worst' (1999: 119). There are sometimes occasions when you are interviewing and a participant says something that requires you to make an in-the-moment decision. In my own research, I remember a boy telling me that he was being bullied. I then had to make the decision of whether to tell his teacher or not. Part of this involved me making a judgement about the nature and the extent of the bullying but I offered him the choice of whether he wanted me to tell his teacher or not. In the end, we left it that I would ask him about it at the next interview (the following term) and suggested that if the problem was still persisting I would then report it.

Connolly and Parkes (2011) from UCL/IOE, researched gang members in London and interviewed about eight people over a six-week period. They had to continually emphasise their distance from the police and that all information would remain completely confidential. An exception to this was if a disclosure was made, such as if they revealed the name of a person who had committed a criminal offence, or even if this was one of them. But doing this was not always easy and split decisions often have to be made in the moment, sometimes based on the perceived seriousness of the offence. For instance, would you report someone to the police if they admitted shoplifting – this may depend on the amount, type and cost of the goods stolen? Almost all of us would not hesitate reporting a person if they confessed to the interviewer that they injured someone and caused them harm, but what about if they said they were carrying a knife, as all their friends in the gang do for their own protection? Despite this being a criminal offence, it is a trickier situation, particularly when the relationship between the interviewer and interviewee has been built up over time and where mutual trust is paramount.

Insider research

Insider research has a series of ethical and methodological issues all to its own. Conducting insider research within her own HE institution, Malone writes about how:

> The participants are increasingly sharing things with me that are very personal and that they inevitably preface with 'You can't write this up.' In some instances, what they tell me only confirms things I have figured out from on-the-record stuff and that's no problem. But in other cases, I'm not sure how to handle it. For instance, a very difficult

situation has developed between one of the students and a professor, a situation that has affected the student so deeply that, for a while, she was almost unable to function professionally ... She used me almost as a therapist, willingly telling me all sorts of things that she obviously does not want made public, but with the tape recorder running throughout. I know these things, but I can't write these things. I don't know what to do with what I know. (2003: 807–8)

This shows the particular problem of trying to guarantee anonymity for insider researchers. If I was a teacher researching in my own school and I mention someone by their title (e.g., the head of science, mathematics coordinator, deputy head teacher, etc.), it is relatively easy for someone to find out who I am talking about: as I have already written, all they have do is look at the person who wrote the thesis, enter them into Google and find the name of the school where they are working. Therefore, researchers should not promise to ensure anonymity when they can't. Malone writes that the promise to protect participants' identities was one of the most 'disingenuous aspects of the informed consent letter' (2003: 809):

I naively and ineffectually offered my participants pseudonyms and promised to make 'every effort' to protect their confidentiality ... What I did not anticipate was that it would also be impossible for me to protect their identities beyond the local community. (Ibid.)

If anonymity cannot be completely guaranteed the participants need to know what the risks are to their privacy and the consequences that might accrue if their name is revealed. This will change the nature of the data that are being collected as participants are likely to be much more cautious in what they tell you, and so this also becomes a methodological issue. For instance, few are going to complain about a member of the senior management team if they think there is a chance that their feelings about them will be revealed. One way around this is for the researcher to allow **member checking** to take place: this involves showing the transcript to the participant, with the promise that they can remove any section which they feel may be controversial. While this may give the participant greater confidence to talk openly it will of course have an irrevocable effect on the data generated and this will need to be acknowledged. Malone (ibid.) originally felt that the chance for her participants to read her interpretations would be a protection against misrepresenting or misinterpreting their views but realised that this also had the potential to be traumatic for them.

Writing about research on the Internet, Whiteman (2012) recounts two contrasting views on whether a researcher is duty bound to reveal names or not in their write-up, which is based on an article by Herring (1996). The first source of evidence Herring quotes comes from those who regard online data as being 'published works and hence protected by copyright law' (ibid.: 154), which maintains that researchers should give full credit to attributed sources and consider revealing names of users and sites. The second position, based on an article by King (1996) in the same journal, advocates that all sources should remain hidden. Whiteman criticises both stances as being based on universal assumptions, which lack an understanding of local contexts that do not take account of a researcher's aims, their methodology, the field they are working in, and so on.

Sometimes, a situation arises where a participant is insistent that they want their own views voiced that their real name is mentioned in the write up. This happened to Mattingly (2005) when conducting research in American hospitals. As her relationship with her participants became closer, so did they become more insistent that their views on the difficulties of caring for ill children were not only voiced but that the voice also had a real name. This can be a difficult decision and my default line is that I generally refuse. However, I have never had a person say they would withdraw from the research if I did not consent and, in all honesty, this might depend on how much I needed them and how good their data was. Crucially, it would also depend on there being no references in the data to other persons (even with pseudonyms) who might be traceable if the interviewee's identity is known. The worst-case scenario might be that, as a result of one known name, other names, perhaps with sensitive or contentious information, are also revealed. So the best advice is to play safe.

However, there was a case with a researcher at UCL/IOE who was interviewing some teenage girls as part of a focus group. They were rightly keen to know what would happen to the data, and who would know about their views. When the researcher explained that they did not need to worry because their names would be changed and their identities anonymised, they became angry and said that they would only continue to take part if their views and associated names were advertised in the public domain such as a social media site like Facebook (see Zimmer, 2009). I am not sure what the outcome was but it shows that promising participants anonymity and confidentiality is not always straightforward.

Sometimes, of course, it is impossible to anonymise a person, for example if you are interviewing the Secretary of State for Education or the Chief Inspector of Schools (also known as the Head of OFSTED[6]). Sometimes, these kinds of (powerful but publically accountable) people insist that they see the transcript before it is published and have the right to remove particular passages. Some people also want to see the questions before the interview and this will have consequences about the data. Sometimes, you may choose to show the questions beforehand because you want the interviewee to give a more considered and reflective response; on other occasions, you want a more immediate, spontaneous reaction, and worry that if the questions are seen before the interview you will get more of a public performance, which is more akin to a public relations exercise.

(v) Avoidance of harm

The avoidance of harm refers to any potential physical or psychological harm, discomfort or stress. Much of this also concerns the level of risk, which is defined:

> by reference to the potential physical or psychological harm, discomfort, stress or reputational risk to human participants (and participating groups, organisations and funders) that a research project might generate. (ESRC, 2015: 27)

6 OFSTED is the Office for Standards in Education, Children's Services and Skills in England. It inspects and regulates services that care for children and young people, and services providing education and skills for learners of all ages. It is a non-ministerial department.

Sometimes, I have had interviewees become tearful when talking about personal issues. In my case, these have been unexpected in that they have not been as a result of a particular question on a particularly sensitive topic. However, harm can also affect the researcher as well as participant and you might have to fill in a personal risk assessment if, say, your research is taking place in a potentially dangerous area such as a conflict zone, or even if you intend to interview your participants in their homes, which may also be in an area of high crime. Some topics are very difficult to research and, for example, many academics are reluctant to carry out research into violence because of the ethical and methodological minefield that surrounds it (e.g., see Connolly and Parkes's research about youth gangs mentioned above). Not only can access be fraught, but the risks of harm are high to both participants and the researchers. Parkes (2010) discusses incidents where, in her attempt to equalise power differentials between adults and adolescent and/or child, her act of not challenging views or behaviours made her complicit in the violence she was attempting to discuss, and she found that once she had relinquished the adult position it was very difficult to invoke or reclaim.

(vi) Data stewardship and security

Some students are a little casual about how they keep their data. It is usually the case that you will store your files on a password-protected computer but I have seen pen-drives (memory sticks) left in computers in the library and so extra care needs to be taken. Some students are a little overcautious with what they write and I have come across assignments that have promised that data will be stored in a password-encrypted computer and hard copies will be stored in a fireproof, locked filing cabinet, for which only two people have the key. Of course, it depends on the sensitivity of the data and there will be occasions when encryptions will be necessary. However, it is also important to recognise a sense of proportion. Although each institution is likely to have its own specific rules about data storage, it is likely in the UK that students will need to confirm that all personal data will be stored and processed in compliance with the Data Protection Act 1998 (DPA, 1998).

Some students change the participants' names immediately on commencing fieldwork and this may sometimes depend on how many people are in the sample. There is, though, a worry that, if you have a large number of participants, you are forever getting confused and when you are writing about Clare, are you referring to Rosanne or do you actually mean Davina? To some extent, when the time arises for you to change names will depend on the type of data that you are collecting and the number of people involved. Yes, it may be good practice to change names as soon as the data is collected and keep a list of pseudonyms but I have known many researchers who only change names at the stage when the data is in the public domain, such as when presenting work at conferences or in a written article.

Another question frequently asked is how long data should be kept before it is destroyed? This will again depend on the nature of the data. The UCL/IOE Research Data Policy specifies that data should be retained for a minimum of ten years, although I have seen many applications that state that data will be deleted much earlier than this.

5.6 INTERNET RESEARCH

As we have seen in Section 5.5 on the right to privacy, researchers have found themselves having to respond to new issues arising from technologically mediated environments, and Whiteman (2012) argues that Internet and new media technologies have been disconcerting for those using more traditional or conventional understandings of what it actually means to be ethical for both researchers and Internet users. Whiteman (2010) points out that this may be a particular concern for Internet researchers, who will often have the added difficulty of having to present and defend arguments, which persuade peers (and perhaps examiners) who have limited or no experience of this type of research in these particular settings (Clark and Sharf, 2007). For further detail of Whiteman's own research, which she conducted at UCL/IOE between 2004 and 2006, see WEBLINK 12.

WEBLINK 12

Whiteman's research on internet-based fan groups

Researchers using social media platforms to carry out research need to be aware that some of them have a dubious ethical record, which they need to be wary of. For example, in 2012, Facebook manipulated nearly 700,000 users' news feeds to see whether it would affect their emotions. There was no informed consent to allow them to decide whether to take part in the study, and the changes to the news feeds were made without the users' knowledge.

There is a mounting literature on ethics in online research which offers guidance and discusses a number of issues, and although the established guidelines do not really deal with the complexities involved in researching online communities, a good starting point is the Association of Internet Researchers (AoIR) 2012 report and the BPS *Ethics Guidelines for Internet-Mediated Research* of 2013.

The AoIR advocate the use of guidelines rather than a code of practice, which is in recognition of the need of the researchers to be adaptable and responsive to diverse contexts and to the continually changing technologies. This is a move away from the top-down regulatory models, and they emphasise the process approach to ethics, which highlights the researchers' own agency and responsibility for making judgements and decisions within highly specific contexts. For the AoIR, the process approach is dialogic, inductive, situated and case-based.

5.7 CONCLUSION

This chapter has looked at and discussed writing an ethical review; the role of RECs and ethical guidance/frameworks; a number of key ethical principles and research using new technologies such as the Internet.

Some people may continue to think that research ethics can somehow be fixed at the beginning of the research, and because it complies with general principles or follows established procedures, it can remain unchanged throughout the project. Although some research designs are, indeed, more stable than others (think of experimental design against ethnography), many researchers (e.g., Robson, 2011; Hammersley and Traianou, 2012; Brooks et al., 2014) are right to point out that the research often has a situated and contingent nature, particularly when it is qualitative, and initial thoughts and designs are likely to be disrupted, undone or challenged by events arising during fieldwork. This fits in with the view that ethics are intrinsic to, or immanent in, the research process, and at least to some extent, conditional upon and responsive to the particularities of the varied contexts in which educational research is conducted. Research ethics should therefore be seen as a 'continuous process of inquiry, interaction and critique throughout the entire research study' (McKee and Porter, 2009: 148).

Although I am arguing that certain ethical principles are also extrinsic and that, as researchers, we need to consider general principles and statements about what constitutes good ethical research practice:

> We know that one size does not fit all, yet we continue to attempt to squeeze our research questions and ethical dilemmas into the framework that does not serve well the researched, the researcher, or the research community. (Malone, 2003: 812)

Whiteman (2012) argues that there needs to be a conceptual shift away from the idea that researchers should be held to account by a set of universal ethical principles towards a move where researchers are more involved in decisions that arise during the research based on the activities they become involved in. In her book *Undoing Ethics*, Whiteman (ibid.) argues for the consideration of two conceptual moves in research ethics, the embedded and/or situated nature and the dynamic process that it often involved. Thus, rather than applying a set of general, predefined and agreed principles, or a set of universal or totalising ethical norms, to research Whiteman (ibid.) argues for an *embedded approach* where the decision-making of the researcher is situated within the local context and is informed by issues which cannot always be anticipated in advance or indeed even be possible to guarantee. For example, 'informed consent must always be obtained' and 'participants must always be anonymised' are not always possible, applicable or even desirable. Second, she also stresses the *dynamic nature* of the research process, which may be ongoing, contingent and fluctuating; in other words, ethical decision-making is usually in motion throughout the research process.

The emergence of RECs in HEs in the first decade of the century has, for some researchers, had a negative effect on the field as debates are 'closed down' and reduced to discussions around a series of, what are becoming, familiar themes. Researchers tick off a list of key ethical principles that they (think) they are going to cover, and this has the danger of reducing debates about more contemporary and everyday issues.

However, I wish to argue that there is a place for a set of guiding principles based on an agreed Code of Conduct, and although they might and cannot always be adhered to, it is surely better to be able to have them for reference and discussion. RECs are a step in the right direction and this includes their function of protecting the researcher, the institution and most importantly, the researched. While doing social and educational research is about more than applying rules, we must not forget that good research demands that ethical concerns should occupy a central place in the whole research process (Ruane, 2005).

━━━ BOX 5.5 ━━━

A summary of the key points

- Ethical issues are often complex and rarely straightforward, and it is important for students (and researchers in general) to talk about them as part of the research community.
- There has been a move away from the authority of the researcher, and a number of key principles have evolved which are enshrined in a number of guidelines and researchers are expected to adhere to them.
- Research is always situated or contextualised to each unique research setting, and this often requires detailed knowledge of the research context.
- The key ethical components involve explanations about what the research is about; informed consent; voluntary participation; rights to privacy; avoidance of harm; and data protection (including stewardship and security).
- There is a lot of guidance available (e.g., from a number of ethical guidelines/frameworks and Research Ethics Committees).
- Writing an ethical review is a research activity in itself and is an ongoing, continuous process.
- Ethical issues are dynamic and are embedded within a particular localised context, and this means researchers often need to be reflective and reflexive.
- Some issues arising from new technologies have disconcerting conventional understandings of more traditional ethical issues.

AREAS FOR DISCUSSION

Here are six scenarios for discussion. What would you do?

Scenario 1

You are conducting research with children who are having difficulties at school. During the course of the research you begin to suspect that one of the children has a serious health condition. You do not know if the family are aware of this. You do some exploration into the condition and it requires medical treatment. In your ethics application, you did not consider this possibility or make any plans relating to disclosure of information gained during the research. You did not state that any research results would be disclosed to the participants' parents. You are concerned about the health and welfare of the child but also do not want to cause undue stress if you are wrong.

Scenario 2

You are conducting observations for your research. During the course of your fieldwork, you are beginning to develop your interest in a different area to the one for which you have ethical approval. Your findings are new and exciting and your observations are giving you plenty of rich data to develop your research in this new area.

Scenario 3

You are conducting a series of interviews with parents for your research. The interviews are in-depth but the topics are not sensitive. During the second meeting with one of your participants, they started to open up to you about their personal situation and show signs of distress during the interview. You think that they are trying to tell you that they are currently in an abusive relationship.

Scenario 4

You are doing your research in school. Your ethics application was commended for being very thorough, detailing clear informed consent procedures with the children. The head teacher at the school to which you have gained access to is very interested in your research and thinks that the findings will be beneficial to the school. It is a very busy time at the school, OFSTED have just been and the inspection did not go well, so morale is low. The head teacher is keen for you to go ahead with the research with as little fuss as possible and without informing the parents and gaining their consent. He does not think that you need to gain the consent of the children either. He says that they are used to having adults in their classroom and it will not affect them. You are concerned about jeopardising the relationship with the head teacher as it has been difficult to negotiate access to schools.

Scenario 5

You are conducting insider research/practitioner research in your place of work. You have informed your colleagues and they have given their consent for you to use data you gain in forthcoming meetings for your research. You are really pleased that your colleagues are supporting you in this. As colleagues have given their consent, you have decided that you will do a comparison of this current data again – data that you already have from meetings that were held last year. This will help you to highlight the impact of policy changes.

ANNOTATED BIBLIOGRAPHY

These are some readings that I have particularly enjoyed:

Alderson, P. and Morrow, V. (2004) *Ethics, Social Research and Consulting with Children and Young People.* **Barkingside: Barnardo's.**
This text has useful suggestions if you are carrying out research with children and young people.

Boddy, J., Jennings, S., Morrow, V., Alderson, P., Neumann, T., Rees, R. and Gibson, W. (2010) *The Research Ethics Guidebook: A Resource for Social Scientists*. Available at: www.ethicsguidebook.ac.uk (accessed 7 July 2016).

The website of this source is also very useful for assisting you to think through the ethical issues arising from your project.

Malone, S. (2003) '"Ethics at Home": Informed consent in your own back yard', *Qualitative Studies in Education*, 16 (6): 797–815.

This article is particularly useful for researchers using insider researcher about their own institution, and the difficulties of guaranteeing their anonymity and protecting their confidentiality.

Robson, C. (2011) *Real World Research: A Resource for Social Scientists and Practitioner Researchers*, 3rd edn. Oxford: Blackwell.

This is clearly written and very accessible, and uses lots of real life examples. It has a very good chapter on 'Ethical and political decisions'.

FURTHER READING

Hammersley, M. and Traianou, A. (2012) *Ethics and Educational Research*. Available at: www.bera.ac.uk/researchers-resources/publications/ethics-and-educational-research (accessed 7 July 2016).

A very accessible article that can be found online: it covers the key ethical principles and interrogates a number of interesting issues, such as how far can informed consent ever actually be informed or free?

Whiteman, N. (2012) *Undoing Ethics: Rethinking Practice in Online Research*. London: Springer.

Drawing from ongoing sociological research into the practices of media cultures online, this book explores contemporary debates regarding the moral, legal and regulative aspects of research ethics. The author proposes that the decisions we make should be informed by the nature of the environments we study and the habits/expectations of participants within them.

PART II

THE APPLICATION OF THE RESEARCH DESIGNS

CHAPTER 6

EXPERIMENTAL DESIGN

Jane Hurry

6.1 INTRODUCTION

Experiment is one of the key research designs in education and social research; it uses a deductive approach and is constructed to address causal questions and to test hypotheses. It is therefore prized by many in the social sciences and is of value both for theoretical purposes and to inform evidence based practice about 'What Works'. The principal forms of experimental design are randomised controlled trial (RCT) and quasi-experiment (similar to RCT, except in the method of assignment to intervention and control groups, discussed below). Experimental designs, particularly RCTs, are often considered to be the most rigorous of all research designs and are seen as the 'gold standard' against which all other designs are judged and measured (e.g., Sherman et al., 1998; Stolberg et al., 2004), a view that will be critically examined in this chapter.

The chapter will cover both the theoretical and the practicalities of conducting experimental studies. Those engaged in research need to be informed both about how to conduct an experiment but also how the design fits into the process of knowledge building. The design, both RCT and quasi-experimental, principally in naturalistic settings, will be critically examined both from the insider perspective of those heavily invested in this methodology and from the outsider perspective.

Experimental designs are quite common amongst psychology doctorates but less so in the other social science disciplines, where sample sizes and resource implications may take them beyond the doctoral student's reach. The examples used in this chapter often draw on psychological examples in the domains of children's reading and education in the criminal justice system, reflecting the author's interests.

6.2 EPISTEMOLOGICAL PRINCIPLES UNDERPINNING EXPERIMENTAL DESIGNS

Experiments hold a special place in Western philosophy and the increasing use of experiments in the sixteenth and seventeenth centuries heralded the emergence of modern science (Hacking, 1983). This involved the deliberate manipulation of something to see what happened later. Francis Bacon first argued at the turn of the seventeenth century that the observation of nature was not enough, we must also manipulate the world to learn its secrets.

The systematisation of experiments developed in the natural sciences over the following centuries, making explicit the need to control test environments in order to isolate causes. The modern theory of experimental control through random assignment, adopted by social scientists, emerged in the twentieth century, particularly in biological research 'in the field'. Researchers wanted to establish the best conditions for crop growth (Fisher, 1925). In order to examine one specific cause (e.g., type of seed, fertiliser or planting time), they had to control for the numerous other factors of influence (rainfall, soil quality, aspect and so forth), but they couldn't control the environment in the way their predecessors had done with bell jars and vacuums. Instead, they cancelled out unwanted environmental factors. They did this by randomly allocating a number of plots to the particular method they were investigating (the intervention, e.g. a new fertiliser) or to the standard method (the control). In this way, other factors influencing crop growth were likely to occur with the same frequency in both intervention and control conditions and so would not explain any significant differences between the groups at the end of the intervention.

Cause and effect, at the heart of the notion of experiment, are complex constructs, even though many of us think we know what they mean. Shadish et al. (2002) observe that a precise definition of cause and effect has eluded philosophers for centuries. Although coverage of these debates is beyond the scope of this chapter, where the emphasis is more practical, Cook and Campbell (1979) give an excellent account of the range of positions from early positivists, such as David Hume (1711–76), who recognised causality but not the notion of experimental manipulation of those causes, through to the later positivist Bertrand Russell (1872–1970), who rejected altogether the need for unobservable concepts such as cause, to John Stuart Mill (1806–73) who proposed three important criteria for inferring cause: '(1) covariation between presumed cause and effect; (2) the temporal precedence of the cause; and (3) the need to use the 'control' concept … to rule out alternative interpretations for a possible cause and effect connection' (Cook and Campbell, 1979: 31). The first two criteria came from Hume but the third underpins the application of experimental design in the twentieth and twenty-first centuries, that is the manipulation of causal agents. Cook and Campbell, whose position is adopted here, take a critical realist stance. They adopt Mill's three criteria but also remind us that experimentation in practice is subject to measurement error, an even greater concern in the social sciences than in the natural sciences. They also embrace aspects of Karl Popper (1902–94), who maintained that scientific knowledge is advanced by developing theories and then testing them by attempting to falsify them. Popper argued that we can never know a theory is true, but we can gain confidence in the theory by seeing how well it resists falsification. Cook and Campbell support the implication from Popper that many tests are needed to explore the strength of a theory, and that 'determinations cannot be made on one or two failures' (1979: 31). See Chapter 4 for a more in-depth discussion of the work of Popper.

The complexity of cause and effect is no abstruse philosophical point, but is of considerable practical significance for experiments. Shadish et al. (2002) give an illuminating example of this complexity, the Inus condition (see Box 6.2), which is 'an *insufficient* but *non-redundant* part of an *unnecessary* but ***sufficient* condition**' (Mackie, 1974: 62).

▬ BOX 6.2 ▬

An illustration of the Inus condition

Dr Folkman's lab developed a drug which shrank cancerous tumours by limiting the blood supply to the tumour (Folkman, 1996, in Shadish et al., 2002: 4–5). Unfortunately, other researchers could not replicate the results until they came to Folkman's lab and learned precisely how to make it, store it and administer it. Only then did they repeat the success of Folkman's team (Shadish et al., 2002: 4–5). The drug was not sufficient to ensure success, there were other factors determining its effectiveness, not understood by its developers. However, under the right conditions it worked, and was *non-redundant*. It was *not necessary* to the shrinking of tumours since it was not the only thing that could cause this effect, but it was *sufficient* under the right conditions, it could do the job.

This is an informative example because it reminds us that whilst we can learn some aspects of causality through one experiment, other factors may remain obscure. A drug can work on one patient but not on another, an educational intervention can work whilst delivered by one teacher whilst making no difference when it is delivered by another. An additional important aspect of the complexity of causality is its reciprocal nature: for example, poor coping strategies can cause depression but depression can also undermine coping strategies; parenting style can influence an adolescent's behaviour but the adolescent's behaviour can also influence parenting style.

The purpose of this preamble is to persuade you that: (1) experiments are a core feature of knowledge building; (2) the nature of causality, which is at the heart of experiment, is complex and should be recognised as such, and therefore; (3) experiments are never enough on their own. The place of experimental design in knowledge generation is outlined in Box 6.3.

━━ BOX 6.3 ━━━

The place of experiment in knowledge generation

- The aim of an experiment is to isolate a cause of an event.
- Typically one is testing a hypothesis.
- The experiment is set up to test whether a putative cause has the predicted effect.

Essentially, you want to assess the proposition (see Box 6.4).

━━ BOX 6.4 ━━━

Assessing the proposition

If X, then Y.

Or, in more colloquial terms: If an intervention is given, then the outcome occurs.

Unfortunately, it's not enough just to show that when the intervention or the treatment occurs the expected outcome also happens. This is because there may be many other reasons, apart from the intervention, for why you observed the outcome. In order to demonstrate that there is a causal relationship, it is necessary to address simultaneously the two propositions (see Box 6.5).

━━ BOX 6.5 ━━━

The need to address the two propositions

If X, then Y and if not X, then not Y.

Or, once again, more colloquially: If the intervention is given, then the outcome occurs and if the intervention is not given, then the outcome does not occur.

If you are able to provide evidence for both of these propositions, you have in effect isolated the intervention from all of the other potential causes of the outcome. You have shown that when the intervention is given the outcome occurs and when it's not present, the outcome doesn't.

Experimental designs typically involve theory testing. This tells us a lot about the circumstances under which experiments should be conducted. The fact that they are designed to test theory means that they are built on a considerable body of previous work, the work that generated the theory. Experiments are not an appropriate design where the underpinning exploratory research has not been conducted, and for sound academic investigation, any proposed hypothesis must be supported by reference to this earlier research.

Mill's three criteria for demonstrating causality are: (i) correlation; (ii) the cause temporally preceding the effect; and (iii) controlled manipulation of the cause producing the effect. These translate into a classic sequence of questions and designs in pursuit of the understanding of causal relationships, the final step being an experimental design (see Box 6.6).

■■■ BOX 6.6 ■■■

Mill's three criteria for demonstrating causality

- Are two variables related – cross-sectional design: (i) correlation.
- Does one variable precede the other – longitudinal design: (ii) temporal precedence.
- Does one variable cause the other – experimental design: (iii) controlled manipulation.

Whilst correlation provides the first foundation for causation, the direction of causality is typically unclear. Longitudinal designs address the direction of causality but cannot rule out the role of some unobserved third variable as the true cause. I provide an example of such a sequence of research below using reading as an example. In research on reading development, it was theorised that an important cause of reading progress was the ability to hear sounds within words, such as rhyme and alliteration, aspects of phonological awareness.

Cross-sectional design

This hypothesis was first tested using cross-sectional designs to see if there was an association between children's reading and their phonological awareness (Bradley and Bryant, 1985). Of the three types of study, cross-sectional is the most straightforward, and it is a **necessary condition** of causality but not a **sufficient** one. For example, the causal connection could work the other way, and reading lots of books could enhance the child's phonological awareness. Indeed, this has been demonstrated in a study of literate and illiterate Portuguese adults (Alegria et al., 1982).

Longitudinal design

A second test used a longitudinal design to see if phonological awareness in young children who had not yet started to read would predict how well they learnt to read.

Phonological awareness turned out to be a reasonably accurate predictor of subsequent reading progress (Bryant and Bradley, 1985), but this still fell short of providing evidence that phonological awareness was a *cause* of reading development. The classic alternative explanation is a third factor, a **confounding variable**, which is associated with both phonological awareness and a child's reading, such as parents frequently reading to their children, the availability of a large number of texts in the home environment, a high IQ or, perhaps, good nutrition. The reason that this was important was because teachers wanted to know how to help their pupils learn to read. If phonological awareness was one of the causal factors in children learning to read then working on their ability to hear the sounds in words would be helpful. If, however, the real cause was, say, exposure to books, which fostered both phonological awareness and reading, placing the focus on children's phonological awareness would have much less of an effect on their reading attainment.

Experimental design

The third test of the theory that phonological awareness was a cause of good reading development was an experiment, which therefore helped find a practical solution to a practical problem. Bryant and Bradley (1985) found that when children were given phonological training they subsequently performed better on reading and spelling tests than similar children not given that training. This has turned out to be a very robust finding, demonstrated by many others (e.g., the National Reading Panel, 2000). I use the Bryant and Bradley study below to illustrate issues to do with control conditions.

I mentioned above that the hypotheses, which underpin an experiment, need to be supported by evidence. This typically takes the form of reference to cross-sectional and longitudinal studies in addition to any theoretical basis.

6.3 KEY FEATURES OF AN EXPERIMENT

There are several key features of an experiment (see Box 6.7).

▬ BOX 6.7 ▬▬▬▬▬▬▬▬▬▬▬▬▬▬▬▬▬▬▬▬▬▬▬▬▬▬▬▬▬

Key features of experimental design

- Intervention (e.g., a drug treatment, an educational intervention) – this is the hypothesised cause, which is operationalised (the **independent variable**).
- An outcome measure, the thing you are interested in influencing, the effect (the **dependent variable**).
- Group comparisons, typically an intervention group and a control group.
- Method of assigning people (or schools, etc.) to intervention and control groups.
- Sample size.

For example, carrying on with the reading analogy, an **intervention** (the independent variable) could be a reading intervention, using greater teaching of phonics, which is hypothesised to lead to higher reading attainment. The **outcome measure** (the dependent variable) is reading attainment. Children of the same age are assigned to comparison groups: an intervention group and a control group who receive standard classroom teaching. The method of assignment should ensure that the children are equivalent on a number of factors related to reading such as the children's reading abilities prior to the intervention, their gender and whether they are socially disadvantaged.

The intervention

Even though you might have good evidence that one thing causes another, operationalising that cause into an intervention often requires care and time. For example, we know a lot about the disease Ebola and its effects, but the development of an effective treatment does not simply follow automatically. Some 'interventions' are very straightforward, though often ingenious. Investigating the psychological power of priming to influence (or 'cause') judgement, Kahneman describes such an intervention, where experienced judges were asked to specify a number of months prison term they would hand down to a hypothetical woman caught shoplifting (2011: 125–6). They were first given a description of the circumstances, then came the treatment. The experimenter rolled a pair of dice, secretly loaded, to land on either 3 or 9. The judges were first asked to say whether they would pass a sentence greater or lesser in months than the number showing on the dice. Finally, they were asked to give a precise prison term. Those who rolled 3 estimated an average prison term of five months, those who rolled 9 estimated eight months. The priming effect of the dice roll had influenced the judges' deliberations.

Frequently, though, the development of an intervention is more difficult and requires previous knowledge of the field. For these complex forms of intervention, a development and piloting phase is essential, or the adoption of an existing intervention. The Vera Institute of Justice in New York conducts multimillion dollar projects for the USA government to improve the way in which offenders are dealt with in the justice system, and for intervention projects they always build in 18 months for the development and piloting of interventions, prior to any evaluation (Jacobson, 2012).

When the intervention relies on human beings, implementation is another issue that needs addressing and I have already mentioned an example of this above is the Inus condition of Folkman's treatment of cancerous tumours. Implementation issues are magnified in educational and social science conditions where treatments rely on the ways in which an intervention is taught or delivered. Least problematic are small-scale experiments, where the research team are responsible for the intervention, but the process of implementation still needs to be documented to enable **replication**, a central feature of rigour in any quantitative research. In large-scale experiments it is additionally desirable to ensure programme fidelity, or at least to document how well interventions have been implemented, since many people may be involved in the delivery. How programme fidelity is ensured will vary according to the complexity of the intervention, from tight scripting to advanced training and monitoring. In an RCT of a web-based literacy programme, Savage et al. (2013) comment that details of implementation too often go unreported. They classified teachers by their ability to implement a web-based programme and showed that better implementation lead to greater progress in reading. The way in which an intervention is implemented can make a difference to the outcome.

Despite, or perhaps because of, the challenges of mounting educational or social science interventions, they often push the boundaries of our knowledge. **Longitudinal research** can identify risk factors but in the process of intervention further factors are revealed. Well-constructed experiments afford the opportunity to deepen understanding of human behaviour. For example, longitudinal research shows educational attainment to be a risk factor for youth offending. Intervention to improve educational attainment may reveal a deep-seated aversion to schooling which introduces a further set of factors to be addressed relating to motivation (Hurry et al., 2008).

The outcome measure

The outcome measure is the operationalised effect. For example, if the theory is that collaborative group work aids children's learning of a mathematical concept, the outcome measures must quantify children's understanding of that concept, and show gains over the course of the intervention. The normal rules of rigorous quantitative measurement apply, that is in demonstrable reliability and validity (Troia, 1999; Robson, 2011). Within experimental design, it is particularly important to get measurement right for two reasons: first, it is often a time and resource hungry method due to the intervention phase; second, the intervention may not work and it is then important to able to convince people that this is a secure finding and not due to measurement error.

The implications of this are that an existing measure of demonstrable reliability and validity is adopted or, where no suitable measure exists, there is a rigorous phase of measurement development. Those working in the natural and medical sciences are familiar with the lengthy processes of devising measurements, e.g. the development of magnetic resonance imaging (MRI) to measure activity in the brain, and the existence of a suitable measure is often part of whether or not a research question is 'researchable'. It is also one of the reasons why working in a research paradigm is so beneficial (Kuhn, 1962), taking advantage of the developmental work of others, and something that I argue should be more forcefully encouraged in educational research and in the social sciences in general.

Working within a theoretical framework has useful practical implications for the selection or development of outcome measures (there may be more than one), as it clarifies the constructs being measured. Take for example the construct of reading where general measures of reading may be quite crude and are often fairly atheoretical. If the theoretical model being tested focuses on a particular aspect of reading, for example, phonological word processing, then this aspect of reading should be measured. It is, however, also probably a good idea to measure reading more broadly conceived because that could support claims for

generalisability of findings. This brings us to the concept of **proximal** and **distal effects**. Proximal effects are those most closely related to treatment, and distal effects are more remote consequences. Sticking with the example of reading, if the theory being tested is that children's understanding of the alphabetic principle (that letters are connected with sounds) enable them to decode (Frith, 1985), then teaching letter sounds should help children decode better. A proximal measure here would be greater letter-sound knowledge but the interest in decoding is the extent to which it helps children read words and texts so it might be important to also test these more distal skills. As a rule of thumb, the largest effects of intervention will be on the proximal measures and, unsurprisingly, there will be smaller effects on distal measures (e.g., Rosenshine et al., 1996; de Boer et al., 2014).

Proximal outcomes are often of interest as mediators of more important, or socially desirable, distal outcomes. An example of this can be found in research on offending (see Box 6.8).

===== BOX6.8 =====

Proximal and distal measures of offending using desistance theory

In research on offending, the main interest to governments and communities is in the distal variable of the reduction of criminal offences. Desistance theory provides a better understanding of how and why people stop offending, and proposes how this can be achieved through proximal variables or mediators, for example through increasing employment, the construction of a non-criminal identity and more stable family relationships (McNeill, 2006; NOMS, 2012).

Since interventions typically target these proximal, mediator variables, this is where the greatest effects are seen and this is useful in gaining confidence that the intervention made some difference. Sometimes, although it is difficult to demonstrate that an intervention will produce effects on a distal variable, such as offending, it is still possible to build a case for the value of the intervention. Tett et al. (2012) attempt to do just that for the value of prison arts projects, such as drama and creative writing, as vehicles not only for promoting literacy development but also desistance. They cite studies, which show the value of art projects for fostering positive relationships between prisoners (Silber, 2005) both with prison staff (Menning, 2010) and with their families (Boswell et al., 2004). They show that the arts can have positive effects on prisoners' personal development as it can enhance their self-confidence (Silber, 2005; Cohen, 2009), develop their communication and social skills (Cohen, 2009), and promote further engagement in education (Anderson and Overy, 2010). They use desistance theory to argue that these positive developments are intermediate or mediating outcomes for prisoners on what may be a complex journey to rehabilitation, although the experimental evidence for that end of the journey is yet to be established (Burrowes et al., 2013) and is currently being based on a number of relatively small qualitative studies.

Theoretical models of mediation, such as that proposed by **desistance theory**, can be tested if proximal and distal outcomes have been measured, using **multiple regression models** (Baron and Kenny, 1986; Kraemer et al., 2001; Gunzler et al., 2013). Unpicking the ways in which interventions cause effects in this way is one technique to look inside the 'black box' of intervention effects (Pawson and Tilley, 1997; Bonell et al., 2012).

It is important to take outcome measures before and after treatment so that the equivalence prior to treatment of the groups being compared can be established and, if necessary, controlled for in analysis. Post-treatment measures should usually be taken soon after the treatment. It is less common to measure long-term effects, and of course some treatments are not expected to have long-term effects, such as insulin or Ritalin. However, in educational and social interventions, the models being tested often propose long-term effects, sometimes referred to as an 'inoculation' model. In inoculation models of causality, long-term effects should be measured, but typically this is only appropriate if short-term effects have been observed first. Although it can be difficult to measure long-term effects due, for example, to a lack of long-term funding, the end of a doctoral project and/or the problems of sample attrition, the availability of existing national data sets (such as in England, the National Pupil Database, which records a range of pupil outcomes for every pupil under school leaving age or the Police National Computer which records every criminal offence by offender) may offer opportunities to harvest data at relatively low cost and with relatively little attrition. If so, this needs to be built into the design from the start to ensure that participants are informed and will give their permission for data to be collected and used from these sources at a later stage.

Group comparisons

Experiment involves the comparison of an outcome variable in the presence and absence of the proposed cause. Typically, but not invariably, this involves the comparison of an intervention and a control group. An example of the advantage of this method over relying on observation and knowledge of practice is given in Box 6.9.

▬ BOX 6.9 ▬▬▬

An example of the benefit of comparison over observation

A few years ago, I was involved in the evaluation of an intensive (and therefore costly) intervention for children who make a relatively slow start in their reading (Hurry and Sylva, 2007). The intervention was the Reading Recovery Programme, which provides daily half-hour sessions with specially trained Reading Recovery teachers for six-year-olds who are in the bottom 20 per cent of their class in terms of reading. Our study compared children who had received the Reading Recovery intervention (the intervention group) with similar children who did not receive the intervention (the comparison group).

Reading Recovery turned out to be particularly effective for the bottom half of the intervention group (i.e., the bottom 10 per cent in the class). There was a statistically significant interaction effect between children's reading levels at the start of the intervention and the benefit they got from the intervention. We could see this because we could compare their progress with the children in the comparison group who did not receive the intervention. Those weakest readers in the comparison group (the bottom 10 per cent of the class) made worryingly little progress over the course of primary school.

However, teachers in the 24 schools using the Reading Recovery Programme sometimes reported that they preferred not to offer the programme to the very weakest, those bottom 10 per cent. They said that the weakest readers took longer to work through the programme than the slightly more competent readers (11-20 percentiles in reading in the class) and generally made poorer progress. Since the programme was an expensive one and only available to a limited number of children, they argued that, based on their observations and local knowledge, focusing on the children who made faster progress under the intervention made more sense and was more cost effective.

Based on their 'observation of nature' the teachers were quite right, but there was a paradox because, although the bottom 10 per cent of readers did, indeed, make the slowest progress, they were also the ones who would make virtually no progress at all without the intervention. In our study, by the age of 10.5 years, without the intervention, the bottom 10 per cent had an average reading age of 7 years 8 months (as opposed to 8 years 2 months with intervention). The slightly better readers actually managed to more or less catch up over the years without the help of the intervention, and so the experiment, with its comparison group, had revealed what observation had missed. Such findings have very practical implications.

Every research design has its core elements. At the heart of experiment is the unambiguous interpretation of findings to test causality (**internal validity**). Differences between intervention and control conditions should be due to the treatment, the whole treatment and nothing but the treatment, and so differences between the conditions, which are not due to the treatment must be kept to the absolute minimum. There are different ways of achieving this.

One method is to compare the same person on the outcome with and without the treatment. For example, how well does someone perform on tests with or without breakfast. The problem here would be that you could not give them the same test on two occasions (following breakfast and without breakfast) and expect performance on the test to be solely due to nutrition. On the second occasion, participants might be expected to do better because they had already seen the test before and thought about the answers. You could give them a different test on the second occasion but would need to be able to demonstrate that the two tests were of equivalent levels of difficulty. Even then, it could be argued that any experience of testing makes it easier to do better the second time around. When employing these techniques, a crossover design should be used to correct for order effects, for example: half the participants have breakfast before the first test and half before the second test. In the analysis, the effect of breakfast on test performance can be inspected and order effects will have been dealt with by sharing them equally between experimental and control conditions. If circumstances permit, this is a good option, but in many situations this is not possible, for example: the intervention may change a person fundamentally, teaching children about letter sounds and names hopefully produces more lasting effects than those that come from whether or not they have breakfast on a given day.

The most common comparison is between two or more different groups, one receiving the intervention and one or more not. The groups need to be as similar as possible before the treatment and I will say more about this in the section on Method of Assignment below. However, even when this is achieved there is a further threat to internal validity, which is the Hawthorne or placebo effect. The term **Hawthorne effect** was coined in the 1950s following a study of the effects of changing the working conditions in the Hawthorne Works in the USA during the 1920s and 1930s. The changes made (i.e., in levels of lighting and heating and the length of the working day) did increase productivity temporarily but the effects were transient. The researchers concluded that the workers were responding to the motivational effects of being part of an experiment, rather than to the specific changes made. Placebo effects have been reported in medicine for well over a century, with the claim being that just the thought of being treated has a curative effect through the power of the mind. Actually, both the existence of the Hawthorne and the placebo effect have been challenged (e.g., Hróbjartsson and Gøtzsche, 2010), and they are most troublesome when the outcome measure is based on participant report rather than observation. Measurement that is blind to the participant's experimental status is preferable wherever possible but, nonetheless, controlling for Hawthorne effects is a standard part of rigorous experiments. In education and social science, the option of a placebo pill is rarely relevant but an alternative is an intervention control group.

The experiment conducted in the UK by Bryant and Bradley (1985), referred to above, provides a good example. They randomly assigned young children to phonological training, which they hypothesised would improve the children's reading and spelling, to a no-intervention control and to an intervention control, which involved training in maths. Their hypothesis was that if improvements in reading and spelling were the result of a Hawthorne effect then the children receiving the maths training should do as well as those receiving the phonological training. They did not, and the children who received the phonological training scored significantly higher on reading and spelling than the children in the other two groups. The other useful element of their design was that they not only tested the desired effects for phonological training but also an unrelated outcome measure, attainment in maths. The fact that the children who received the phonological training did not do better in maths, but that the children in the maths group did, provided further support for the internal validity of the experiment (see Table 6.1).

The use of an intervention control group strengthens an experimental design and can address concerns about the ethics (discussed further in Section 6.5) of providing special input to only one group, since the intervention control group also receive extra input. You may be surprised at the small sample size in this experiment of 13 children per group but this is not uncommon in psychological experiments, and I discuss this later on in a separate section on sample size at the end of this section.

Single-subject experimental studies are a variant of experimental design and are useful in particular circumstances. They involve making repeated measures of an individual on and off the intervention programme and comparing performance in the different conditions. Cook et al. (2015) have developed some useful evidence standards in the area of Special Educational Need, which cover single-case study designs and set out quality indicators (Qis) in eight areas (see Box 6.9). The majority of Qis for single-case study designs are the same as for group

Table 6.1 A test of the effect of phonological training on reading and spelling

Outcome measure	Phonological training N = 13	Maths training N = 13	No training N = 13
Spelling	Significantly better attainment than both other groups	No different from no treatment control	No different from maths group
Reading	Significantly better attainment than both other groups	No different from no treatment control	No different from maths group
Maths	No different from no treatment control	Significantly better attainment than both other groups	No different from phonological group

Source: Bryant and Bradley (1985).

comparisons but under internal validity there are three additional elements: (1) that there should be at least three demonstrations of experimental effects at different times; (2) that there should be a baseline phase for each of these data points (exceptions are discussed); and (3) the design should control for common threats to internal validity, for example using commonly accepted designs such as ABAB (a non-intervention phase followed by intervention, followed by non-intervention, followed by intervention).

▬▬ BOX 6.10 ▬▬▬▬▬▬▬▬▬▬▬▬▬▬▬▬▬▬▬▬▬▬▬▬▬▬▬▬▬▬▬

Eight areas for quality indicators in a group comparison and single-case studies (Cook et al., 2015)

- Context and setting.
- Participants.
- Intervention agents (the people delivering the intervention).
- Description of practice (the intervention).
- Implementation fidelity.
- Internal validity.
- Outcome measures.
- Data Analysis.

Methods of assignment

The best way to ensure intervention and control groups only differ in terms of the treatment is to randomly assign group members to the intervention condition. This is the RCT. As long as the sample size is big enough, random assignment should ensure group equivalence in both observable and unobservable characteristics. However, in addition to sample size, there is a further proviso, that the attrition rate from the beginning to the end of the experiment is low and is not substantially higher in the control than experimental group because unequal attrition undermines group equivalence. As in the example of Bryant and Bradley's experiment above, sample sizes may often be quite small and are particularly common in psychology experiments. In such cases, it is advisable to match pairs on key observable dimensions related to the theoretical model being tested before random assignment. For example, Bryant and Bradley matched pairs of children on gender and phonological awareness before the treatment and then one of the matched pair was randomly assigned to the intervention group and the other to the control group. This process improves the chances of achieving well-matched groups in small samples.

If RCTs were easy to conduct a student's and/or researcher's life would be much simpler, and providing robust evidence for practice would be easier and more straightforward. However, RCTs are often difficult and expensive to mount, and this can make running one particularly difficult for doctoral students. Although certain systematic reviews, especially in medicine (e.g., the Cochrane Collaboration), will only include studies, which have employed this methodology, in education and social science RCTs may be impractical or too expensive to run. Medical research tends to attract more funding than social science research and, for example, in the UK Allocation of Science and Research Funding 2015/16, the ESRC was allocated £153.2 million compared to the Medical Research Council allocation of £580.3 million. This may be one reason why RCTs are rarer in the social sciences than in medicine. In one systematic review of educational interventions, Seethaler and Fuchs (2005) found only 34 of 806 relevant articles in five journals (4.2 per cent) used random allocation, indicating a 'drop in the bucket' in terms of evidence based on this method.

This has led to much discussion of how to proceed where an RCT is neither practicable nor possible. A widely accepted second best alternative is to use a quasi-experimental design (Cook and Campbell, 1979), which involves treatment, outcome measures and comparison groups, but does not use random assignment to those groups. In quasi-experimental design, the group that does not receive treatment is referred to as the comparison group rather than the control group. Faithful to the sine qua non of experiment, intervention and comparison groups should be as well matched as possible, ideally on baseline measures of the outcome variable, but if that is not possible on some proxy measure of the outcome variable. For example, in the research on the effectiveness of the reading intervention, **Reading Recovery**, the intervention schools had elected to fund this costly intervention and the experimental study was taking advantage of this rather than having to pay for the intervention. Schools in the intervention comparison condition (phonological training) and the comparison condition (standard school practice) were selected from schools matched with the intervention schools on the basis of the proportion of children taking free school meals (a variable associated with reading attainment) and the schools' performance on national tests – i.e., the percentage of children achieving Levels 2 and 3 on the Standard Assessment Tests (SATs) – at the age of 7.

The second method of ensuring that group differences following treatment are the result of the treatment rather than any pre-existing differences is to control for baseline measurement of the outcome variable during analysis. Whether random or non-random allocation has been used, experiments in social science should report group differences at baseline, and control for these in the analysis, but this is essential in quasi-experimental designs. However, even when intervention and comparison groups are well-matched on the outcome measure at baseline there may be other differences between the groups that might be responsible for the improved performance of the intervention group, such as enthusiasm for the intervention. That is why random assignment is seen as the superior design, since all group differences are random.

The closeness of the match between intervention and comparison groups is important in terms of the credibility of the evidence. There are a number of scales of the adequacy of research designs, particularly employed with 'What Works' investigations: for example, see the Institute of Education Sciences: What Works Clearinghouse on WEBLINK 1. One of the earlier examples is the Maryland Scale of Scientific Methods, devised by Lawrence Sherman et al. (1998) to classify the strength of evidence for different methods of crime prevention, and building on standard methods texts, notably Cook and Campbell (1979) (see Box 6.11). Level 5, RCT, is the strongest level of evidence on the scale. Level 4 is the next best with a quasi-experimental design and well-matched treatment and comparison groups. Level 3 refers to quasi-experimental designs with unmatched treatment and comparison groups.

WEBLINK 1

What Works
Clearinghouse
website

BOX 6.11

Maryland Scale of scientific methods to classify strength of evidence (Sherman et al., 1998)

Level 1: Correlation between a crime prevention program and a measure of crime or crime risk factors at a single point in time.

Level 2: Temporal sequence between the program and the crime or risk outcome clearly observed, or the presence of a comparison group without demonstrated comparability to the treatment group.

Level 3: A comparison between two or more comparable units of analysis, one with and one without the program.

Level 4: Comparison between multiple units with and without the program, controlling for other factors, or using comparison units that evidence only minor differences.

Level 5: Random assignment and analysis of comparable units to program and comparison groups.

An example of some of the dangers that can arise from a poorly matched comparison groups can be seen in Box 6.12.

The risks that may result from badly matched comparison groups

A Canadian study by Porporino and Robinson (1992) illustrates the dangers of Level 3 quasi-experimental designs. They conducted one of the largest studies of the impact of education on re-offending. Readmissions to prison of people (n = 1736) who had participated in Adult Basic Education (ABE) were monitored for just over a year. They were classified into three groups according to their participation in ABE: those who had completed ABE; those who were released before completing ABE; and those who withdrew from ABE. Of those completers, 30 per cent had readmissions in the follow-up period, compared with 35 per cent of those released before completion and 42 per cent of those who withdrew. It is tempting to conclude that ABE reduces re-entry to prison. However, the group who withdrew from ABE were self-selected and were older and had more previous custodial sentences than the completers. It may be these factors, rather than the ABE programme, that explains prisoners' higher readmission rate, and so the results are inconclusive because of the limitations of the design.

An alternative to an RCT that can avoid some of the problems of quasi-experimental design is a Waiting List design. In Waiting List designs, participants are selected from a pool of participants who will receive the intervention. Some are selected to receive it first and they become the experimental/treatment group, and the others become the 'Waiting List group'. Both groups are assessed at baseline and again at the end of the treatment period but the Waiting List group will not yet have received the treatment and so provide a control group. The Waiting List group subsequently receive the treatment and this avoids any differences caused by self-selection and may also address ethical problems associated with giving one group and not another access to a potentially beneficial intervention. An alternative Waiting List design is to monitor participants on the outcome variable over a fixed period and then subsequently over the same amount of time under an intervention condition. However, in a Waiting List design, long-term follow-up is not possible since everyone receives the treatment in the end.

Sample size

Sample size should reflect the expected impact of the treatment and the heterogeneity of the groups. The smaller the expected impact and the greater within group variation, the larger the sample size that is needed. This is because statistically significant group differences are influenced by the magnitude of group differences, the size of the groups and the amount of variability between participants on the outcome variable. Experiments in cognitive psychology often have small samples: the interventions are typically targeted in the sense that the outcome variables are closely related to the intervention (therefore larger treatment effects can be anticipated) and there is limited naturally occurring variation in the participants. This provides the right conditions for finding significant results with small samples. Social interventions frequently have more general interventions and more distal outcome measures, for example, interventions to reduce offending (therefore smaller treatment effects can be anticipated), and, in this case, sample sizes need to be larger to deliver statistically significant intervention effects.

The appropriate sample size to test a hypothesis can be calculated by a fairly simple procedure called 'power analysis'. Unfortunately, many education and social science researchers frequently do not use calculations to determine their sample size. Nobel Prize winning psychologist Daniel Kahneman confessed that 'like most research psychologists, I had routinely chosen samples that were too small and had often obtained results that made no sense' (2011: 112). There is a range of software programmes available to make formal **power calculations** of the required sample size (e.g., Power and Precision; Stata, Clustersampsi). In order to use these programmes, the researcher needs to make some decisions. Box 6.13 outlines the decisions required and some conventions typically adopted. The alpha level referred to in the box is the probability of incorrectly rejecting the null hypothesis when it is actually true, referred to as a Type I error. In other words it is the likelihood of saying there is a difference between an intervention and control group when there is no difference: for example that an intervention for maths works when it does not. A Type II error, β, is the likelihood of accepting the null hypothesis when it is false; saying that that maths intervention does not work when it does. The probability of (correctly) rejecting the null hypotheses when it is false $(1-\beta)$, in other words avoiding a Type II error, is referred to as the level of power. The **effect size** does what it says on the tin, it tells you the size of the effect of that maths intervention, quantifying the difference between intervention and control groups on the outcome. The Cohen's d effect size is just the standardised mean difference between two groups. A Cohen's $d = 1$ signifies that intervention and control group means differ by one standard deviation.

━━━ BOX 6.13 ━━━

Calculating your sample size using power analysis

- Alpha level, α (level of statistical significance, usually less than a 5% chance of making a Type 1 error, $p < 0.05$).
- An acceptable level of power error rate (usually 80%, i.e. less than a 20% chance of making a Type II error; see Cohen, 1988; Mazen et al., 1987).
- The effect size required. This will vary depending on the experiment but the lowest effect size (Cohen's d) required would typically be 0.20. Effect sizes below this are considered small (Cohen, 1988). Hattie (2009) provides an informative discussion of effect sizes in educational interventions.
- As an illustration, if alpha is set at 5%, power at 80% and the anticipated effect size of *d* is 0.33, the sample size will need to be 72 (Howell, 2009).

Two more subtle but important factors influencing sample size are: (1) whether or not samples are clustered; and (2) the amount of variance that might be explained by baseline measurement on the outcome variable. In education and social science research, participants are often clustered (e.g., in schools, hospitals, neighbourhoods, etc.). Participants within a cluster typically share a range of characteristics (e.g., age, ethnicity, social class) that may be related to the outcome variable of interest. Usually **cluster sampling** should be avoided but this is often impractical and therefore larger samples should be recruited to account for this. Sometimes, researchers are specifically interested in variations between clusters. For example, a study may be interested in finding out whether an intervention is more successful in some schools than in others or in some neighbourhoods than in others. In these cases, the research design will include multilevel sampling and multilevel analysis. A pre-test is typically found to be a major predictor of subsequent performance and this increases the power of a study since it reduces the amount of variance to be explained by any intervention (Cohen, 1988). Including a pre-test in statistical analyses reduces the required sample size for a given power.

6.4 ANALYSIS, INTERPRETATION AND WRITING UP

In common with other fixed designs (Robson, 2011), experiments are designed to make analysis and interpretation transparent and straightforward. Both analysis and writing up should follow clear conventions (see Box 6.14).

▰▰▰ BOX 6.14 ▰▰▰▰▰▰▰▰▰▰▰▰▰▰▰▰▰▰▰▰▰▰▰▰▰▰▰▰▰▰▰▰▰▰

The two main aspects of analysis

Descriptive statistics, in particular checking the equivalence of experimental groups at baseline.

Hypotheses testing, establishing any statistically significant differences between experimental groups on the outcome measure following intervention. The statistical tests used are typically: **T-tests**, **Analysis of Variance** or **multiple regression**, tests which require the outcome measure (dependent variable) to be on the interval scale of measurement (e.g., score on a maths test, a self-esteem scale, height or weight). Control for baseline is also advisable.

To make the interpretation of results unequivocal, the analysis should demonstrate group equivalence at baseline before reporting group difference at outcome. Where groups are not equivalent at baseline, they would be graded Level 3 on the Maryland Scale (see Box 6.11), which undermines their value as evidence since differences in the outcome could be due to group differences at baseline. Irrespective of equivalence at baseline, it is advisable to control for baseline scores on the outcome measure when testing hypothesised differences between intervention and control groups following intervention.

Models of writing up experiments can be found in relevant journals but need to be as transparent as possible. They typically have the structure shown in Box 6.15.

━━ BOX 6.15 ━━━

A typical structure for writing up results from an experiment

Introduction/background: A focused coverage of the relevant literature, which provides an evidenced rationale for the experiment and a theoretical and/or empirical basis for the hypotheses.

Methods: A transparent account of how the experiment was conducted, sufficient to enable replication. Sub-sections typically include a description of: the design (to include method of assignment); participants; measures that include information on their reliability and validity; procedures; details of the intervention and, if appropriate, intervention control and control conditions (e.g., standard practice); ethics.

Results: Descriptive statistics followed by hypothesis testing. Results should be presented in accordance with an appropriate set of conventions - e.g., American Psychological Association (APA) - and should be a straightforward, factual description of findings.

Discussion: Typically the discussion starts with a summary of the findings, i.e. whether or not hypotheses were upheld or rejected. This is followed by the author's (or researcher's) interpretation of the findings and a discussion of how this adds to existing knowledge. Limitations should be considered and, indeed, some journals specify that a certain number of limitations should be enumerated. Finally, a concluding paragraph that addresses the overarching questions raised in the study.

6.5 ETHICAL ISSUES

In common with any empirical work, published ethical guidelines provide a framework, for example those of the British Educational Research Association, the British Psychological Society or the British Sociological Association (see Chapter 5). These cover the central issues of confidentiality, consent and the avoidance of harm. Ethical issues particularly associated with experimental designs relate to the allocation of interventions to some participants and not others. It may be argued that those not receiving an intervention are losing out and that this is therefore unethical. This position is held by those responsible for the reading intervention Reading Recovery and has meant that there are no studies of children in one school randomly allocated to Reading Recovery or control conditions.

One solution to this issue is to employ a Waiting List design, which I described in Section 6.3, where all participants are monitored for progress on the outcome variable (before and after intervention) and all eventually receive the intervention. In one such study that I carried out about ten years ago, children's spelling was tested at the beginning and end of one term to assess progress. The following term, they were taught about **morphemes**, important in spelling, and their spelling progress in the second term was compared to their progress in the first. The progress was found to be greater in the term in which they received instruction on morphemes (Hurry et al., 2005), but as I have already written, unfortunately this particular design precludes long-term follow-up.

Another good strategy to use is to compare two useful interventions, as employed by Bryant and Bradley (1985), who, as we saw in Section 6.3, gave one group of children a phonological intervention whilst another group received a maths intervention. This combines a sound ethical approach with a strong research design (the treatment control).

There is also an argument that failure to use random allocation, where such a design is practical, is itself ethically suspect. Ann Oakley et al. (1995) argued that it is acknowledged in medicine that treatments should be assessed using RCTs and that this should be no less true in education. They liken educational intervention without rigorous testing (RCT) to 'knitting without a pattern' (ibid.: 161). It is revealing that most of us would expect medicines to be exhaustively tested, using RCTs, but many are reluctant to subject educational interventions to the same tests. It would seem that we recognise that drugs can cause harm as well as good but do not have the same concerns about educational interventions. That would be a mistake. A recent example of an educational intervention which might be assumed without questioning to be a good thing can be found in the deployment of Teaching Assistants (TA) to assist children with special educational needs. Subjected to rigorous research, Blatchford et al. (2012) found in a large-scale British study that pupils with a TA actually made less progress than similar children without a TA. It is worth pointing out, however, that often the reason that researchers use quasi-experimental designs is that RCTs are impractical in social sciences, and very expensive. In education for example, schools are reluctant to be used as control groups if they can't see any benefits.

Interventions should not intentionally cause harm. An infamous example of such an important experiment is one that was conducted by Stanley Milgram (1974) at Yale University in the early 1960s. Stimulated by the Adolf Eichmann trial in 1961, Milgram was interested in the extent to which people would obey orders even when they thought that they would seriously harm someone. To test his hypothesis, he misled male participants into thinking that they were administering increasingly painful electric shocks to people who failed to learn something. It is worth looking up footage of this on YouTube (see WEBLINK 2), where you can see that some of the participants seem very distressed. Such experiments would not pass a Research Ethics Panel today, although they have partially been replicated in TV game shows.

WEBLINK 2

The Milgram
experiments

6.6 ADVANTAGES AND DISADVANTAGES OF CARRYING OUT EXPERIMENTAL RESEARCH

Well-designed experiments have high credibility with policy-makers because of their methodological robustness, their practical application and their demonstration of the achievability of desirable outcomes. Social scientists value them as the most demanding test of theory (see Box 6.16).

━━ BOX 6.16 ━━━

Advantages of experimental designs

- Potential unambiguous identification of causes.
- Practical testing of theoretically sound interventions.
- The cornerstone for evidenced-based practice.

___

However, they also have a number of important disadvantages, listed in Box 6.17. In a critique of a systematic review of RCTs in adult literacy, numeracy and language, John Hattie (2002) comments on a range of problems which can accompany this 'gold standard' design, including overly small sample sizes (average group size 26), high attrition (average 66 per cent) and pre-test differences.

━━ BOX 6.17 ━━━

Disadvantages of experimental designs

- Can be challenging to do in the messy area of social science.
- Highly focused and do not address outcomes which are difficult to measure quantitatively.
- They tend not to explain why interventions fail.
- They can minimise or ignore context.
- They focus on group differences, not individual differences.

___

Experiment should be seen as one of a range of designs to inform education and social science research, to be applied to the right kind of research questions. There is far too little replication of experiments in education and social science. In the natural sciences, replication is an expectation and this is all the more important in education and social science where outcomes are hard to measure and contextual effects are influential and hard to control. However, it is also the case that it is very difficult for researchers to obtain funding to replicate their own or other studies and originality is overly prized. A project, known as the Reproducibility Project: Psychology, undertook to replicate previously published work in psychology. Only 36 of the 100 replication studies found significant effects and the effect sizes found were on average of half the effect sizes reported in the original studies (Open Science Collaboration, 2016).

6.7 A CHECKLIST FOR RESEARCH QUESTIONS THAT CAN BE USED IN EXPERIMENTAL DESIGN

The final section in this chapter provides a checklist for research questions for experimental designs, including some possible questions that I see as being particularly appropriate for using this design (see Box 6.18).

▬ BOX 6.18 ▬▬▬▬▬▬▬▬▬▬▬▬▬▬▬▬▬▬▬▬▬▬▬▬▬▬▬▬▬▬▬▬▬▬▬

Possible research questions that are suitable to use in experimental design

A checklist for research questions suitable for experimental designs

- Are you investigating causality? *Does the improvement of young offenders' literacy and numeracy reduce their re-offending?*
- Are you testing theory? (this is not essential but it is helpful) *Does phonological awareness underpin reading development?*
- Is there existing evidence from *correlational* and *longitudinal* studies that support your hypotheses of cause and effect? Is there an association between phonological awareness and reading (correlation)? Does phonological awareness predict subsequent reading abilty?
- Do suitable interventions, which operationalise the proposed cause, exist or can they be developed within the available resources? *Can you devise a literacy and numeracy intervention for young offenders which matches their abilities and which will engage them as learners?*
- Are the proposed effects measurable using rigorous quantitative measures? *Can you measure literacy and numeracy gains?*

▬ BOX 6.19 ▬▬▬▬▬▬▬▬▬▬▬▬▬▬▬▬▬▬▬▬▬▬▬▬▬▬▬▬▬▬▬▬▬▬▬

A summary of the key points

- Experimental designs have been developed to tests causality. They do this by manipulating causes through a treatment or intervention and comparing groups with and without intervention.
- They sit well within a critical realist epistemology.
- Within this framework Mills proposes three criteria for the demonstration of causality: (i) correlation; (ii) the cause temporally preceding the effect; and (iii) controlled manipulation of the cause producing the effect.
- These criteria map onto three research designs, the last of which is experiment: correlational design; longitudinal design; experimental design.
- Experimental designs require substantial knowledge of the chosen area. Hypotheses should draw on theory and evidence, where possible from correlational and longitudinal studies.
- Interventions should be practical and also a good operationalisation of the proposed cause.
- Intervention and control groups should be similar except for the intervention. The best way of achieving this is through random assignment to groups (an RCT). An alternative is to compare groups, which are similar although not randomly assigned (a quasi-experimental design).
- Outcome measures should operationalise the proposed effect; they are typically quantitative and should be of demonstrable reliability and validity.
- Sample sizes should be sufficient to detect the expected effect and power analysis is a useful method of estimating the necessary sample size.
- Analysis should demonstrate the similarity between comparison groups at baseline and the difference between groups following intervention.

- Writing up should start with a justification of the hypothesis being tested, followed by a methods section, which enables replication, a results section, which states the findings without interpretation and a discussion section, which interprets the results.
- The particular ethical issue of experiment relates to intervention. An intervention should not cause harm. More commonly, there are debates about the ethics of denying the comparison group a potentially helpful intervention.
- Experimental designs work very well under the right conditions and are highly prized by policy-makers and theoreticians. They are not good in under-researched fields, in assessing effects, which are hard to measure using rigorous quantitative techniques, in looking at individual differences or at the effects of context.

AREAS FOR DISCUSSION

- What are the potential merits and weaknesses of experimental designs?
- Select a research question of interest and identify the proposed cause and the proposed intervention. Is the intervention and effect operationalisation of the cause? Does the intervention include elements that do not relate to the cause?
- For the same question, or a new one, are the measurable effects key to the area of study? Are there effects, which are harder to measure, which are likely to be important?
- What are the problems of a self-selected intervention group and in what ways could random allocation be made more possible?
- How would you prepare to conduct an experimental study? Could this be a piece of research of itself?
- Is random assignment to an educational intervention ethical?
- What are some of the practical problems that researchers encounter when they try and use an RCT design in education?

ANNOTATED BIBLIOGRAPHY

Hattie, J. (2002) 'What are the attributes of excellent teachers?', in B. Webber (ed.), *Teachers Make a Difference: What is the Research Evidence?*. Wellington: New Zealand Council for Educational Research (NZCER).

An important meta-analysis of 800 educational interventions using effect sizes to enable comparison.

Pawson, R. and Tilley, N. (1997) *Realistic Evaluation.* London: Sage.

A discussion of experimental designs in evaluation work with a useful focus on the role of mediating variables or mechanisms.

Robson, C. (2011) *Real World Research*, 3rd edn. Oxford: Blackwell.

A clear chapter on experimental designs in real world settings, covers both the more common group designs but also with an additional useful section on single case designs.

Shadish, W.R., Cook, T.D. and Campbell, D.T. (2002) *Experimental and Quasi-Experimental Designs for Generalized Causal Inferences*. Boston, MA: Houghton Mifflin. Available at: http://impact.cgiar.org/experimental-and-quasi-experimental-designs-generalized-causal-inference (accessed 10 January 2016).

Update of Cook and Campbell's seminal book on quasi-experimental design.

FURTHER READING

Cook, B., Buysse, V., Klinger, J., Landrum, T., McWilliam, R., Tankersley M. and Test, D. (2015) 'CEC's standards for classifying the evidence base of practices in Special Education', *Remedial and Special Education*, 36 (4): 220–34.

A useful text for those interested in single-case studies in an experimental context.

Cook, T.D. and Campbell, D.T. (1979) *Quasi-Experimentation: Design and Analysis Issues for Field Settings*. Boston, MA: Houghton Mifflin.

Seminal book on the principles and practice of quasi-experimental design.

Howell, D. (2009) *Statistical Methods for Psychology*, 7th edn. Belmont, CA: Wadsworth.

Useful text for the statistical side of experimental design, including a discussion of power analysis.

CHAPTER 7

SURVEYS

Charlie Owen

━━ BOX 7.1 ━━━━━━━━━━━━━━━━━━━━━━━━━━━━━━━━━━━━━

Overview of chapter

This chapter includes:

- Epistemological principles underpinning surveys.
- Definitions of surveys.
- How surveys are designed.
- Different ways of sampling.
- Real life examples of survey research.
- Advantages and disadvantages of probability sampling.
- Key methods of data collection used in survey research.
- Further issues around data collection, including validity.
- Differences between correlation and causation in data analysis.
- Some of the main points students need to consider when conducting a survey.

7.1 INTRODUCTION

We are all familiar with surveys, and most of us have been approached by someone in the street asking if we have a few minutes to take part in a survey, or someone telephoning us with the same question – even though it may turn out they are selling something. We are also used to hearing reports of surveys in the media – especially when the results are 'shocking'. It is this commercial misuse of surveys and the selective reporting and sensationalisation of results that have sometimes given surveys a bad name.

In this chapter, I will investigate the use of surveys for social and educational research. I will look at how surveys are designed, how the data are collected and how they are analysed. I will also consider their strengths and weaknesses, and I shall look at examples of surveys, including surveys of voting intentions, primary education and child poverty, amongst others. When you have completed reading this chapter, you should be in a better position to understand surveys and to judge whether using one is appropriate for your research. You should also be better able to evaluate reports of surveys – whether scientific or the more sensational kind.

7.2 EPISTEMOLOGICAL PRINCIPLES

Surveys are a quantitative method, relying on counting. Their epistemological position is towards the positivist end of the spectrum of approaches (see Chapter 4; and Crotty, 1998). This means that surveys have an objectivist approach, which assumes there are real social phenomena, and that surveys are able to try to capture some of what they are. Although the phenomena themselves might be subjective (such as attitudes, beliefs, opinions), the assumption is that we can try to understand them by assessing them in a more objective way. However, we can never achieve complete objectivity, as we use our own subjectivity to collect and interpret our data. It is the social scientist's role to step back and reflect upon the rigour and adequacy of their own methodology. This is what the philosopher Pierre Bourdieu called the 'objectification of the act of objectification' (Jenkins, 2002: 47).

It is difficult, these days, to find someone who defines themselves as a positivist. One reason for this might be, as the sociologist Anthony Giddens puts it:

> The word 'positivist' … has become more of a derogatory epithet than a useful descriptive concept, and consequently has become largely stripped of whatever agreed meaning it may once have had. (1974: ix)

As we have seen in Chapter 4, currently most social scientists who identify themselves with this philosophical position refer to themselves as being 'post-positivists' (Kuhn, 1962; Popper, 2002/1934).

To remind readers, positivism is characterised by a commitment to empirical observation, and disputes about the nature of reality are to be resolved not by appeals to authority or by rational argument, but by observation, or what Kolakowski (1972) has called the 'rule of phenomenalism'. A modern example concerns advice on the position for babies to sleep. The standard advice, included in the bestselling Dr Spock's *The Common Sense Book of Baby and Child Care* (1958), was to lay the baby on their front (prone). This seemed logical, as, for example, if the baby were to vomit whilst asleep, they would be less likely to choke. However, reviews of empirical studies of the association between sleep position and the sudden infant death syndrome (SIDS) concluded that placing the baby on their back (supine) was much safer (e.g., Gilbert et al., 2005). One observer concluded, 'We now know that the advice promulgated so successfully in Spock's book led to thousands, if not tens of thousands, of avoidable cot deaths' (Chalmers, 2001: 998).

Observation as a way of establishing knowledge requires that people agree on what they have observed, which means that operational criteria have to be established. This is a form of intersubjectivity, meaning that my experience is shared with others, because we agree on the criteria, and for surveys this means researchers have to agree on how surveys should be conducted and what questions should be asked. Survey researchers spend a lot of effort examining their methods and refining their questions. Whilst this is no guarantee of validity, and all research is fallible, this reflexivity on methods is what characterises social science.

7.3 DEFINITIONS: WHAT IS A SURVEY?

The key feature of a survey is that it is a method of making **inferences** about some 'population' based on information collected from a sample. By an inference I mean that we want to be able to draw some conclusions from the data. These conclusions are often about the amount of something: for example, what percentage of pupils is regularly absent from school? Or how many hours per week (on average) do students spend on the Internet? Or what percentage of students believes university prospectuses give a misleading impression of their university? More often, the conclusions we want to draw are about the relations between things: for example, are boys more likely to be absent from school than girls? Or do master's students spend more time on the Internet than undergraduates? Or do science students feel that prospectuses are less misleading than other students? The relationships about which social scientists are interested in drawing inferences are very often inferences about causation: for example, does watching more television cause children to be absent from school; or does spending more time on the Internet cause students to write better assignments; or do students who are failing on their courses tend to think university prospectuses are more misleading? In practice, surveys can only observe that things go together, although the ultimate aim is usually to establish some kind of causal relationship.

For a summary, see Box 7.2.

━━ BOX 7.2 ━━

The definition of a survey

A survey is a methodology that aims to gain information about a specific group by asking questions of a representative sample of that group.

Results are typically used to understand the attitudes, beliefs, or knowledge of a particular group, and sometimes to suggest a causal relationship.

Population

Surveys sample a population, which does not have to be a geographically defined group but is defined by having some feature or characteristic(s) in common. For example, it might be the population of school pupils in England (or in just one school), the population of undergraduate students in physics in the world (or at one university), or the population of prisoners undertaking remedial English classes in the United Kingdom. Populations also do not have to be people: a population might be all primary schools in England or all universities in Japan.

If we want to know something about this population, then the most thorough and complete way of gaining the information would be to contact every member: that would be a **census**. Most countries in the world carry out a population census every ten years, with active encouragement from the United Nations (UN). However, for most purposes, a census would be too time consuming and too expensive. Instead, researchers will gather information from a sample of the population – that is a subset of all the people who make up the population. On the basis of the results from the sample, we then make inferences about the population, and the way in which we make these inferences, and the confidence we can have in them, depends upon the way in which the sample is selected from the population. It is vital that our sample is representative of the population, and there are well-established ways of selecting representative samples from which we can feel confident that our findings are generalisable to a wider population.

The inferences that we seek to make from our sample to the population are the generalisations that we seek to make from behaviour (including expressed attitudes or beliefs) in the survey to behaviour in the real world. Our theory says that these generalisations will only be valid if the people in the sample are representative of the population.

It is easy, or intuitive, to believe that large samples are always more likely to be representative of the wider population, than surveys that have smaller numbers. However, the importance of selecting a representative sample was demonstrated long ago in a famous example, the *Literary Digest* poll to predict the results of the USA presidential election. In 1936, the *Literary Digest* distributed over 10 million straw vote ballots, and got back over 2.3 million – a huge sample. However, their prediction of the result was spectacularly wrong. The poll predicted a victory for the Republican candidate, with 55 per cent of the vote, when in fact the Democrat candidate, Franklin D. Roosevelt, was returned, with 61 per cent, the Republican getting just 37 per cent. The reason for this failure was bias in the sampling: 'bias' means some kind of systematic error in the way elements from the population are chosen for the sample. In this case, 'The sample was drawn primarily from automobile registration lists and telephone books' (Squire, 1988: 126–7). Unfortunately for the pollsters, people who owned cars and telephones in 1936 were not representative of the whole population, and in a follow-up survey, Squire found that people with a car and/or a telephone were much more likely to vote for the Republican candidate than those who had neither. Consequently, they were more likely to be included in the sample, and this bias was more than enough to eliminate the advantages of the very large sample size. This demonstrates the important role of having a sound sampling strategy to obtain a representative sample.

Another more recent example of surveys failing to predict the results of an election concern the UK general election in 2015. The polls, even on the day of the election, had the two main parties in the election, the Conservative and Labour parties, neck and neck on 34 per cent each, and saying the result was too close to call. When the votes were counted, the Conservative Party had won an outright victory, with a 7 per cent margin over Labour and an overall majority of Members of Parliament (330/650). Very soon after the result, there were a number of investigations into how all the polls had failed to detect this huge lead. Many possibilities have been suggested: these include a late swing to the Conservatives, suggesting that the polls were correct at the time they were taken; 'shy Tories' (Conservatives) who were reluctant to admit to pollsters that they were voting Conservative; 'lazy' Labour voters, who said they would vote but then stayed at home. However, none of these stood up to scrutiny (Wells, 2015; Sturgis, 2016). In particular, some polling organisations followed up the samples they had used before the election to ask how they had actually voted, and they got the same (inaccurate) result as the pre-election polls. This indicates that it was not the answers that people gave that were misleading, but the sample itself was at fault. YouGov, one of the leading polling agencies, published its own review of what went wrong and concluded that: 'neither late swing nor misreporting provide a satisfactory explanation for the polling error in 2015' (Rivers and Wells, 2015: 17). Instead, they concluded, there was something at fault with their sampling. All the polls used the same way of identifying a sample: they used pre-established panels from which to select. These panels are self-selecting and agree to take part in surveys for a small reward. The survey company selects from the panel to try to make the sample representative of the population (see **quota sampling** below), but if the people who join the panel are not like the general population, then this might not be enough. In the last four days before the election, eight major polling organisations between them interviewed over 29,000 people with YouGov alone interviewing approximately 2,000 people a day, selected from a pool of approximately 34,000 panelists. (For more information about the 2015 UK general election see WEBLINK 1.) But as with the *Literary Digest*, sample size cannot compensate for lack of representativeness in the sample.

WEBLINK 1

2015 UK
general election
information

The British Election Study (BES) used a different sampling methodology: they took a **random sample** of households. The BES then made strenuous efforts to contact all the sampled households, calling up to nine times, and they also interviewed people face to face, rather than with an online survey. When this sample was asked (after the election) how they had voted, the result was very close to the actual result: the BES sample gave the Conservatives a lead of 7.78 per cent, when the actual result was 6.51 per cent (Mellon and Prosser, 2015: 11).

Another regular survey, the British Social Attitudes survey (BSA), also asked its 4,328 respondents whether and how they had voted. In contrast to the polls, the BSA matched the outcome of the election quite closely. Amongst those who said they had voted, support for the Conservatives was 6.1 per cent higher than that for Labour, very close to the 6.6 per cent lead actually recorded in the election (Curtice, 2016: 10). It is worth noting that Labour was six points ahead among respondents who answered the door at the first visit, almost exactly the same as the polls using quota samples. This suggests that those who are hard to contact were different from those who were easy to contact, and not including them in the quota samples led to a bias.

BSA, like the BES, conducted face-to-face interviews with a sample chosen at random. The success of these two surveys in matching the actual election outcome, in contrast to the other polls, suggests it was not respondents' failure to give valid answers that made the difference, but the way the samples were chosen, and that random samples proved superior to quota samples.

7.4 SAMPLING

There are two broad categories of sampling strategy. These are '**probability sampling**' and **non-probability sampling**. Each have their merits, but probability samples give more robust ways of making inferences, simply because they provide researchers with a better understanding of the relationship between the sample and the population. For a list of techniques that each of these two modes of sampling typically use, see Box 7.3.

▰▰▰ BOX 7.3 ▰▰

Probability and non-probability sampling

In *probability sampling*, the probability of selection of each participant is known – typical probability sampling techniques include:

- Simple random samples.
- Systematic random samples.
- Stratified random samples.
- Cluster samples.

In *non-probability sampling*, the probability of selection of each participant is unknown – typical non-probability sampling techniques include:

- Quota samples.
- Purposive samples.
- Snowball samples.
- Convenience or opportunity samples.

Probability sampling

For probability sampling we need to know the probability that each member of the population will be in the sample. The easiest probability sample is the simple random sample, where everyone has the same probability, or equal chance of being selected.

An example of a simple random sample is a raffle where all the ticket stubs are put into a container, shaken up, and then one or more is chosen at random. Each ticket has the same probability of being selected; however, if the shaking was not very thorough the tickets put in last would be nearer the top, and so would have a higher chance of being selected: this is called a **biased sample**, because the probabilities of being chosen are not equal. A biased sample is not simply unrepresentative, it is systematically inclined in one direction, and the whole aim of sampling strategies is to avoid bias.

If I were interested in estimating the satisfaction of students on a particular course, I could draw a random sample of students and get them to complete a student satisfaction questionnaire. Imagine that there were 100 students on the course and I wanted a sample of 20. To get a simple random sample, I might write all their names on slips of paper, mix them up and pick out 20. Each student would have the same probability of being chosen, namely 1 in 5 (20/100). I could reduce the work involved in sampling a little: if I were supplied with a list of names by the administration, rather than writing the names out I could choose them from the list. If I took every fifth student (being careful to choose a random starting point in the list) I would still get a random sample. This would be called a 'systematic random sample', as there is some system or logic in the choice. The key point is that every student still has the same probability of being selected.

However, random samples do not always require equal probability of selection – as long as the probability is known. For example, I may suspect that male and female students have different degrees of satisfaction, so I want to be sure to get a mix in my sample. With a simple random sample I will probably get a mix, but not necessarily – especially if the gender balance in the group is very uneven. Imagine there are 70 female students in my group and 30 male: it would be very unlikely that a sample of 20 would have no male students, but it could happen, or the number might be small. If instead I split the population into a female group and a male group, I could sample from each and be sure of getting a mixture. I would then have to split my register into a female group and a male group and randomly select from each group. These two groups are called 'strata' and such this sample is called a 'stratified random sample'.

Female and male students do not have the same probability of being in the sample, but all female students have the same probability as each other and all male students have the same probability as each other. If the sampling probabilities for females and males were kept the same, then we would end up with 14 females and 6 males, so that the sample would have the same proportions as the student population. This is a common practice, and it makes interpretation of results for the whole sample very straightforward. However, if we wanted to compare females and males, then it would be better to have equal numbers (i.e., 10 of each), as the **power** of the comparison depends on the size of the smallest group. Issues of power are dealt with in more detail later. Stratifying the sample is a good strategy as it makes the sampling more efficient, but it does require that you have some information in advance (which is not always available), and it does require an extra effort of subdividing the population.

In all of these strategies, before I could make my selection, I would need a complete list of the population, and this is called the **sampling frame**. For probability samples, we always need a sampling frame, and although generating such a frame can be time consuming and expensive, it is a necessary feature of probability samples. However, there may be some possible shortcuts. Imagine my exercise of measuring student satisfaction became known about in my university, and it was decided that I might extend the exercise to the whole student body. Drawing up a complete list of all the students could be quite a task. I might decide that rather than sample randomly across all students, I might instead select a sample of courses, and only include students on those courses. That would also save a lot of time and effort, as instead of dashing about all over the campus, I could just concentrate on the courses I had selected.

I would, of course, need a sampling frame of courses, but that is easier to compile than a complete list of students. This is known as a 'cluster sample', with each course representing a cluster.

I would still need a sampling strategy for the clusters: I could choose a simple random sample, or a systematic random sample from the list supplied by the registry. I might even want to stratify the courses, for example into arts and science courses, or into full-time and part-time courses. Having selected the courses, I then need to decide on a further strategy for selecting students within courses. I might include all students on a course, or I might have a simple random sample, a **systematic sample** or even a **stratified sample**. In this way I would have a multi-stage sampling strategy. Much of research involves accommodating competing alternatives: cluster samples increase sampling error, because people within a cluster are generally more alike than individuals chosen at random, but the savings in time and effort gained by cluster sampling means that more data can be collected, compensating for the greater sampling error by the increased sample size. This makes it a very effective strategy.

Non-probability sampling

The time and effort needed to compile a sampling frame in order to draw a probability sample can make non-probability sampling more attractive – indeed, sometimes, it is simply impossible to compile a frame, as no such list exists. A sampling method often used in market research and opinion polling is quota sampling, where the sample attempts to gain representativeness by matching the proportions of known characteristics of the total population with the proportions in the sample – for example, the proportions of male and female or of different age or ethnic groups.

In order to get a representative sample, the population is categorised into sub-groups and a sample chosen with numbers in those groups in proportion to their numbers in the population. So, in my group of 70 female students and 30 male students, for a sample of 20 my quotas would be 14 female students and 6 male. For a quota sample, I would make sure I administered questionnaires to the right number of female and male students. Although I would need to know the relative numbers in the sub-groups, I would not need any further information – I would not need a list of names.

In other words, I would not need to draw up a sampling frame. For a population of 100 this is not a huge effort but, for a large and dispersed population, not having to generate a sampling frame can be a large saving. Imagine again that I want to distribute student satisfaction questionnaires across the university. Instead of getting lists of courses and lists of students, the university registry might tell me that 60 per cent of students were taking arts courses and 40 per cent were doing science. If I decided on a sample size of 200, that would mean I needed 120 arts students and 80 science students. I could approach students in some public area and ask them if they were doing arts or science or, better still, with the tutor's or lecturer's permission, I could attend student classes and then give out my questionnaires to the right numbers to meet my quotas.

Quota samples superficially resemble stratified random samples. The main difference between them is that in the stratified random sample it is the population that is stratified and in the quota sample it is the sample that is stratified. This means that for a stratified random sample the elements are assigned to strata in advance of sampling, whereas in quota samples elements are added to the quota only as they occur.

The theory behind the quota sample is that people selected to match certain criteria, such as gender, age, social status, etc., will have similar views, so as long as our quotas match the population, the sample will be representative. Polling organisations tend to use quota samples and one attraction is that they are much cheaper to conduct than probability samples. They can also be conducted much more quickly, especially when samples are drawn from a pre-existing panel, such as the polls for the 2015 general election described above. However, there is a danger that quota samples will not be representative, even when the quotas match the population. Although interviewers are given quotas to interview, the final selection of who to interview is left to the interviewer, and there is no **a priori reason** why such a selection method should lead to representative samples. One potential cause of selection bias stems from refusals to take part. Refusal rates in quota samples tend to be very high in comparison with most random samples. For example, Jowell et al. (1993) cite a number of studies with refusal rates of the order of 45 per cent. Furthermore, interviewers only approach those who are available, and are not required to search out those not immediately available. Thus, refusal and non-contact will potentially bias quota samples: the samples will be biased towards those whom interviewers feel comfortable approaching, those who are available and those who are willing to take part on the first encounter.

A random sample tries to be representative by fixing the probabilities of being in the sample to give everyone an equal chance of being selected; a quota sample tries to be representative by matching the balance of key characteristics in the population. Because of the need for a sampling frame, a random sample can be difficult to set up, whereas a quota sample can be defined with very little information. The time saved in developing the sampling frame, and in recruiting the people selected from it, can be used instead to recruit a bigger quota sample. However, size cannot compensate for bias (remember the *Literary Digest*), and recruiting to fixed quotas cannot be sure to eliminate bias from quota samples. However, whilst probability samples are unbiased, if those sampled do not take part in the survey there is a risk that the achieved sample is still biased, and to an unknown degree. Squire's (1988) follow-up to the *Literary Digest* survey found that even amongst those receiving an invitation to take part, Democrat voters were much less likely to respond than Republican voters, and this non-response bias contributed to the error of the prediction. However, probability samples are also subject to non-response biases, and low response rates undermine their representativeness. A number of studies have compared results from probability samples and quota samples, and Cumming concluded that: 'unless a very high response rate can be achieved, quota sample surveys with age and sex quota controls may be an acceptable alternative to probability sample surveys' (1990: 132).

A different way of trying to achieve a representative sample is the purposive sample.

For such a sample, people are chosen on purpose, because they meet some prespecified criteria. Most commonly, they are selected because they are deemed to be 'typical' of the population. So if the typical student in my university were a woman in her early twenties doing media studies, then I might just need a few of them to get a good view of student satisfaction. Of course, I wouldn't have much idea of the range of opinion, or if it differed by subject of study, as I would have already factored that out. Sometimes a purposive sample is chosen not to be typical, but to include extremes, so as to get a variety of views. So, we might choose a few students known to be very satisfied and a few known to be very dissatisfied and ask them our questions. That might give some information on the range of views, but it would be of little use for monitoring changes in the overall level of satisfaction over time, as the sample was never representative. The key message is that different strategies are appropriate for different purposes.

There are times when we might want to research something for which no sampling frame exists, or could possibly exist, and about which we cannot even know what quotas there are or who is typical. For these circumstances, a different strategy is required. Imagine we wanted to conduct some research on drug dealers. It is no good asking for a list from which to take a sample! However, it is often a reasonable assumption that people in the population of interest know other people in the group. In theory, if you can make contact with one person – or, better still, a small number of people – your initial contacts should be able to put you into contact with others. They in turn will introduce you to further members, and so on. This form of sampling is known as a '**snowball sample**', using the metaphor of the cartoon snowball that picks up volume as it rolls down the hill.

There are a number of problems with the method: the initial contacts might be difficult to make; the initial contacts might be reluctant to identify others, especially if illegal activity is involved; and the achieved sample is potentially highly unrepresentative of the population. Nevertheless, it can be the only practical method when working in some completely unknown area or when it is impossible to know who the population are. A few years ago, I heard of a PhD student who was exploring the lives of men who were HIV positive. He began his research by attending a clinic and the sample grew from the point after he befriended a patient.

A very popular strategy is that of the **convenience sample**, sometimes called an **opportunity sample**.

This barely merits the status of its own title, as it means little more than the people you can happen to get hold of – nothing could be more convenient than that. Although such a sample should not be used for a main research study, it can nevertheless be helpful for testing out an idea or even for piloting your research.

7.5 SOME EXAMPLES OF SURVEY RESEARCH

The next section presents and discusses issues arising from four examples of surveys, each using a different method of sampling frame.

1. The role of private education in the goal of achieving universal primary education (2003): stratified random sample

The focus of the research reported by Tooley et al. (2007) was the role of private education in meeting the UN Millennium Development Goal (MDG) of universal primary education. The research was conducted in the District of Hyderabad in the state of Andhra Pradesh in India. Tooley et al. report that the district has a population of 3.83 million and that nearly half of the population live in 'notified slums' (ibid.: 541). They selected three zones in the District for data collection, with a total population of about 800,000 (ibid.: 542).

They described three types of school management: government school (managed either by the state or local government); private aided schools (managed privately although teacher salaries and other expenses are government funded); and private unaided (PUA) schools (managed and funded entirely privately).

The main focus of their study was the private unaided schools: 'PUA schools are of two types, recognised and unrecognised. The former have purportedly met the regulatory requirements of the state' (ibid.: 541). The researchers were particularly interested in the unrecognised PUAs. However, there was no list of these, so the team had to construct their own. They did this by conducting a census of schools in the three zones:

> A team of eight researchers recruited from a local non-government organisation ... were asked to physically visit every street and alleyway in the area, ... looking for all schools, primary and secondary. (Ibid.: 542)

This is clearly a very difficult and laborious process. The total number of schools located was 918. Of these, 34.9 per cent (320) were government schools, 5.3 per cent (49) were private aided, 23.3 per cent (214) were recognised PUA schools were and 36.5 per cent (335) were unrecognised PUA. Some data were collected for each of these schools, but the main data collection was for a *stratified random sample* of 153 schools. Schools were stratified into approximate size bands and three management categories: PUA (unrecognised), PUA (recognised), and government (the few private aided schools were not included). Since differences on the basis of the school management was an important part of the research, it made sense to stratify on this basis, so as to be sure of getting a balance in the sample. School size was also felt to be a possible influence on school performance, so that this was also an important source of variation for stratification. Remember, stratification is always beneficial for the sample as it is making use of information already available. In this case, the information about management and school size were collected during the census and were available for sample selection.

2. The Young Lives project investigating child poverty (2002): purposive and probability sampling

In the example above, a census was conducted in a small area in order to generate a sampling frame. However, sometimes even this is impossible, and other strategies have to be employed. This is illustrated in the Young Lives project, which was 'a collaborative study investigating childhood poverty in four countries – Peru, Vietnam, Ethiopia and India (Andhra Pradesh State) – through follow-up of cohorts of children over time' (Wilson et al., 2006: 352). The initial aim of the project was 'to measure and find out about what happens to children born into poverty in the millennium' (ibid.: 355). Consequently, a 'representative' sample of the population would not provide a sufficient focus on the poor. There were no frames in any of the countries that would have enabled accurate targeting of poor families, so alternative strategies were required. Initial sites were chosen **purposively**, on the basis of detailed local knowledge. These were referred to as 'sentinel' sites, and then at the household level the research teams constructed lists of household members, which acted as sampling frames from which to select suitable children:

> The Young Lives sampling design uses both purposive and probability sampling methods – purposive in that the sentinel sites were selected on the basis of considerable thought, largely focused on their poverty status ... Households within the sites were selected by a method equivalent to random sampling ..., according to local conditions, which suggests that whilst the samples may not be nationally representative they should be representative of the site from which they were selected. (Ibid.: 356)

Sample size is very much related to cost, and there is a necessary trade-off between coverage and cost. For the Young Lives study it was important that the children should be in geographically compact areas, as the sites were also intended to provide suitable settings for a range of complementary studies. It was decided to sample 20 sentinel sites in each of the four countries, selected in a purposive way. This number was thought to give enough diversity without making data collection too costly. At each site, the project drew up lists of households with children aged between 6 and 17 months and 100 households were selected, with procedures to over-sample poorer households. From each household one child was chosen, at random if there was more than one eligible child. In this way, each country had a sample of 2,000 children.

3. Choosing to work in childcare (2001): a multi-stage strategy including a stratified random sample, a cluster sample and a simple random sample

A study known as *Entry, Retention and Loss*, conducted on behalf of the former Department for Education and Skills (DfES), and of which I was part, was concerned with why people choose to work in childcare, why they stay and what makes them leave (Cameron et al., 2001). Part of the study involved a survey of nursery workers in independent (private or voluntary) day nurseries in England. We wanted to choose a representative sample of these workers, and we wanted it to be a probability sample, for the reasons I have already mentioned above, namely that probability samples are unbiased and can be used to generalise to the wider population. So, the first thing we needed was a sampling frame. Although there was no list of all nursery staff, there were lists of nurseries because, under the Children Act 1989, all independent nurseries were required to register with their local authority. At that time, there were 150 local authorities in England, and as each had a list of registered nurseries in their area, this was the starting point for constructing the sampling frame.

We could have chosen to visit every local authority (LA), but that would have been very expensive since such a widely dispersed sample would have required a lot of travelling. Instead we chose to sample a selection of LAs. As there are different types of authority, which might differ in their availability of childcare and of employment, we decided to stratify LAs. The strata were as follows: Inner London, Outer London, Metropolitan (large conurbations like Manchester and Liverpool), Unitary (smaller urban areas like Bristol and Brighton) and Two-Tier (or Shire Counties, which include rural areas, such as Essex and Cornwall). We decided to select 16 LAs – 3 from each stratum plus an extra for Inner London as this had a large number of nurseries. The figure of 16 that was chosen was large enough to give a good spread (about 10 per cent of LAs), but reasonable in terms of logistics. Within each stratum, LAs were chosen at random. These 16 local authorities therefore constituted a stratified random sample of all LAs.

A list of all registered nurseries was obtained from each LA. It would have been possible to contact all the nurseries in the sampled authorities, but, again, to cut down on the amount of work involved in getting cooperation and in travelling to the nurseries, a sub-sample was chosen. From each list, a simple random sample of nurseries was chosen. A total of 441 nurseries were selected. When we tried to arrange the interviews, we found that 10 per cent of selected nurseries could not be contacted, which we concluded in most cases were likely to have ceased operation since being registered. Of the remaining, 396,145 (36 per cent) refused to take part in the study but 251 (64 per cent) agreed. This is not a bad refusal rate, but there is always a concern with any survey that the non-respondents might be systematically different from the respondents, and so introduce bias into the sample.

These nurseries form a cluster sample, since each nursery included a 'cluster' of nursery workers. Each nursery was visited and up to 10 staff were interviewed. Where a nursery had 10 or fewer staff, all were interviewed; and where there were more than 10, a simple random sample was chosen from the staff list, using random number tables. In total 2,060 staff from 251 nurseries were included in the final sample.

So, there was a multi-stage sampling strategy: a stratified random sample of LAs, a cluster sample of nurseries and a simple random sample of staff.

4. Teachers' attitudes towards inclusion (2000): a non-probability example using purposive, self-selected (or voluntary)

Not all surveys of course use probability samples, and indeed it is probably only a minority of surveys which do. The next example used a non-probability sampling strategy. Avramidis et al. (2000) reported on a study of mainstream teachers' attitudes towards the inclusion of children with special educational needs. They did this by selecting one local education authority (LEA)[1] in South-West England. The authority was identified purposively as one 'where considerable progress [in promoting inclusive education] has been made over the last few years' (ibid.: 195). Thus, the LEA was not chosen to be 'representative' of the whole country, but as one where particular efforts had been made with regard to inclusive education.

The actual survey was conducted in a subset of schools within the LEA, although the report does not give much detail on the sampling strategy employed:

> The survey involved 23 mainstream schools, 14 primary and nine secondary, representing urban, suburban and rural areas of the LEA. Seven primary schools and four secondary were chosen because the LEA had identified them as examples of good inclusive practice … These schools were self-selected. The sample was balanced with another seven primary and five secondary schools randomly selected across the rest of the LEA. (Ibid.: 198)

Thus, there would seem to have been some stratification by type of area, but this is not made explicit and the criteria for assignment to an area type are not given. Some of the schools were chosen in a purposive way – 'as examples of good inclusive practice' – but the rest were 'randomly selected'. It is not clear what is meant in the quotation above by 'self-selected', but generally getting a volunteer sample is to be avoided, as volunteers are likely to differ significantly from the general population. Consequently, volunteer samples are likely to be biased (Rosenthal and Rosnow, 1975).

As is usual, not everyone selected into the sample agreed to take part:

> Of the initial sample, seven schools (five secondary and two primary) opted out … The overall sample thus represented 16 schools participating in the survey (12 primary and four secondary). (Ibid.: 198)

---

1 Prior to 1 April 2009, Local Education Authorities (LEA) were the bodies responsible for the local administration of state sector education services in England and Wales. These bodies are now been subsumed under local authorities (LAs).

This refusal is a form of non-response, and again might be expected to introduce bias into the sample, as those who refuse to take part are likely to differ from those who do take part. The issue of non-response is dealt with in the next section.

7.6 ADVANTAGES AND DISADVANTAGES OF PROBABILITY SAMPLES

As I have already written, the huge advantage of a probability sample is that it is unbiased, but we cannot know about the degree of bias in non-probability samples. However, probability samples have two major disadvantages. One involves the need to have a sampling frame and the other is the impact of non-response.

The need for a sampling frame

Probability samples always require a sampling frame – a list. Sometimes, these lists already exist and can be accessed. For example, it is easy to get a list of universities in Japan (it is available from Wikipedia, for instance) or a list of primary schools in England (from the Department for Education: EduBase2) or a list of private household addresses in the UK (the Postcode Address File, or PAF, maintained by the Royal Mail) for conducting household surveys. However, other populations may have no list: for example, private unaided schools in India (see the example above) or educational psychologists offering cognitive behaviour therapy (CBT). To select a probability sample in these circumstances requires some preliminary work to generate a frame. This can be very expensive and time consuming. Moreover, as we have already seen, it may be the case that it is simply impossible to create a frame and a non-probability sample is the best (and sometimes the only) solution.

Non-response

A second disadvantage is that having selected a sample from a frame the elements have to be identified and located. If I wanted to estimate student satisfaction in a particular university, the university registry might supply a list of all their students and I could use that to draw a sample. However, I would then have to find each student selected into the sample and get them to take part in the survey. That can be enormously difficult: imagine how much easier it would be to select a few classes – in a purposive or opportunistic way – and to visit them during a session and to invite the students to take part. This leads into the difficult issue of non-response, where a selected member of the sample does not take part in the survey. There are two types of non-response: non-contact and refusal. Non-contact is where a sampled element cannot be located: for example, a student's address may be out of date or a selected address from the PAF never has anyone who answers the door. The other form of non-response is refusal, which is where a sampled person is located but they decline to take part in the survey.

The concern over non-response is that it might introduce bias into the sample if those not contacted or who refuse differ systematically from those who take part. This I why my advice to survey researchers has always been to maximise the response rates, and, in particular, to try and work on persuading contacts who are reluctant to take part:

> an important rationale for wanting to maximise response rate is an assumption that this will bring greater gains in accuracy of estimation than simply increasing the selected sample size. In other words, it is assumed that adding in hard-to-get respondents will not merely improve precision, but will reduce non-response bias. (Lynn et al., 2002: 135)

It is always difficult to estimate non-response bias because, by definition, you cannot collect information from those who do not take part. However, a number of studies have looked at the impact of non-response by comparing initial participants (the easy-to-get) with later ones, either through repeated efforts to contact (the difficult-to-contact) or through efforts to persuade initial refusers (the reluctant). The assumption has been that refusers are more liable to be different from the easy-to-get than are the difficult-to-contact, and it is easy to see how this might be the case. Take the example of the student satisfaction survey: it might well be the case that students who were satisfied with their course may feel well disposed to the organisers and willing to share their approval, whilst those who were dissatisfied may feel no inclination to be helpful, and this would introduce a bias in favour of satisfaction. On the other hand, it might be that those who were dissatisfied feel this is their opportunity to voice their anger and so return their questionnaires at a high rate whilst those who were satisfied do not reply as they feel little needs to improve. That would produce a bias in favour of dissatisfaction.

It is more difficult to find out about refusers than the difficult-to-contact, as by definition they have refused to take part. However, some studies have collected data on refusers: for example, Foster (1996) reported on a study conducted by the Government Statistical Service. Interviewers for the *Family Expenditure Survey* called at sampled addresses. Where a household refused to take part, their recent census data was accessed, and in that way it was possible to compare the characteristics of those who took part in the survey with those who refused. These studies suggest that the difficult-to-contact may have more differences between them and those who took part than did the refusers:

> This would appear to suggest that resources for extended efforts might be better concentrated upon making contact with difficult-to-contact ... than upon attempting refusal conversions. (Lynn et al., 2002: 142)

Furthermore, studies suggest that efforts to reduce non-response may have little impact on the conclusions from a survey:

> Unquestionably, the highest possible response rates, legitimately obtained and within the bounds of the project at hand, are desirable in survey research.
> But ... a higher response rate is not automatically indicative of better data.
> (Langer, 2003: 18)

Of course, non-response is also an issue for non-probability samples, but in those cases it is much more difficult to quantify, as people are not pre-selected for the sample. In some cases a refusal rate could be calculated, but the crucial non-contact rate is impossible to calculate. However, the reason that non-response is a particular issue for probability samples is that it undermines their basis for a claim to representativeness.

Response rates to surveys have been falling: 'response rates across all modes of survey administration have declined, in some cases precipitously' (American Association for Public Opinion Research, 2013). The UK Office of National Statistics reported a decline in the response rates for its regular household surveys: the response rate for the Labour Force Survey went down from 74 per cent in 2005 to 60 per cent in 2008 (Betts and Lound, 2010). This means that the representative samples carefully selected by probability samples are potentially undermined. It has led to some questions about the utility of the extra effort involved in drawing probability samples if the representativeness of their achieved samples is reduced. For example, Groves has speculated as follows:

> Many nonprobability sample designs attempt to balance respondents on a set
> of attributes correlated with the survey variables, thus assuring that respondents
> resemble population distributions on those variables. This balancing is
> obtained by quotas or other mechanisms to achieve the targeted number of
> interviews, with relatively little effort at follow-up or refusal conversion.
> With probability sampling, both repeated callbacks and refusal conversion are
> required. But given the rising costs of achieving higher response rates and the
> findings of few non-response biases in lower response rate surveys, some in the
> field are questioning the value of the probability sampling framework for surveys.
> (Groves, 2006: 667)

WEBLINK 2

Non-response
rates
information

There is an extensive literature on non-response bias (e.g., Groves et al., 2002; American Association for Public Opinion Research, 2013), which goes beyond this chapter. For more information about this topic see WEBLINK 2.

7.7 METHODS OF DATA COLLECTION

The typical methods of data collection for surveys are interviews and questionnaires. An interview is usually conducted one-to-one, and this may be face-to-face or by telephone. There are some advantages to the interview as a method of data collection. Since there is a personal invitation to take part, people find it more difficult to refuse, so the response rate for an interview is generally higher than for a questionnaire. Also, if an interviewee finds a question difficult to understand, then the interviewer can clarify it, and this is not possible with a questionnaire. However, it is important for the reliability of the survey that questions are asked in a consistent way: if there is more than one interviewer, then the answers they get should not depend on who asks the questions. Consequently, interviews for surveys are almost always highly structured, and interviewers generally work from of strict, predetermined, text – essentially reading out a questionnaire – which ensures a consistency of delivery across interviewers.

More common as a means of data collection is the questionnaire, which again is typically highly structured, mostly consisting of closed questions. Great care has to be taken in constructing questions for questionnaires, as the wording has to be unambiguous and easy to understand. This is because questionnaires are usually completed alone, with no one to clarify the meaning of questions if there are any ambiguities. On the other hand, it is an advantage for questionnaires that the questions can be carefully crafted and refined, with pre-testing, or pilot, being an essential part of the research process to iron out any imprecision or uncertainties. There is a lot of guidance on writing good questions (see, e.g., Oppenheim, 1992; Foddy, 1993).

A big advantage of the questionnaire is that it can be distributed to a large number of people very easily. It can be given out by hand, delivered by post or distributed via the Internet. The use of the web to deliver questionnaires is becoming increasingly popular, partly because it is so cheap and easy to deliver large numbers of questionnaires quickly.

The disadvantage of questionnaires is that response rates can be low: a meta-analysis of return rates for 39 surveys which compared postal and Internet questionnaires found an average response rate for postal questionnaires of 45 per cent, but with many below 20 per cent, and web-based questionnaires with an average of 34 per cent, but with many much lower (Shih and Xitao, 2008), and as we have seen low response rates always raise concerns about the representativeness of the achieved sample. Response rates for web-based surveys are typically lower than for postal questionnaires, but strategies have been developed to increase response rates (Fan and Yan, 2010). In particular, it was consistently found that sending a pre-notification before sending out the survey and at least two reminders afterwards was effective in increasing response rates – even in some instances doubling them (Cook et al., 2000).

7.8 FURTHER ISSUES AROUND DATA COLLECTION
Validity

So now we know how to select samples and how to collect data, but are surveys a valid way of gathering data about social activities? In social research, the term 'validity' is used to mean the extent to which a procedure measures what it is intended to measure. There are two aspects to validity: internal and external. 'Internal validity' means whether the survey was conducted rigorously, or if there were particular features about it that would undermine its validity. One factor that could reduce validity would be if the sample did not accurately represent the population. In addition, the questions have to be framed so that they are clearly understood by the participants. The participants also have to be able and willing to answer the questions. The **external validity** of a survey means the extent to which the findings can be generalised to the population. A survey that is poorly designed and conducted – that is, with a low internal validity – will almost certainly lead to misleading inferences, and so have a low external validity. However, a survey with a high internal validity may nevertheless still have a low external validity, which could be because the answers people give in a survey may not be good predictors of their behaviour.

Survey interviews and questionnaires tend to have high **face validity**, that is to say they appear to be about what they are actually about – generally there is no attempt to trick or deceive the people taking part. If I ask you about your satisfaction with a particular course, it is because this is what I want to know about; or, if I ask nursery staff how much they are paid, it is because I want to know about the pay for this group of workers – there is no hidden agenda.

One problem is whether people give valid answers and there are many reasons why people may not. First of all, people may simply not want to tell the truth: people generally want to give a good impression, and so they might distort their answers to make themselves look better. So, if I ask students how many hours they spend studying each week, they might exaggerate and answer more hours than they actually do. Or, if I ask them how much alcohol they drink, they might tend to understate that. However, one study found the opposite bias: in a follow-up to a survey on alcohol consumption, Lahaut et al. (2002) found that non-drinkers were less likely to respond to the original survey, so that rates of alcohol consumption were overestimated. In another example, surveys have been found to underestimate abortion rates, both because of underreporting by respondents and by selective non-response (Peytchev et al., 2010).

Another reason people may give false answers is because they are trying to be helpful. Often, when asked a question in a survey, people will assume there is something else behind the question: they will ask themselves, what does he/she *really* want to know? They try to work out the situation, and then answer accordingly. When our interviewers ask nursery staff if they were thinking of leaving, they started to think like this: if she is asking that, it means she thinks that people will want to leave, so I should say I am thinking of leaving. This has been called the **demand characteristics** of the situation (Orne, 1962). The simple act of asking the questions sets up expectations in the person being asked, which can produce invalid responses. Sometimes people do not have a view, but they may feel that, having been asked, they need to give an answer. The tendency for people to behave differently from how they usually behave, and improve a particular aspect of their behaviour, is sometimes known as the 'Hawthorne effect' (which we have come across in Chapter 6), after the phenomenon was noticed in some industrial experiments in a factory in Hawthorne, USA, in the 1920s and 1930s (Dowling and Brown, 2010: 46–7).

Asking a question can have another effect: it might be that before you asked, the person did not have a view but the very act of making the respondent think about the question may cause them to reconsider their position (see, e.g., Krosnick, 2002). For example, when we asked nursery staff if they were thinking about leaving their job this may have set off this particular thought process: *well, I hadn't thought about it, but now that I do, I realise there are lots of things I don't like about this job – I think I'll look for another*. So, when they answered, 'Yes, I am thinking of leaving,' this was a true answer but it was not true before they were asked the question. Therefore, we can see that a survey should not be regarded as always being an inert measuring instrument; it may change the very thing it is trying to measure.

Yet another reason people may not give a valid answer is because they do not know the answer: this may be because they do not have the information (e.g., they may not know their hourly pay) or they may not be aware of the true answer. According to the advertising industry, in the USA in 2014 carmakers spent $14.1 billion on advertising. (See WEBLINK 3 for more information about advertising expenditure in the USA.) Yet, if you ask people why they bought the car they have, they will give you many good reasons – about emissions, miles per gallon, safety, etc. – but no one will say it was because they thought there was a good advert for the car. Why do car companies spend so much on advertising if none of us are influenced by it? A survey which asked people if the advertising influenced their choice of car might well suggest that the advertising budget is wasted, but, given the amount of money that car makers invest in promoting their products, this seems highly unlikely to be true.

WEBLINK 3

Advertising
expenditure in
the USA

7.9 DIFFERENCES BETWEEN CORRELATION AND CAUSATION IN DATA ANALYSIS

Surveys observe people where they are: if two things tend to go together, then we only know they are correlated, not that one causes the other. For example, if we find that people who work longer hours report more stress, we cannot assume that the long hours are causing the stress. It might be the other way round: people who are stressed choose to work more hours, perhaps as a way of relieving their stress. Or, both might be caused by a third factor: people with unsatisfactory home lives might be more stressed and choose to work more hours to avoid being at home. Only an experiment, which varies one factor and observes the effect on the other, can establish causation. Nevertheless, there is a very strong temptation in surveys to argue, and make the leap, from correlation to causation. A recent report from the think tank Bright Blue reviewed evidence for a relationship between poverty and having diverse social networks, for 'disadvantaged people from ethnic minority groups' (Shorthouse, 2015). The report cites evidence from surveys that there is a correlation between having two or more close friends and a lower likelihood of being in poverty. But, Shorthouse makes the elision from correlation to causation when he concludes that 'strong social networks play some role in reducing poverty' (ibid.: 3) and that 'the diversity of individuals' social networks – in regards to socio-economic and ethnic diversity – could help lessen poverty' (ibid.: 4). The proposition could easily be the other way round: that the poor cannot afford to socialise with friends and so their social networks are weaker. The temptation to argue from correlation to causation is strong, but it is not valid.

7.10 WHAT DO STUDENTS NEED TO CONSIDER WHEN CONDUCTING A SURVEY?

Carrying out a sound and rigorous survey involves a number of steps and decisions. Some of the main points that a student will need to consider are listed in Box 7.4.

BOX 7.4

The main points and issues that students need to think about

- What is the question(s) that I am interested in?
- What is my population going to be? Who am I going to survey?
- How will I gain access to the sample?
- What kind of sampling am I going to use?
- What are the main methods or instruments that I am going to use?
- How will these methods be administered?
- How am I going to pilot my methods?
- What skills am I going to need, including the methods of analysis?
- What are the ethical considerations that I will need to consider?
- What am I going to do if I do not get a high enough response rate?
- How am I going to ensure that my survey has a high validity?
- How am I going to manage data that I collect?

7.11 CONCLUSION

Surveys are a familiar form of data collection in social science, both from personal experience and from the media, but they are not as simple to execute or to understand as they first appear. They can vary in their level of complexity from those that present simple frequency counts to those that provide relational and/causal relational analysis (Cohen et al., 2011). Where it is possible, it is vital to have some strategy for generating a representative sample, but even defining 'representative' is not straightforward. Once a sample has been selected, there are threats to validity from non-response rates and further threats to validity come from the way people answer our questions. Yet, despite these difficulties, I argue that surveys remain one of the most important and commonly used social science methodologies.

BOX 7.5

A summary of the key points

- Surveys are a quantitative method, relying on counting. Their epistemological position is towards the positivist end of the spectrum of approaches and they aim towards objectivity.
- Survey researchers spend a lot of effort examining their methods and refining their questions in order to try and achieve a high internal, external and face validity.
- The key feature of a survey is that it is a method of making inferences about a population based on information collected from a sample.
- A survey is a methodology that includes at least one question that aims to gain specific information about a specific group by collecting data from a representative sample that is generalisable. Results are typically used to understand the behaviour, attitudes, beliefs or knowledge of a particular group, and sometimes to suggest a causal relationship.
- It is important to try and achieve a sample that is representative of the wider population.
- There are two broad categories of sampling strategy: probability sampling and non-probability sampling. Each have their merits, but probability samples give more robust ways of making inferences.
- The easiest probability sample is the simple random sample, where everyone has the same probability, or equal chance of being selected.
- Probability sampling uses random sampling and the main techniques used are simple random sampling, systematic sampling, stratified sampling and cluster sampling. These all require a sampling frame or a list of the population to be surveyed.
- Non-probability sampling techniques include quota sampling, purposive sampling, convenience sampling and snowball sampling.
- One of the main disadvantages of probability sampling is that it requires a sampling frame, which can be difficult find or does not exist, and some surveys using this technique have a high non-response rate.
- Non-probability sampling does not require a sampling frame.

- The main methods of data collection for surveys are interviews and questionnaires, and each has its advantages and disadvantages.
- Researchers need to be careful of mistaking correlation for causation.

AREAS FOR DISCUSSION

- What are the main points that you need to think about when you are planning to conduct a survey?
- What are some of the advantages and disadvantages of using surveys?
- How do I know if my sample is large enough?
- What happens if I cannot find, or do not know, what the sampling frame is?
- What are the particular personal skills and/or attributes that a survey researcher needs to conduct survey research?
- How objective are surveys?
- What are the particular merits of using interviews or questionnaires in survey research?

ANNOTATED BIBLIOGRAPHY

Callegaro, M., Baker, R., Bethlehem, J., Goritz, A.S., Krosnick, J.A. and Lavrakas, P.J. (eds) (2014) *Online Panel Research: A Data Quality Perspective.* Chichester: Wiley.
The use of panels for online surveys is becoming increasingly popular. This book is a state-of-the-art review.

de Leeuw, E.D., Hox, J.J. and Dillman, D.A. (eds) (2008) *International Handbook of Survey Methodology.* New York and London: Lawrence Erlbaum.
A comprehensive handbook covering methodological and statistical issues.

de Vaus, D.A. (2013) *Surveys in Social Research*, 6th edn. London: Routledge.
This is a very clear and thorough introduction to surveys.

Engel, U., Jann, B., Lynn, P., Scherpenzeel, A. and Sturgis, P. (eds) (2014) *Improving Survey Methods: Lessons from Recent Research.* London: Routledge.
A comprehensive review of new developments in survey methods.

Groves, R.M., Dillman, D.A., Eltinge, J.L. and Little, R.J.A. (eds) (2002) *Survey Nonresponse.* New York: Wiley.
Thorough coverage of issues around non-response.

Lohr, S.L. (2010) *Sampling: Design and Analysis*, 2nd edn. Boston, MA: Brooks/Cole.
Highly technical treatment of sampling issues in both design and analysis, especially for complex surveys. Requires high levels of statistical competence, but is extremely thorough.

Oppenheim, A.N. (1992) *Questionnaire Design, Interviewing and Attitude Measurement*, 2nd edn. London: Pinter.

Rather old, but thorough and readable.

FURTHER READING

Converse, J.M. and Presser, S. (1986). *Survey Questions: Handcrafting the Standardized Questionnaire*. London: Sage.

Fan, W. and Yan, Z. (2010) 'Factors affecting response rates of the web survey: A systematic review', *Computers in Human Behavior*, 26 (2): 132–9.

Gillham, B. (2008) *Small-Scale Social Survey Methods*. London: Continuum.

Public Opinion Quarterly (2006) *Nonresponse Bias in Household Surveys*, Special Issue. Available at: http://poq.oxfordjournals.org/content/vol70/issue5/#ARTICLES (accessed 7 July 2016).

CHAPTER 8

ETHNOGRAPHY

Rebecca O'Connell

▆▆ BOX 8.1 ▆▆▆▆▆▆▆▆▆▆▆▆▆▆▆▆▆▆▆▆▆▆▆▆▆▆▆▆▆▆▆

Overview of chapter

This chapter includes:

- Definitions of ethnography.
- Epistemological principles underpinning ethnographic research.
- Key methods used in ethnographic research.
- Key features of the research design.
- Analysis, interpretation and writing up.
- Practical issues, including roles.
- Advantages and disadvantages of carrying out ethnographic research.
- Two examples of PhD theses that have used an ethnographic design.

8.1 HISTORICAL ORIGINS AND DEFINITIONS OF ETHNOGRAPHY

Creation myths are common to most cultures and social anthropologists trace the origins of ethnography – our discipline's defining method – to the story of Bronisław Malinowski (1884–1942) and his stay in Melanesia. Sociologists tend to trace the origins of 'their' ethnography to the urban ethnography of the Chicago School's William Foot Whyte (1955/1943) and others. Whilst there are differences in emphases between the two disciplines, the underlying principles and methodological approaches are broadly the same. Nevertheless, the account of ethnography given in this chapter is that of a social anthropologist and is therefore skewed as well as partial.

When the First World War broke out, Malinowski was studying in the Trobriand Islands. Unable to return to the UK, and wringing virtue out of necessity as any good researcher

Figure 8.1 Malinowski in the Trobriand Islands, 1918

must, he developed a research approach based on long-term immersion in a culture. Its aim was to try to understand social life from the perspective of the indigenous people themselves or, in the language of the time, 'from the native's point of view' (1922: 25). Malinowski's 'fieldwork' method, the hallmark of which was participant observation, was in contrast to that of the earlier so-called 'armchair anthropologists' who relied heavily for their theorising on the second-hand reports of missionaries and others (Figure 8.1).

A number of sources attempt to define what ethnography is (e.g., see the core feature listed by Massey and Walford (1998) on WEBLINK 1) but, in brief, ethnography may be described as a methodological approach that involves 'the extended involvement of the researcher in the social life of those he or she studies' (Bryman, 2004: 291). A classic example is Edward Evans-Pritchard's *The Nuer* (1940), an account of the modes of livelihood and political institutions of a Nilotic people, that is, people indigenous to the Nile Valley who speak Nilotic languages. The ethnography describes the Nuer using the organising principles of **structural functionalist** anthropology: ecology, kinship, lineage, religion and politics. For more information about the Nuer, see WEBLINK 2.

The idea that a holistic account of a particular people or place was desirable and possible rested to a large degree on the supposed unchangingness and boundedness[1] of that community. With the decline of structural functionalism, the 'disappearance' of 'remote' societies and the recognition that there is no such thing as 'a people without history' (Wolf, 1982), this notion gave way as recognition of social change and internal variation supplanted models of ordered equilibrium. However, the attempt to understand and describe human behaviour 'holistically', in its social context, remains a hallmark of ethnographic accounts.

WEBLINK 1

Characteristics of ethnographic research by Massey & Walford

WEBLINK 2

Evans-Pritchard's research about 'The Nuer'

---

1 Boundedness is a concept that will be defined in more detail in Chapter 9.

Ethnographic approaches have been popular within the field of education and schools, with classroom research blossoming in Britain in the 1970s (Gordon et al., 2001: 188). My own ethnographic research, conducted for my doctorate between 2003 and 2005, concerned the work of registered childminders (home-based childcarers who are members of the Early Years Education and Care workforce) in Inner London (O'Connell, 2008, 2010, 2011). My research was carried out in the context of the professionalisation of childminding and its increasing incorporation into the education sector, including inspection by OFSTED. I set out to explore what childminding was 'like' from the childminders' perspectives, rather than from the perspectives of the early years education 'experts' whose evaluations had previously dominated research on childminding. I was interested in how childminders' perspectives of quality compared to new quality standards and how childminders negotiated competing agendas. I was also interested in the points of view of parents and childminding support workers.

8.2 EPISTEMOLOGICAL PRINCIPLES UNDERPINNING ETHNOGRAPHIC RESEARCH

In attending to context, ethnographers assume implicitly or explicitly that there is a need to make connections between phenomena, rather than as Agar (1994: 112) expresses it, 'tearing them into pieces' (cited in Wolcott, 2008: 79). Underlying this ethnographic 'way of seeing' (ibid.) is a concern to make sense of social action in the terms of the actors' social situation; to understand social life from the 'native's point of view'. Some suggest that this means ethnography as a method is closely linked epistemologically to 'anti-positivist' phenomenological and interpretive approaches. However, as outlined in Chapter 4, the opposition between positivism and constructionism (and so on) has been shown to be overly simplistic. In fact, one of the potential advantages of an ethnographic approach may be that it is able to capture a multiplicity of perspectives and represent the subjective and objective (or **emic/etic**, that is, insider/outsider) as two sides of the same coin (see Bourdieu, 1977).

Reflecting this, Martyn Hammersley argues for an ethnographic epistemology which adopts what he calls 'a subtle form of realism' (1992: 50–4). The implications of his approach for ethnographic practice are that the ethnographer must attend to issues of 'truth' (or perhaps reality) where these are relevant. This depends on the task at hand. For example, informants' accounts may be collected for various reasons and interpreted in a number of ways. In interpreting informants' accounts, the issue of 'truth' is irrelevant if one is interested in such accounts as 'indicators of cultural perspectives held by the people producing them' (ibid.: 53). On the other hand, if one is using the accounts as a source of information about phenomena, for example an event to which access is not possible, the accuracy of the account is important. In this case, its veracity must be assessed by cross-referencing it with other accounts, for example, or different sorts of data.

8.3 KEY METHODS

Ethnography may and often does involve the use of multiple research methods and the collection of many sorts of data. Whilst ethnography is often viewed as existing within the qualitative tradition, ethnographers also collect quantitative data, taking measurements and conducting surveys, in fact, 'counting what can be counted'. As Hammersley and Atkinson suggest, ethnography involves using whatever methods, and taking whatever data are available, to shine a light on the research problem (see Box 8.2).

BOX 8.2

Definition of ethnography

In its most characteristic form [ethnography] involves the ethnographer participating, overtly or covertly, in people's daily lives for an extended period of time, watching what happens, listening to what is said, asking questions – in fact, collecting whatever data are available to throw light on the issues that are the focus of the research. (Hammersley and Atkinson, 1995: 1)

In addition, methods from the ethnographic repertoire have been developed and applied in various guises and contexts, including, for example, in international development work (Chambers, 1994) and research with pre-school children in early years settings (Clark and Moss, 2007). This said, the 'hallmark' of ethnography is generally understood to be participant observation (Hammersley and Atkinson, 2007).

In my research with childminders, I carried out a small survey, conducted informal and formal interviews, did some photography, monitored online childminding forums and collected ephemera (e.g., 'Thank you' cards from parents to childminders). However, the bulk of my research was carried out via participant observation. In addition to working with childminders at home, I spent a total of about 140 hours in 13 drop-ins (communal facilities where childminders socialised and children could play collectively), with most of my time being spent at three sites in distinct regions. I also participated in a range of training and networking opportunities, including various non-routine outings and social events. I trained and registered as a childminder (completing an Initial OFSTED Inspection, the home visit required to ensure that a registered childminder met and/or was working towards safety and training standards), observed one inspection and received feedback from childminders on many more.

Participant observation

Most social research, for example using interviews or surveys, focuses on internal states and reported behaviour. Participant observation allows for a much richer understanding of people and social life (Bernard, 2006). Making the case for participant observation and expressing caution about dependence on accounts of behaviour, Daniel Miller, Professor of Material Culture at the Department of Anthropology at University College London, argues that: '[i]t is better to be immersed in people's everyday life and also listen in to the conversations they have with the people they live with, rather than carrying out the artificial procedure that we call an interview' (Miller, cited in Baker and Edwards, 2012: 31).

Whilst many talk of becoming 'immersed' in a culture, participant observation is a method that involves the researcher assuming a role that is simultaneously inside and outside the setting she or he is researching. It 'involves getting close to people and making them feel comfortable in your presence so that you can observe and record information about their lives' (Bernard, 2006: 342). As a method, participant observation may be understood as a continuum, at one pole of which is complete participation (active research, as well as **auto-ethnography**) and at the other, complete observation (passive watching). The participant observer occupies a position somewhere between these two poles and the degree of participation or observation may vary depending on the situation. To see an example of a study that has used full participation, see WEBLINK 3.

WEBLINK 3

Example study using 'full' participation

Traditionally, anthropology has involved the study of an/other culture. The participant observer's position as a 'stranger' to the culture in question, and his or her gradual learning to behave in ways which are appropriate until he or she becomes 'a knowing member of the community' (Blommaert and Jie, 2010: 32), has been understood as a tool for understanding how that culture 'works' (Schutz, 1944). Learning to 'see' in one's own culture or society can be more difficult because much more is taken for granted, but many doctoral EdD students have used ethnographic approaches within their own institutions, such as schools and hospitals. Given that we all have multiple identities, we are often to some extent outsiders in many social situations. Furthermore, it is possible to learn to 'defamiliarise' oneself, so that, with practice, we become more adept at observing with fresh eyes even those aspects of social life with which we are familiar. Spradley (1980) calls this developing 'explicit awareness' and suggests this attentiveness to the details of everyday life can be developed through practicing. Participant observation means that the researcher and the participants are in social contexts governed by rules, codes and values and both are co-constructors of meanings. However, shared contexts do not necessarily mean shared meanings and researchers interpret situations through the lens of their own biographical experience.

Fieldnotes

The data collected by participant observers typically take the form of fieldnotes (Emerson et al., 1995). Ethnography literally means 'writing culture' and ethnographers 'are those who write things down at the end of the day' (Jackson, 1990: 15). The researcher watches what is going on, takes part where he or she can, and asks questions if and when appropriate. She or he more or less explicitly makes notes in a notebook. These may comprise only a word or a phrase that is needed to jog a memory. These 'scratch notes' or 'jottings' are fleshed out later in the day as fieldnotes to provide a sense of the social context and social meaning. Pelto and

Gretel (1993) caution against using as low a level of abstraction as possible when reporting concrete events because they may be difficult to interpret later on (see Box 8.3).

BOX 8.3

An example of 'thick description'

For example, rather than writing:

> A showed hostility to B

it is better to record:

> A scowled and spoke harshly to B, saying a number of number of things, including 'Get the hell out of here, Mr B!' He then shook his fist in B's face and walked out of the room.

The ethnographer is aiming for what anthropologist Clifford Geertz (1973) calls **thick description**, that is, a description that provides the context of a social behaviour so that it becomes meaningful to an outsider.

A book (or more usually a folder on a computer) of fieldnotes may be kept along with (usually separate) analytical notes, methodological notes and a fieldwork 'log', the latter being a record of where the participant observer has been and who he or she has seen and what he or she has done. Reflective notes about the thoughts and feelings the research brings up for the researcher are also essential. They record the often emotional and difficult process of being both an 'insider' and an 'outsider' and are important for understanding how the researcher interprets phenomena as well as serving as an important source of data in their own right. For example, the degree to which it is more or less difficult to 'penetrate' a particular group might provide insights about its boundedness. Analytical notes or memos are also essential. These are notes of emerging analyses and insights that develop as the research progresses and may be confirmed, refined or dispensed with as more data are collected. Some ethnographers also keep separate methodological notes, which record changes in research design or direction since, as outlined below, the 'iterative' nature of ethnographic research means that it does not follow the idealised process of design – data collection – analysis. Fieldnotes also need to be filed systematically to make reviewing them easier. It is vital to consider these issues when designing ethnographic research, in particular so that enough time is built into the research plan for writing as well as observing. In my ethnographic study, I used a digital recorder for some interviews and transcribed them in part or in full but, generally when conducting participant observation, I made fieldnotes in a notebook and wrote them up as soon as possible afterwards, usually in the evenings. I used Atlas.ti to code notes and as a systematic method of storage and retrieval. To see some examples of my own fieldnotes from my PhD (discussed earlier in the section), and some from Jon's PhD see WEBLINK 4.

WEBLINK 4

Two fieldnotes examples

Interviews

Participant observation usually includes and/or is combined with interviewing. Interviews range from informal, unstructured, semi-structured to structured (Figure 8.2), but sometimes the majority of the data will come from informal conversations, e.g. while walking down a corridor, sitting in a café or talking in a market or shop. However, these conversations always have an ulterior motive in that the researcher is trying to elicit information and Burgess (1988) refers to these as 'conversations with a purpose' (for ethical implications of this kind of 'deception', see Section 8.6). With increasing structure comes increasing control by the researcher.

Informal →→ Unstructured →→ Semi-structured →→ Structured

Participant control ◄————————————————► Researcher control

Figure 8.2   Types of interview and locus of control

Note: Based on Bernard (2006: 210-15).

Ethnographic interviews are usually fairly unstructured, but may take the shape of beginning with a 'grand tour question', that is, an invitation to give a broad overview, for example of a place, people, set of activities or group of objects, followed up by further questions which focus in on the topic of interest, asking for examples and experiences (Spradley, 1979). Others suggest that ethnographers should '[g]et people onto a topic of interest and get out of the way' (Bernard, 2006: 216). Which kinds of interview one uses will depend on the purposes of the interview, the relationship to the interviewee, and the context in which the interview is conducted. For example, when interviewing a professional he or she may expect the interview to be somewhat more structured than when interviewing a key informant whilst undertaking a task together. Since the interview setting (e.g., public space), interviewee (e.g., more or less 'powerful' or 'elite'; confidentiality restriction) constrains what may be said, the interview situation must be taken into account when interpreting the data (e.g., Kvale, 1996). So, too, should the way the interview is framed by the researcher and the questions he or she asks. A sound piece of advice from Harry Wolcott is to 'pay as much attention to your own words as the words of your respondents' (1995: 102). There are no rules about when particular types of interviewing may be appropriate; however, informal interviews may be useful in the early stages of research to build rapport and establish research topics, whilst more formal methods such as structured interviews, questionnaires or cultural domain analyses (see, e.g., Borgatti, 1993/1994) may enable the ethnographer to test out the degree to which particular ideas are held by wider groups of people, that is to help generalise from more in-depth interviews and observations.

Other methods of data collection

Whilst there is an emphasis on participant observation and interviewing in ethnographic research, other methods of data collection or data generation are also widely employed (see Box 8.4).

Other ethnographic methods of collecting data

- Surveys (e.g., Wallman, 1984).
- Archival research and analysis of documents and ephemera (e.g., Brettell, 1998).
- Secondary analysis of research and documents – e.g., school reports (e.g., Woods, 1979), OFSTED reports, policy documents.
- Online research – e.g., chat rooms, online communities (e.g., Domínguez et al., 2007).
- Visual approaches – e.g., photography, video, sketches, maps (e.g., Rich and Chalfen, 1999; Pink, 2001; Radley and Taylor, 2003).
- Participatory approaches – e.g., mapping, walks, sorting/ranking exercises (e.g., Chambers, 1994; Wallman, 1984).
- 'Innovative' approaches – e.g., debate, raffle, drama, football (e.g., Gillies and Robinson, 2012).

Participatory Rapid Rural Appraisal (PRRA) takes a number of these methods and applies them to collect ethnographic data about a particular group or community in a relatively short space of time. This approach was developed in applied anthropology and has been used to address many particular and practical problems, for example to establish on behalf of an aid agency where to locate a village well to meet the needs of different social groups and interests (Chambers, 1994). As introduced below, the approach has also been usefully employed in education settings with young children, to inform the design of a new building. PRRA techniques include the 'transect walk', 'walking and taking' or the 'go along' (Kusenbach, 2003), in which the researcher is given a guided tour along a particular route by a local person (or a number of walks by a number of different people from different interest groups) to learn about features of the physical and social setting. The group of techniques also involves participatory map making and 'pile sorting' or ranking exercises, both of which may generate different sorts of data. For example, the 'products' of the methods may include not only the physical maps or ranks of particular issues but also important insights drawn from the talk, gestures, and so forth which surround the mapping or ranking exercise and provide insights into the range of different views held. Techniques such as these have been adapted and applied in early years settings, for example in an interactive research strategy known as the Mosaic Approach, used to seek the views of young children (under 5 years) on the spaces they inhabit (Clark and Moss, 2007). Further information about the PRRA approach based on Clark's study can be seen on WEBLINK 5.

WEBLINK 5

Example of the PRRA approach

8.4 THE RESEARCH DESIGN: KEY FEATURES

A key feature of ethnographic research design is its iterative nature. In this respect, it is similar to other crafts and creative endeavours, as Elliot Eisner, Professor of Art and Education, wrote:

In the process of writing, in the process of painting, and in the process of researching, ideas emerge which become leading ideas, which then direct the course of action. Sometimes these ideas are accidental, they are unanticipated. You write yourself clear. You see what you said. This is a goal seeking behaviour. In a much vaguer sense it's 'muddling through' and it's an important kind of activity. (1985: 66)

Whereas an idealisation of research often assumes the model:

Theory > research questions > design > fieldwork > analysis

such a model, which is of questionable validity in research generally, is even less appropriate to ethnographic research.

It is common to suggest that ethnography and qualitative research more generally are inductive rather than deductive; that they do not set out to test theory but rather to generate it. Whilst it is probably true that ethnography is not the foremost approach for testing the validity of a certain hypothesis, it is also not the case that it never does so. Indeed, ethnographic research as a whole generates new knowledge and tests theory by adding cases to the body of knowledge, which demonstrate situations in which particular theories do and do not apply. Furthermore, strictly 'inductive' approaches, that demand that theory only follows data (as, for example, in some versions of grounded theory), suppose that the researcher becomes some sort of tabula rasa in a way that is, in reality, not achievable. We are all positioned in relation to the world in particular ways and it is not possible to entirely bracket, that is ignore or somehow escape, our preconceived ideas. What we must strive to do, however, is to be aware of how our positioning and preconceived ideas affect what we choose to study and how we interpret it; we must be prepared to hold ourselves and our ideas up to the light, in order to take account of the impact these have on our data and what we make of them. For these reasons, ethnography is an inherently reflexive process (see Chapters 4 and 5), and the making of systematic reflective notes is a vital part of the ethnographic research process.

Ethnographers do not begin without any ideas about what they may find, then, but neither do they typically begin with a fully developed research question. Malinowski (1922) suggested that ethnographic research begins with a 'foreshadowed problem', which Hammersley and Atkinson (2007) call 'a hunch'. The problem or hunch may be theoretical, for example a gap in knowledge, a lack of a particular approach to a particular phenomenon, or puzzling research results. However, it may also be a personal, practical or political topic that interests the researcher, a problem grounded in his or her own experience which he or she wants to investigate empirically through conducting research. The problem or question may also jump out at the researcher, taking the form of 'opportunistic' research, for example the opening of a new superstore in a locality or the building of a bridge linking a previously remote community. Thus, research problems or questions may be generic (formal) or topical (substantive). Either way, the problem is unlikely to be fully formulated in advance as a research question. In the initial stages, early ideas are modified in response to the situation and new information and there is a progressive focusing on the topic.

In my research on childminding, my initial interest ('foreshadowed problem') was to explore what childminding was 'like', from childminders' perspectives. I selected the topic because it interested me as a mother of young children who were cared for by a childminder – and my mother had been a childminder. An iterative approach informed a progressive focusing in on the 'qualities' (in the substantive sense) of childminding and the relationship of these to 'quality' (in the evaluative) (Moss, 1994: 1).

The first stage in the research is to carry out a process of what Bernard (2006) calls 'casing the joint'. This 'casing' may take the form of a pilot study. It is likely to include gathering information about potential settings, refining problems and revisiting assumptions about categories of sites. A main aim of this stage of the research is developing the foreshadowed problem and establishing that it is researchable. For example, Bernard (ibid.: 70) suggests adopting 'a realistic approach' and asking oneself the questions that are listed in Box 8.5.

▬▬ BOX 8.5 ▬▬▬▬▬▬▬▬▬▬▬▬▬▬▬▬▬▬▬▬▬▬▬▬▬▬▬▬▬▬▬▬▬

Questions used in a 'realistic approach'

1 Does this topic (or research site, or data collection method) really interest me?
2 Is this a problem that is amenable to scientific enquiry?
3 Are adequate resources (time, money, people) available to study this topic?
4 Does my research question, or the methods I want to use, enable me to resolve ongoing ethical problems?
5 Is the topic of theoretical or practical interest?

If the answers to these questions are 'yes', then the next step is to select places/people/ settings/ situations for the study. This is 'sampling'.

Sampling, validity and generalisability

Quantitative research that aims at making generalisations beyond the particular population studied usually calls for 'probability sampling' (see Chapter 7). However, the claims made by and for ethnography do not generally rest on being able to make these kind of statistical generalisations. Contrary to some accounts, this does not mean that ethnographic or other forms of research, such as case studies, cannot generalise from their findings. What it does mean, however, is that such generalisations will not be statistical ones. In order to generalise (in a non-statistical sense), it is important to know the particular characteristics of the case or cases selected so that one can say something about the likelihood or not of findings being applicable in other social contexts that share some of the same features.

Some of the methods I employed in my ethnographic study of childminders enabled me to situate the childminders with whom I worked within a wider context. For example, childminders' online forums revealed a widespread discontent with processes of professionalisation, suggesting this was not particular to the local area in which I worked (O'Connell, 2011).

Sampling involves the selection of phenomena for study. These phenomena exist at different scales. An ethnographic study of a secondary school (e.g., Ball, 1981), for example, involves the selection of a particular region, an institution within that region, and people within that institution such as managers, teachers and pupils. Selecting a setting for the study may be the first sampling task; however, sampling takes place within the case in relation to people, places and times.

Because no setting is socially homogenous, sampling of people needs to be undertaken within any social context. In ethnographic research, sampling informants is often a combination of convenience sampling (in which participants are selected because of their accessibility to the researcher) and snowball sampling (whereby one research participant leads on to the identification of further participants) (Bryman, 2004: 304). One advantage of ethnographic research is that it can aid in the identification of meaningful categories of informants or participants from which to sample. A research design using the 'face sheet characteristics' researchers bring with them to the field for classifying people, for example social class, ethnicity and gender, might involve selecting equal numbers of male and female teachers, for example, or including white British and black British pupils. However, 'member defined categories' or 'researcher identified categories' (Loftland, 1976), might be somewhat different and more meaningful and, depending on the research question, provide a better basis for selection of participants. For example, the ethnographic researcher might discover that teachers of particular subjects are marginalised in a school, or that pupils living in particular geographical regions are disadvantaged in relation to accessing particular aspects of the curriculum. The flexibility of ethnographic research allows for such information to be incorporated into the design.

Traditionally, ethnography involves long-term immersion in a particular setting. One rationale for fieldwork being undertaken over a minimum of one calendar year is that it enables the researcher to observe all events within an annual cycle. This is as important for ethnographers studying a school setting, for example, as for anthropologists studying 'traditional' agricultural communities. However, sampling also involves selecting in time. Even if we have the luxury of conducting fieldwork over the period of a year or more (note that, with the exception of research students, this is becoming increasingly unlikely) we cannot be present all the time. Therefore, different moments of a day, term, month or year are necessarily selected for study for different reasons.

The time demands of conventional ethnographic research have led to worries about gaining funding from bodies that may be seeking 'value for money' that comes from less time-consuming research (Jeffrey and Troman, 2010). It is noticeable that many of the 'classic' ethnographies, and my own, were originally conducted as doctorates (e.g., see Hargreaves, 1967; Lacey, 1979; Ball, 1981; Aggleston, 1987; Carspecken, 1991; O'Connell, 2008). However, an ideal length for fieldwork is difficult to establish. Walford (1995: 77) advocates a period of two years, while some earlier anthropologists specified a minimum of 12 months was needed to understand the complexities of what is happening in social situations. My own research was conducted over a period of two years, including a break of 4 months of maternity leave. As described below, my time was spread between different activities including visits to childminders' homes, attendance at childminder drop-ins and activities, participating in training, and interviewing other professionals and parents. Jon's research was over a school year but only usually involved him spending three days a week between September and July – so, roughly 110 days.

Jeffrey and Troman (2010) propose three models, or strategies, which they have used to address the time demands of ethnographic research. All of them involve shorter periods of fieldwork, which still attempt to encompass the nature and principles of ethnographic practice (see Table 8.1). Bernard (2006: 353) also argues that, 'if you have a clear question and a few, clearly defined variables, you can produce quality work in a lot less time than you might imagine', especially if one is conducting 'native ethnography' at home.

Regarding sampling in my ethnographic research, I chose the setting (an Inner London borough) because it was convenient (where I lived), it was mixed in terms of social class and ethnicity and I had established contacts with childminders and a childminding support worker there. To some degree, then, the selection of the study area was opportunistic. I also sampled people and in time, as Figure 8.3 shows, the childminders who took part included ten 'main' participants: two who cared (consecutively) for my own children (pseudonyms Maureen and Wendy) and eight 'in-depth' childminders whom I visited at least once a month, on different days and at different times, for a year. Sampling temporally allowed me to observe how the work changed according to the season (winter is much harder work for childminders who have to dress multiple small children in coat and hats) and the time of day (mornings and evenings when children are dropped off and collected are busy and important times in which childminders and parents exchanged information and negotiated arrangements). I also visited another 22 childminders at home at least once and I got to know a greater number of women through drop-ins, training and social events. In addition, I interviewed parents and childminding support workers. All the childminders who took part were women and most were working class, defined in terms of income and education. The 'in-depth' childminders tended to be experienced and/or mature. There was variation in the sample (which, as illustrated in Figure 8.3, increased in inverse relation to

Table 8.1 Three strategies for shorter-term ethnographic research

Strategy	Compressed	Selective-Intermittent	Recurrent
Time demands	Short, highly concentrated, intense period of fieldwork from anything up to a month	Flexible approach of visits building up to progressive focusing based on particular analytical categories, from around three months to up to two years	Structured around temporal phrases - e.g., beginning and ends of terms, exam periods, or regular specific time periods, irrespective of event

Source: Jeffrey and Troman (2010).

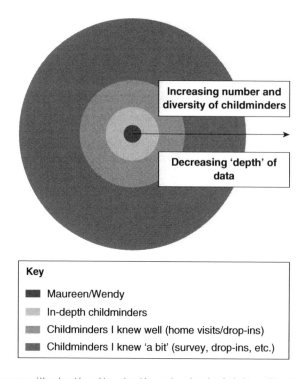

Increasing number and diversity of childminders

Decreasing 'depth' of data

Key

■ Maureen/Wendy

▨ In-depth childminders

▨ Childminders I knew well (home visits/drop-ins)

■ Childminders I knew 'a bit' (survey, drop-ins, etc.)

Figure 8.3   Diagram illustrating the depth and extent of data collection

'depth' of data) in terms of ethnicity, age, marital status, age of children, length of time childminding and houseform (whether the childminder lived in a flat or a house). Childminders were recruited face-to-face at 'drop-ins' and training, as well as through key 'gatekeepers' (those who control access to the research field(s)) and via 'snowballing'.

There have also been a number of other doctoral students who argue that while the period of their research means that they are wary of calling their study 'an ethnography', they are still using certain or particular 'ethnographic principles' such as in-depth interviewing and generating data through informal conversations through (at least to some extent) participant observations.

8.5 ANALYSIS, INTERPRETATION AND WRITING UP

Analysis in ethnographic research is not distinct from data collection. As in other qualitative research it is also not distinct from writing up (Van Maanen, 1988; Wolcott, 2009; Smart, 2010). In short, in ethnography, data are used in the early stages 'to think with' (Hammersley and Atkinson, 2007: 163) and in the later stages 'to write with' (Smart, 2010). In ethnographic research, because writing is part of the process of analysis, it may only be at the writing up stage that the research problem is finally clarified. In my doctoral thesis, it wasn't until close to the end of the PhD that I realised that it was my interest in the contradictions which are at the heart of paid care work that were driving my research interests. I wrote in my thesis that:

> Perhaps it is only now that I can begin to fully recognise that fieldwork was, in fact, foreshadowed by an exploration of my own nascent sense of the contradictions between care and justice and 'what is at stake'. What I have perhaps come to 'know' most fully is what I thought I knew in theory: that such contradictions may not be resolvable. I do not pretend to have resolved them here (for me or anyone else). Rather … I have tried to begin to unpick and explore some of the intricate and intimate negotiations of a reality, which is characterised by such tensions. (O'Connell, 2008: 72)

Despite the fact that analysis takes place throughout the research process, there is, however, likely to be a phase in the research which is focused on analysis, interpretation and writing up. At this stage, the ethnographer reviews and codes fieldnotes, analytical notes, makes new memos and so forth with a view to 'making sense' of the data in relation to the research problem or questions.

The first method to use is that of 'the ocular scan' (Bernard, 2006: 304). This involves reading one's notes, looking at one's pictures and highlighting what seems important and interesting. The ethnographer makes analytic notes and memos and identifies and codes useful concepts. Codes may be deductive, that is, applied to the data from outside (such as theoretical categories) or inductive, involving ideas that emerge from the data, including **InVivo** (observer identified) concepts, that is, codes that attempt to retain participants' own terms that are deemed meaningful:

> Reading through the corpus of data and generating concepts which make sense of it are the initial stages of ethnographic analysis … The immediate aim is to reach a position where one has a set of promising categories and has carried out a systematic coding of all the data in terms of those categories. (Hammersley and Atkinson, 2007: 164)

Codes and categories identified by the researcher may range from the mundane or concrete to more abstract and analytic. It is a good idea to try not to start with too many. Moving from description (fieldnotes and narratives) to interpretation via analysis involves increasing abstraction; analysis involves making sense of local cultures and actions in terms that relate to wider analytical perspectives (ibid.: 189).

Making interpretations of the data may be understood as drawing inferences from them. Discussing the validity of ethnographic research, Hammersley and Atkinson suggest that, '[d]ata in themselves cannot be valid or invalid; what is at issue are the inferences drawn from them' (ibid.: 177). To be valid, these inferences should take into account the social context in which the data were gathered; time dimensions; the persons from whom data was gathered (if relevant) and (as discussed in Section 8.2) whether an 'account' is being analysed as a source of 'information' or as data about a person's 'perspective' (or both). Part of ensuring the validity of inferences or interpretations involves considering alternative interpretations. Inferences can be confirmed or refuted by revisiting the data and, in some cases, by collecting additional data. More direct ways of testing relationships between concepts and indicators include **triangulation** – a term 'taken from navigation and surveying in which different bearings are taken in order to arrive at a precise physical location' (Brannen, 2005: 12) – with other data sources or types (for example maps, surveys), or the respondent validation method in which informants are asked to verify the plausibility of the ethnographer's interpretations. The triangulation approach has been critiqued (ibid.:12), however, and there are limits to 'native exegesis' (see, e.g., Charsley, 1987). It is important to remember that all interpretations are partial and provisional (Thomson and Holland, 2003). However, this does not mean interpretations should be slapdash. As Hammersley (1992) argues, against relativism, there *are* better and worse accounts.

Writing with data is common to qualitative approaches (see, e.g., Holliday, 2007). The nature of the data collected in an ethnographic study is often somewhat different to those more commonly collected in interview-based studies. The number of participants is likely to be smaller and data may generally comprise of fieldnotes. Whilst it is common to include 'quotes' from participants in the writing-up of qualitative research based on interviews, much of what constitutes ethnographic research 'evidence' may not include spoken words or, if it does, may concern the context in which words are said, or nuanced interpretations about the ways in which words are used in particular situations. Other findings may have little to do with words at all but be observations of mundane or everyday behaviours. What constitutes 'evidence' in support of interpretations is thus somewhat different. **The literary turn** in social anthropology involved reflective critique of the techniques used by ethnographers to convince readers of the veracity of their interpretations (e.g., Clifford and Marcus, 1986). Re-analysis of some classic ethnographies found that a number of literary tropes were common, and that a key technique employed was that of convincing the reader of the ethnographer having 'been there'. It is true that being able to 'speak from the gut' about a particular social situation helps convince the reader. However, theoretical, political and ethical issues regarding textual strategies and the crisis of representation are important to consider, albeit that they are common to other disciplines and approaches.

Practically, there are many ways in which to structure the final account. However, Jackson (2000) suggests a few strategies for shaping how the data are written up. One option is to 'tell a story': e.g., a 'natural history' (of the research process and findings). Another is to structure the account according to inductive or deductive themes. A more abstract account, which links to theory or theories might structure the writing according to meta-themes (ibid.). A common strategy in writing up ethnographic (and other predominantly qualitative research) is to adopt the 'hourglass model' in which findings of the particular study are 'nested' or framed within a wider theoretical and empirical context, to which the findings are referred back at the end (see Figure 8.4).

This 'hourglass approach' presupposes that the ethnographer has collected plenty of contextual information in order to situate the particular study. Of course, as Wolcott (1994) suggests, the question of writing strategy can only be resolved when we are clear what the research questions are, why we are writing and, importantly, for whom we are writing.

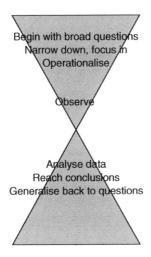

Figure 8.4 The hourglass model of research

Source: Trochim (2006).

8.6 ETHICAL AND PRACTICAL ISSUES

Although the principles of ethical research practice are set out in Chapter 5, this section focuses on what is particular about ethical research practice in ethnography, for while the problem of how ethical procedures may transform the research process is a challenge for all social scientists, 'it represents a particularly severe challenge for ethnographic work' (Hamersley and Atkinson, 2007: 227; for a discussion of how Research Ethics Committees have shaped and influenced health-based ethnographic studies, see Crabtree, 2012). This section discusses the particular ethical issues of informed consent, 'assumed' privacy, possible deception and the 'interpretative authority' of the researcher.

It has been argued that in ethnographic research informed consent 'is neither achievable nor demonstrable in the terms set by anticipatory regulatory regimes that take clinical research or biomedical experimentation as their paradigm cases' (Murphy and Dingwall, 2007: 2223). Given that the research design is not determined at the outset but develops and often changes over time, it may not be possible to provide full information in advance about what the study entails and the topics it will cover.

Another issue is that the ethnographer does not have complete control over the settings in which he or she is researching. This may mean, for example, that people who are not (or were not) the focus of the research become included in it, by virtue of entering a room in which the researcher is observing, for example. There are no clear rules regarding whether that person should be informed about the study or whether his or her consent should be sought. Such issues link to the concept of 'assumed privacy'. Whilst some argue that observing people who may not believe they are being observed but are in public places does not represent an ethical problem because it does not invade 'assumed pri-vacy', for others this is more complicated. The question of 'assumed privacy' and the expectations of those being observed is a particularly 'hot' issue in relation to online environments and the status of publicly available information as potential research data (e.g., see AoIR, 2012). See Chapter 5 for a more in-depth discussion on the ethics of online research.

A further important issue relates to that of deception. Ethical regulations insist that research participants are made aware of the research being conducted. However, the premise of participant observation rests on the establishment of rapport and the development of a situation in which the ethnographer hopes to become less visible over time, so that people go about their business as if the ethnographer was not there. For example, in her ethnography of dual earner couples, *The Second Shift*, American ethnographer Arlie R. Hochschild (1989) sought to become 'like the family dog'. This may be regarded by some as passive deception – but it is a key part of successful ethnographic practice. As Bernard says:

> [O]nly by confronting the truth about participant observation – that it involves deception and impression management – can we hope to conduct ourselves ethically in fieldwork. (2006: 342)

Finally, although it is not always discussed as an ethical issue, the notion of 'interpretive authority' (the power to analyse and represent people and their lives) is also of particular relevance to ethnography. Given that the ethnographer claims to speak 'from the native's point of view', one question is to what degree the researcher should seek the participation of informants in making interpretations about them? It is common practice in some 'participatory' research designs to suggest that research participants will be able to review, approve or edit research outputs about them. However, this is not straightforward and does not necessarily resolve the ethical dilemma of unequal power relations. As Rachel Thomson (2007) has shown, participants do not always recognise themselves or appreciate what they may experience as the objectification of themselves and their story. Moreover, many people may be met on an on–off basis and the researcher will not be able to trace them anyway, even if he or she wished to.

Whether a particular research practice is ethical or not depends on the context, the research questions, and much more besides. Many dilemmas in ethnographic research must be resolved on a case-by-case basis. However, such issues should not be taken lightly and decisions about what to do should be guided by the ethnical codes of conduct of the relevant scholarly society, for example the Association of Social Anthropologists (2011) (see WEBLINK 6). Ethnographers, like other researchers, have a responsibility to their participants and to other researchers to prioritise ethical research practice.

WEBLINK 6

Association
of Social
Anthropologists

Conducting fieldwork: practical issues

Key practical issues in carrying out fieldwork include those to do with accessing and entering the field, field relations and field roles. Accessing the field site is a somewhat risky process in that it may determine or at least colour the possibilities for the development of field relations. It should therefore be thought through carefully. How one gains access to a setting, for example, through which gatekeepers, may impact in important ways on the individuals to whom the researcher subsequently gains access. Plenty of documentation and information about the study should be provided at this stage. Even if one cannot formulate the exact research questions, the researcher should be able to explain the broad focus of the research and, importantly, explain to a lay audience what ethnographic research involves. It is important to remember that entering the field is not only a practical issue but is also likely to generate important data about the social organisation of a setting. It is therefore important to document the process, relations between yourself and those you meet, how you are introduced to new informants, and your own feelings.

Relations

Field relations are important and Woods (1996) points out the significance of the research-er's sociability in carrying out ethnographic research where interaction has a critical role. 'In the end, ethnographic fieldwork stands or falls on building mutually supportive relations with a few key people' (Bernard, 2006: 199). In social anthropology, such key people are generally referred to as 'informants'. Bernard (ibid.) distinguishes between 'key informants' and 'specialised informants'. The ethnographer finds key informants who know a lot about their culture or way of life and are willing to share it. Specialised informants have particular competence in some particular domain. It is recommended that one does not choose key informants too quickly; as discussed above in relation to entering the field, their status and social relations may prevent the researcher from gaining access to other informants who may also be important.

Roles

In the field, the ethnographer may adopt a range of 'roles' in his or her interactions with others. As discussed above, these may range from complete participant to complete observer and anywhere in between. This may differ, depending on the stage of the research, or the particular site, or the activity being undertaken. With the emergence of the EdD degree it is not uncommon for researchers to be 'insiders', for example teachers. **Insider ethnographies** (see O' Reilly, 2009), in which educational settings such as schools and colleges become the research site, raise particular 'epistemological, methodological, political and ethical dilemmas' for researchers (Anderson and Jones, 2000: 430; see also Mercer, 2007). For information and a more in-depth discussion about the concept of insider research, based on O'Reilly's study see WEBLINK 7.

WEBLINK 7

O'Reilly
on insider
research

The researcher will also engage in 'identity work', or what Goffman (2007/1959) calls 'impression management', manipulating his or her persona to facilitate the collection of useful data. In part, which role she or he adopts is determined by the purposes of the research, but it is also influenced by the researcher and the participants. In some situations and settings, the researcher may adopt the role of, and be seen as, an 'expert' whilst in others the same researcher may be regarded as and/or adopt the role of the 'novice' (e.g., Ozga and Gewirtz, 1994; Ozga, and Walker, 1999). Carrying out longitudinal ethnographic research (that is, research involving data collection from the same individuals over time) with apprentices, Brockmann (2011) writes about the different roles that she employed in the workplace, and builds on the work of Adler and Adler (1998) who distinguish between 'active member' and 'peripheral' member roles, depending on how centrally the researcher participates in the activities of the community. For more information about longitudinal research, see WEBLINK 8. In terms of field roles in my own ethnographic research, as a young mother of young children, I generally adopted the role of a novice. In my relations with childcare professionals my status as a postgraduate researcher was foregrounded.

WEBLINK 8

John Bynner
on longitudinal
research

Whilst the ethnographer may manipulate his or her identity to gain acceptance or access to different sorts of information in different kinds of settings, research participants will also construct the researcher role, meaning that how one is seen is not entirely within one's control. In the past, anthropologists have been viewed (not without good reason in some cases) as suspicious characters and, not uncommonly, as spies.

In terms of managing personal characteristics, researchers sometimes manipulate or falsify aspects of their identity. For example, some women pretend to have marital status in contexts where being an unmarried woman inhibits the researcher's acceptance into a community as a fully social adult. However, there are limits to impression management and identity work. Whilst personal characteristics such as age, ethnicity and gender may help or hinder in accessing particular sites or information, as well as how the researcher is perceived by and perceives others, they may also be tricky to manipulate. Such issues should be considered when embarking on a field of study; whilst there are advantages to straddling the position of insider/outsider there is probably little point in trying to do participant observation among a group to which access will never be allowed. It is important to reflect upon and monitor the identity work one does because it may have important effects upon the data collected and how it may be interpreted.

8.7 ADVANTAGES AND DISADVANTAGES OF CARRYING OUT ETHNOGRAPHIC RESEARCH

As a methodological strategy, ethnography allows for a more holistic approach to the study of social behaviour than other methods such as individual interviews or surveys. The focus on a particular setting or a small sample size may allow for an exploration of the interconnections between social phenomena. Ethnography also allows for a large degree of flexibility and, as noted above, the research design is altered in response to the circumstances of fieldwork. The employment of ethnographic research methods facilitates the exploration of emic accounts. It is also efficient because data are gathered in situ. Importantly, compared to approaches which focus solely on accounts of behaviour, participant observation may allow ethnographers to explore distinctions between **normative**

statements and actual practice – in other words, between what people say they do and what they actually do (see Miller, cited in Baker and Edwards, 2012: 31; Bourdieu, 1977).

On the other hand, since the ethnographer is *the* research tool, ethnographic research typically involves a large investment of time. As outlined above, anthropological ethnographic studies are classically thought to involve a period of a year or more, to allow for familiarising oneself with the setting, observing events in an annual calendar and, in some cases, learning a new language. This said, ethnographic studies 'at home' may be undertaken in much shorter periods as discussed in Section 8.4.

Conducting research in a setting with which one is familiar is, however, challenging in its own ways: familiarity may serve to obscure the everyday. As outlined above ethnographers must, for this reason, learn to defamiliarise themselves. This is a craft, which is principally learned through practice; in which the act of repeatedly observing, recording and writing up help foster some sense of objectivity and develop an ethnographic 'way of seeing'. Whilst it is impossible to become 'neutral' one may learn to 'suspend active judgement' (Bernard, 2006: 280).

One consideration that is not always noted is that, since ethnographic research requires the investment of the researcher as a person, it demands a good deal of emotional energy and is very tiring. Furthermore the need to systematically write up and file fieldnotes at the end of the day requires organisation, commitment and diligence. It also takes time, which must be built into the research plan. On the plus side, since the researcher 'is the tool', ethnography usually requires little in terms of other kinds of research resources. The ethnographer Paul Willis (1977) also pointed out that another difficulty for the ethnographer is making and justifying the selections they make. In a lecture at the UCL/IOE in 2000, he talked about the problem of selecting the one per cent of material that will appear in the thesis from the field data that itself represents one per cent of the possible data that could have been gathered from the setting. The point is that, however long ethnographers spend in a particular setting, the data that they collect and then write up represents a tiny fraction of what they might have observed, gathered, analysed and presented.

An important point that Hammersley and Atkinson (2007) make is that in many respects ethnography is the most basic form of social research because it bears a close resemblance to the routine ways in which people make sense of the world in everyday life. Some see this as a strength and others as a weakness. Potential disadvantages include that the 'subjective' nature of the data and interpretations may be considered by some as problematic. Some also criticise a lack of transparency in how research findings are established. This lack of clarity undermines ethnographic research, making it difficult to judge whether an account is a good one and the basis for interpretive claims. The issue of 'generalisability' may also be considered problematic by some, and is hotly debated, since reliance on a small sample size raises questions about the degree to which the research findings are typical or representative of a broader population (see for example Bassey, 1999; Gomm et al. 2000; Hammersley, 2001). Finally, the political issue of the 'weight' of data is an important consideration: whilst ethnographic data may be rich and have high validity, this is of little good if it is regarded as 'unscientific' and anecdotal by research funders or other stakeholders. Ways of addressing these last issues include combining ethnographic research with other methodological approaches as part of a mixed methods design and clearly situating the ethnographic research in relation to the wider context.

Whilst ethnography can make generalising claims, it is probably the case that ethnographic research is better at answering questions about 'how' and 'why', rather than 'how many' or 'how likely'. However, neither this, nor any of the advantages or disadvantages above is meaningful in and of itself. What is important is that the methodology is suited to the research problem and audience to be addressed. Research designs are not good or bad in and of themselves; they are more or less appropriate for answering particular empirical research questions and for particular purposes (Brannen and O'Connell, 2015).

8.8 AN EXAMPLE OF AN ETHNOGRAPHY: WAITE(2003)

Another example of a doctoral thesis that uses ethnography also comes from a former presenter for CDR, Edmund R.T. Waite. Like me, Waite is an anthropologist and gained his PhD from Cambridge University (2003). He became interested in the Uyghur people in China's Xinjiang region ('Chinese Central Asia') and spent about 15 months living amongst them in the mid-1990s, returning in 2004–05 to carry out post-doctoral research. The Uyghurs are Muslims, one of five recognised religions in China, and as a minority religion their way of life has recently been subjected to stringent political controls. Waite's research interests and aims were initially framed in quite general terms (relating to the issue of how Muslim Uyghurs have been affected by the experience of living in a secular state), but as his fieldwork progressed, his research questions began to have a greater focus on the issue of religious orthodoxy and local struggles to define what is the correct version of Islam.

Waite was based at a teacher training college in the oasis city of Kashgar. The college was aware of and fully supported his anthropological research. He was advised to phrase his research aims in terms of a study of 'religious customs' since this was deemed to be an acceptable topic at the time by government authorities. The language spoken by the Uyghurs is a variety of the Turkic language and before he began his fieldwork Waite took classes at London University's School of Oriental and African Studies (SOAS). By the time he arrived in China, he had a working knowledge of, and was able to communicate in, basic everyday language, although obviously his language skills developed considerably as he spent time in the field.

Carrying out research in another country presents challenges and, for Waite, it would have been extremely difficult without any knowledge of the language. Even with his good working knowledge of Uyghur, he acknowledges that he must have missed many of the subtleties or nuances in many of the conversations. This also limited themes and areas he could explore, and invariably changed the nature of the data he collected, which needed to be acknowledged. Like all ethnographers, he also needed to be continually reflexive and be aware of the influence of his own background, perceptions, values and interests on the research process.

The people were very welcoming and hospitable and Waite was invited to family gatherings, weddings and other communal celebrations. His research design was open and flexible and his main method of data collection was, again, participant observation. He spent his time in the streets and marketplaces and visited mosques, teahouses, farms and rural households. Waite was an outsider and, therefore, not a full participant, and his role as observer changed between times and places: sometimes he was a passive observer, sitting, watching and not engaging; at other times he was actively joining in with practices such as eating meals, and attending local community celebrations. Most of his data was generated through informal conversations and participant observation with and of people he struck up conversations with in the rural communities. But he also had about ten key informants, such as staff and students at the training college and local religious leaders, and these acted as gatekeepers to gain access to other local people whom he felt were able to provide him with good data. It was a snowball sample, with each participant recommending another person to talk to and learn from. Eventually, Waite reckons that he probably gathered data from about 150 people in the community and the notes that he wrote up each evening filled five thick volumes of field diaries. You can see that one of the difficulties for ethnographers is the selections they need to make and justify from such a large data set.

In addition to the informal conversations, he also carried out more formal interviews with around a dozen people (not all of these were the key informants mentioned above), where he would sit down with a series of well thought out questions, and which he recorded. The way in which Waite conducted his fieldwork poses various ethical problems. For instance, he was hardly likely to walk around with a set of consent forms, asking people to sign one every time be began to talk to them. Very few of the participants knew what the research was really about and neither of course did Waite, at least in the early stages. However, the very fact that he was a white European made him stand out; he was different and most people knew he was researcher and so the process was **overt**.

In his CDR session Waite tells a story that illustrates the need to be cautious about what people tell you during interviews for, as Douglas (1976) reminds us, people are either evasive, give misinformation (intentionally or not), put up a front which conceals their real feelings or puts them in a more favourable light, or they deliberately tell lies. In this case, one young man presented himself and is family as being very pious and dutiful and told Waite that they were religiously devout and attended the mosque every day without fail. Several months later Waite learned from a neighbour that the young man was involved in selling drugs, his sister worked as a prostitute and the family as a whole never attended the local mosque, which illustrates nicely the need to try and triangulate the data with other sources, and certainly reminds us of the need to be cautious about taking what people say at face value. Although, of course, it is not always possible to cross-check everything you are told, being in the field for a long time may make cross-checking easier and is therefore one of the advantages of ethnography.

One of the differences between Waite's (and O'Connell's) work which distinguishes it from the journalism that Will Gibson alluded to in Chapter 4, is that they are both underwritten by theory/theories and, despite their appearance of openness and an almost casual approach, are actually systematic, in that a lot of the people Waite spoke to would be planned and he would carry out 'conversations with a purpose' (Burgess, 1984) to pursue themes that he was interested in. There had been precious little research undertaken (at least by Europeans) in this area of China but his methodology used established ethnographic techniques and his research built on, and added to, other findings about religious customs in other areas of the world.

Publications from Waite's research can be found in the References (2006a, 2006b, 2007).

8.9 A SHORT REVIEW OF SOME CLASSIC ETHNOGRAPHIES IN SOCIAL RESEARCH

Ball, S. (1981) *Beachside Comprehensive A Case Study of Secondary Schooling.* **Cambridge and New York: Cambridge University Press.**
This account of the experiences of schooling of the pupils in a single comprehensive school is based on three years' fieldwork which Stephen Ball spent as participant observer at Beachside Comprehensive.

Evans-Pritchard, E.E. (1940) *The Nuer: A Description of the Modes of Livelihood and Political Institutions of a Nilotic People.* **Oxford: Clarendon Press.**
This classic ethnography describes the culture of a group of East African pastoralists. One chapter is devoted to each major social institution of the Nuer.

Foote Whyte, W. (1955/1943) *Street Corner Society: The Social Structure of an Italian Slum.* **Chicago, IL: University of Chicago Press.**
Through this book, based on fieldwork over three-and-a-half years, including 18 months spent with an Italian family, Whyte became a pioneer in participant observation and a founding figure in sociological ethnography.

Hochschild, A.R. (1989) *The Second Shift.* **New York: Viking.**
Based on interviews with 50 couples and observations of family life in a dozen homes, the book focuses on the stories of 11 couples to illuminate the ways in which women and men in two-career marriages juggle work and family life.

Malinowski, B. (1922) *The Argonauts of the Western Pacific.* **London: Routledge and Kegan Paul.**
Considered by many to be the first modern ethnography, *Argonauts* is the first of a trilogy about the Trobriand people.

Mead, M. (1928) *Coming of Age in Samoa: A Psychological Study of Primitive Youth for Western Civilisation.* **New York: Morrow.**

Mead's ethnography focuses mainly on adolescent girls and the struggles they face while growing up. The book sparked debates about the accuracy of her research and remains controversial.

Skeggs, B. (1997) *Formations of Class and Gender.* **London: Sage.**
Using detailed ethnographic research, the book explains how women inhabit and occupy the social and cultural positions of class, femininity and sexuality.

Willis, P. (1977) *Learning to Labour: How Working Class Kids Get Working Class Jobs.* **Farnborough: Saxon House.**
Based on in-depth ethnography, including interviews and observations of a set of working class 'lads' in a school in a West Midlands town, the book aims to illuminate how and why 'working-class kids get working-class jobs'.

■■■ BOX 8.6 ■■■

A summary of the key points

- The attempt to understand and describe human behaviour 'holistically', in its social context, is characteristic of ethnographic accounts.
- Ethnography generally involves the researcher being involved in people's daily lives for an extended period of time.
- Ethnography tries to see situations from participants' viewpoints.
- Although participant observation is the hallmark of ethnographic research, ethnographers may use a variety of different methods to generate data.
- In ethnography, the researcher is the principal 'tool' or 'instrument' of data collection.
- Ethnographic research is an iterative process, where initial theories and ideas are modified in the light of new information gathered.
- Ethnography raises particular considerations regarding research ethics, in part because the questions are rarely fully formulated in advance.

AREAS FOR DISCUSSION

- What are the potential merits and weaknesses of ethnographic research?
- What are the particular personal skills and/or attributes that an ethnographer needs to conduct their research?
- Is ethnographic research just a collection of stories?
- Does it matter in ethnography that different researchers may come to different conclusions?
- Is it possible to judge quality and veracity, i.e. can we distinguish a 'good' from a 'bad' ethnographic account?
- If the researcher is the tool, how much is it appropriate to reveal about his or her identity?

ANNOTATED BIBLIOGRAPHY

Brockmann, M. (2011) 'Problematising short-term participant observation and multi-method ethnographic studies', *Ethnography and Education*, 6 (2): 229–43.
Based on ethnographic research undertaken as part of a mixed methods study of apprentices in England and Germany, the article reflects on the identity and role of the researcher and the complementarity of observational and interview data.

Geertz, C. (1973) 'Thick description', in C. Geertz (ed.), *The Interpretation of Cultures: Selected Essays*. New York: Basic Books.
An important chapter, which describes Geertz's approach to ethnography and emphasises the importance of describing human behaviour in its context in order to convey its meaning.

Humphreys, L. (1970) *Tearoom Trade: A Study of Homosexual Encounters in Public Places*. New York: Aldine de Gruyter.
A controversial study in which the author infringed the privacy (but did not disclose the identity) of his research subjects when he conducted covert ethnographic research on gay sex in public toilets.

Wallman, S. (1984) *Eight London Households*. London: Tavistock.
Looks in detail at the pattern of life in eight households, through detailed descriptions and analysis of their resource systems.

FURTHER READING

Charsley, S. (1987) 'Interpretation and custom: The case of the wedding cake', *Man*, New Series, 22 (1): 93–110.
Based on an ethnography of first marriages and the wedding industry in Glasgow, the paper argues for an understanding of anthropological interpretation, not as a quest for true meaning but as a matter of eliciting readings which are possible within, and part of, the cultural context studied.

Clifford, J. and Marcus, G. (eds) (1986) *Writing Culture: The Poetics and Politics of Ethnography*. Berkeley, CA: University of California Press.
A very influential collection of articles from the height of the 'literary turn', which considers various aspects of ethnography as text. See also Marcus and Fischer (1986).

CHAPTER 9

CASE STUDIES

Mano Candappa

BOX 9.1

Overview of chapter

This chapter includes:

- A discussion of case study research as the study of the particular, and its essential features.
- Key debates around and epistemological principles underpinning case study research.
- Discussion around the concept of 'boundedness'.
- Types and purposes of case studies.
- Case selection and design issues.
- Classic and more contemporary examples of case study research.

> The quintessential characteristic of case studies is that they strive towards a relatively holistic understanding of cultural systems of action.
>
> (Snow and Anderson, 1991: 152)

9.1 INTRODUCTION

The use of case studies in social research has a long history and has been a familiar research approach in sociology, psychology, political science and business, among others. Within sociology, it is often linked to divisions amongst sociologists who argued for qualitative methodologies and techniques of enquiry such as observation and verbal types of analysis, rather than quantitative methodologies and survey techniques in investigating social phenomena. While these lively debates appear to have decreased in mainstream sociological circles from around the mid-1950s, as Mitchell (1983) maintains, interest in case study research has survived and remains popular in education research.

The turn to case study research in education has, in part, been largely associated with a need to explore processes and dynamics of practice. At a different level, the growth of sociological case studies in schooling, particularly in the UK, was fostered through varieties of symbolic interactionism, phenomenology and ethnomethodology, which resulted in increased support for approaches to research that 'acknowledge the capacity of individuals to interpret social events and to attribute personal meanings to the world in which they function' (Crossley and Vulliamy, 1984: 194). The corollary of this, which forms the premise of case study research, is that any unit of investigation in which persons are involved can only be understood if the perspectives of those involved are taken into account (Pring, 2000). Therefore, whilst case studies are not essentially qualitative, their logic derives from the worldview of qualitative research.

9.2 WHAT IS A CASE STUDY?

One of the main difficulties with case study research is that there is little consensus on what actually constitutes a case study, and the term is used in a variety of circumstances and contexts with different meanings. For example, professionals such as doctors, lawyers, psychologists and social workers, as well as business and management, study 'cases' (usually individual people, groups, organisations, etc.); additionally, some teaching devices are called 'case studies'. As a teaching tool, a 'case' is usually a framework for discussion among students and, in contrast to case study research, does not have to be an accurate and fair presentation of actual data. Case studies for research purposes do not have a generally agreed definition either, further confusing the issue. However, most researchers seem to agree that case study is not a method or methodology, but a flexible strategy for doing research. Yin, for example, takes this further and identifies key elements of case study research as:

> An empirical enquiry that investigates 'a contemporary phenomenon (the "case") in depth and within its real world context'. (2014: 16)

We find this view also echoed in Pring (2000), when he describes case study research as the study of a unique case or particular instant in a natural setting. In studying the case, the researcher engages in in-depth data collection over time using *multiple sources of evidence*.

Within this broad understanding of case studies, several key authors seem to agree that a fundamental feature of case studies is that:

> the case is a *bounded system*. Stake elaborates: 'the case has working parts; it is purposive; it often has a self. It is an integrated system'. (2003: 135)

This distinctive characteristic of boundedness separates case studies from other forms of qualitative enquiry. The boundaries of the case are established through the research questions around which the study is organised. Case studies ask 'how?' and 'why?' questions, which centre on issues along thematic lines, rather than simple information questions. Stake (2003: 142) gives the example of a case study research question such as: 'In what ways did the change in hiring policy require a change in performance standards?' as opposed to the information question, 'Who influenced her career choice?'

The case boundaries circumscribe 'what is deemed vital and important within those boundaries ... [and] usually determines what the study is about' (Stake, 1978: 2) and what its unit of analysis will be. The unit might be a person, a group, an institution, or a collection of institutions – the larger the unit, the more complex the analysis will become (I discuss these aspects of case study research further in Sections 9.4 and 9.5).

In addition to their boundedness, most researchers agree that other essential features of case studies are that they are:

- *Particularistic*: they focus on a particular phenomenon, situation, event or programme.
- *Descriptive*:– 'the end product of a case study is a rich, "thick" description of the phenomenon under study ... Case studies include as many variables as possible and portray their interaction, often over a period of time' (Merriam, 1988/1991: 13).
- *Heuristic*: they illuminate the reader's understanding of the phenomenon being studied, bringing about new meanings, extending experience or confirming what is known.
- *Inductive*: data is grounded in the context, there is no privileging of theory: theory should follow from the research, not precede it.

(Following Merriam, 1988/1991: 12–13)

Apart from these essential features, case studies might usefully also be described in relation to type and purpose. As Flyvbjerg (among others) notes, it has mistakenly been thought that case studies are useful mainly for generating hypotheses and for the first stages of a research project, a position that he refutes, arguing that: 'the case study is useful for both generating and testing of hypotheses but is not limited to these activities alone' (2006: 229). Indeed, case studies can prove insightful in research for the purposes listed in Box 9.2.

BOX 9.2

Types of case study

- *Exploratory*: often identified with the exploratory stage of an investigation.

They can also be:

- *Descriptive*: exemplified by famous case studies such as Whyte's (1955/1943) *Street Corner Society*, in which he studied a disadvantaged Italian immigrant neighbourhood in Boston, USA, living within the community over a three-and-a-half-year period, and discovered key phenomena relating to group and social structure (see WEBLINK 1 for more information about this case study).
- *Explanatory*: such as Allison's (1971) best-selling study of events around the 1962 Cuban missile crisis – a 13-day confrontation between the USA and the USSR over Soviet nuclear missiles placed in Cuba, 90 miles away from the USA mainland. (See WEBLINK 2 for more information about this case study.)

WEBLINK 1

A descriptive case study

WEBLINK 2

An explanatory case study

(Continued)

(Continued)

As well as being increasingly:

- *Evaluative*: used in policy research to study specific projects, programmes, interventions and initiatives. As evaluations, case studies can be used to interrogate implementation processes ('formative' or 'process' evaluations), as well as to analyse outcomes and make judgements on effectiveness ('summative' evaluations).

(For more examples of descriptive and explanatory case studies, see Yin, 2012, 2014.)

In terms of main types of case study, Stake (2005: 445–7) identifies three: the intrinsic, the instrumental, and the collective (see Box 9.3).

▬▬ BOX 9.3 ▬▬▬▬▬▬▬▬▬▬▬▬▬▬▬▬▬▬▬▬▬▬▬▬▬▬▬▬▬▬

Stake's three types of case studies

The *intrinsic* case study is one undertaken because the researcher wants a better understanding of a particular case: 'this case itself is of interest' (ibid.: 445). Biographies and most programme evaluations can be seen as examples of intrinsic case studies.

The *instrumental* case study, by contrast, is examined mainly to provide insight into an issue or to redraw a generalisation. The case facilitates our understanding of something else. So, while an intrinsic case would be undertaken because of an interest in a specific person or thing for its own sake, rather than as an instance of a wider phenomenon, in the instrumental study the case is of secondary interest. An example of a classic instrumental case study is Becker et al.'s (1961) pioneering USA study, *Boys in White: Student Culture in Medical School*, which explores how medical students became doctors. Whilst based in a single medical school, the interest and focus of the study was not in the particular medical school itself but in the process of transition from a young aspiring doctor to a skilled and confident physician. (See WEBLINK 3 for more information about this case study.)

WEBLINK 3

An instrumental case study

The *collective* case study is the joint study of a number of cases selected in order to investigate a phenomenon. It is an instrumental case study extended to several cases. The logic underlying collective case studies is replication (discussed further in Section 9.4). An excellent example of a collective case study based on replication logic is Szanton's (1981) *Not Well Advised*, which reviews university-based attempts to advise local governments in New York and six other USA cities (see also Yin, 2014). (See WEBLINK 4 for more information about this case study.)

WEBLINK 4

A collective case study

These main types of case study design are diagrammatically represented in Figure 9.1.

As Stake (2003) is at pains to point out, however, case studies often do not fit into such neat or discrete categories, so these should be seen as heuristic rather than determinative.

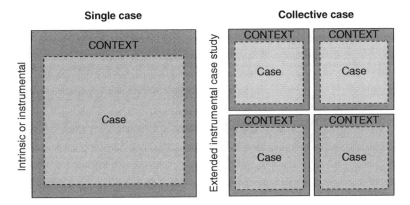

Figure 9.1 Basic case study designs

Source: Adapted from Yin (2014: 50).

Indeed it is possible for case studies to be of intrinsic as well as of instrumental interest, and also studied as a collective.

Case studies can be categorised in other ways, too, and I am particularly interested in what has been called the *ethnographic case study*, which has come up for discussion with students from time to time. Whilst agreeing with Stake (2005: 433) that 'as a form of research, case study is defined by interest in an individual case, not by the methods of inquiry used', it would be useful to acknowledge this type of case study to differentiate it from traditional ethnographic research. As Simons (2009) notes, the ethnographic case study focuses on a specific project or programme and uses qualitative methods, but draws on a wider range of methods than in classic ethnography.

9.3 ONTOLOGICAL AND EPISTEMOLOGICAL CLAIMS OF CASE STUDIES

It seems useful to pause to consider the nature of social reality implicit in the case study approach and the types of knowledge that case studies generate. Given the logic on which case studies are based (which I referred to earlier), the case study researcher posits – whilst not denying the existence of sensory knowledge – that the reality being researched is a reality defined by the participants, and that there are multiple realities. These realities do not exist independently of the researcher and the researched, and the case study would seek to preserve the wholeness within real life settings. This sets the case study approach within a social constructionist epistemological framework and, I would argue, a depth realist ontology (see Bhaskar, 1978; Blaikie, 2007).

Whilst this guiding epistemological assumption is often seen as a strength, the question of knowledge and generalisability from a single or small number of cases is a point of criticism. However, as Mitchell convincingly argues, much of this criticism rests 'on a misconception of the basis upon which the analyst may justifiably extrapolate from an individual case study to the social process in general' (1983: 207). The criticism would be valid if case studies sought to generalise to populations, which they do not: case studies seek to generalise to the building of theory. As Mitchell (ibid.) points out, there is an epistemological difference between logical and statistical inference, and inference from case studies is logical or causal and cannot be statistical. To further elaborate, he quotes Znaniecki (1934), who states that, 'enumerative induction abstracts by generalisation, whereas analytical induction generalises by abstracting ... [it] abstracts from the given concrete case characters that are essential to it and generalises them' (in Mitchell, 1983: 201). The validity of the arguments and inferences in case studies would therefore rest on the strength of the theoretical reasoning advanced.

9.4 STUDYING THE CASE

Mitchell's defence of the case study's knowledge claims above is founded upon the validity of the analysis, which in turn will be determined by robustness of research design, sufficiency of the data gathered and the rigour of the research process. This leads us to the question of how we should conduct a case study in order to fulfil these conditions, and to which I now turn.

Case boundaries and research questions

Of first importance is the research question(s), which lies at the heart of a case study's conceptual structure. As I have mentioned, these would be 'how' and 'why' questions drawn along thematic lines, which will determine the conceptual boundaries of the case. As with all social research, the research question therefore defines the study and needs to be approached with thought and care following a thorough review of the literature. How to pose case study research questions can perhaps be best explained through illustration, and I give below examples of research questions devised by students using case study in their research.[1]

▬ BOX 9.4 ▬▬▬▬▬▬▬▬▬▬▬▬▬▬▬▬▬▬▬▬▬▬▬▬▬▬▬▬▬

Examples of students' research questions when using a case study approach

a. A study of teacher professionalism:

 o How is teacher professionalism understood and enacted in a school setting?

  o How are governmental notions of teacher professionalism and professional standards articulated at a school level?
  o Is there a tension between teacher autonomy and accountability, and how is this manifested in a school setting?
  o How do teachers' views of professionalism translate into enacted teacher professionalism (teaching practice)?

1 Thanks to former research students Martyn Keys, Ian McGimpsey, Ben Major and Allan Hamilton for kind permission to reproduce their respective research questions in this paper.

b. An exploration of the role of youth workers:

   o How are youth worker roles constituted in youth service settings?

      o What affects the constitution of youth workers' roles in youth service provision, and in what ways are these effects more or less powerful?

      o How do youth workers and young people, as central participants in the youth service, understand the role of professionals in supporting young people?

c. An exploration of the construction of the geography curriculum in a secondary school:

   o In what ways do personal, institutional and political factors influence the development and implementation of the geography curriculum in a secondary school geography department?

d. A study of working life prospects within a local authority:

   o How does work-based experience and learning compare with more formal qualifications in facilitating employees' career prospects within the workplace?

As I have already indicated, case studies can be researched as a single case or as a collective, and it will be seen that while examples 'c' and 'd' above seem to relate to a specific single case, examples 'a' and 'b' could equally be studied as a single or as a collective (or multiple). Case study designs can also involve cases-within-the-case or embedded units – as I represent below – where the researcher decides to focus additionally and in detail on further units (persons, events, etc.) within the case to gain deeper and more nuanced understandings.

So, taking examples 'a', 'b' and 'd' above, one can see how embedded units of selected teachers/youth workers/employees could enrich the study of the case. Therefore, how to research the case – the research design – comes down again to the research question.

Case selection

Once the research question has been crafted, a key consideration in conducting case studies must surely be the *selection of the case* for study, and case study researchers often worry over questions about how typical their case is, how representative of a possible population of cases. Here again, however, the question seems to follow a different logic, one which relates to principles of statistical induction. In contrast, in case studies, the justification in selecting a case for study will be in terms of its *potential for learning*, its *explanatory power* (see Mitchell, 1983; Stake, 2005). In fact, the most significant case might well be the atypical case where events can throw underlying principles into sharp relief. As Flyvbjerg points out, atypical cases 'often reveal more information because they activate more actors and more basic mechanisms in the situation studied' (2006: 229). What we should be looking for, then, is what Mitchell calls the 'telling case', where 'particular circumstances surrounding a case [can] serve to make previously obscure theoretical relationships ... apparent' (Mitchell, 1987: 239). Focusing on the 'telling' case is both a way of seeing how theory and concepts are manifested in a particular case and of drawing out concepts and theory from the case.

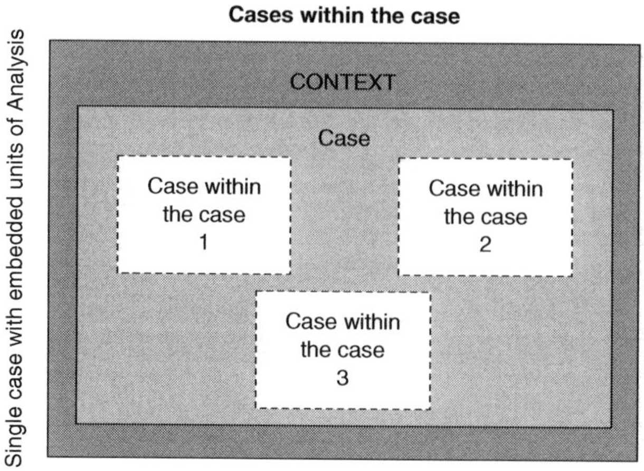

Cases within the case

Figure 9.2 More complex case study design

Source: Adapted from Yin (2014: 50).

Useful discussions on how and when to select cases for single-case study designs are found in Flyvbjerg (2006: 229–33) and Yin (2014: 51–6), considered in terms of 'information rich', 'significant' or 'critical' cases. In Box 9.5, I will focus on three, which seem also to suggest different types of 'telling' cases.

▬ BOX 9.5 ▬▬▬▬▬▬▬▬▬▬▬▬▬▬▬▬▬▬▬▬▬▬▬▬▬▬▬▬

Three 'telling' cases

The critical case

Such a case would be apt in testing a well-formulated theory with clear propositions as well as circumstances where these propositions hold true. A case meeting all these conditions – the critical case – could confirm, challenge, or extend the theory, using logical deduction of the form 'if this is (not) true for this case then it applies to all (no) cases'. When looking for critical cases Flyvbjerg's (2006) advice is to look for 'most likely' or 'least likely' cases citing Whyte's (1955/1943) *Street Corner Society* as one example. There contemporary theory suggested a slum neighbourhood that was socially disorganised which was the rationale for selection; however, through the case study the opposite was shown.

The extreme, unique or deviant case

These would be unusual cases, well-suited to getting a point across in a dramatic way; Flyvbjerg (2006) suggests Foucault's (1979) 'Panoptican' as an example. Yin (2014) reports extreme **cases** or unique cases being studied in clinical psychology, where an injury or disorder might be so rare to be worth documenting and analysing.

The revelatory case

This would be one where a researcher has access to a situation previously inaccessible to scientific study, so much so that 'the descriptive information alone will be revelatory' (Yin, 2014: 52). A classic study that Yin uses as an example is Liebow's (1967) *Tally's Corner* about a group of African American men living in a poor inner-city area of Washington, DC; there, Liebow had the opportunity to study the everyday lives of unemployed Black men which few social scientists previously had, even though such situations were common across the country. The study provided important insights into problems of unemployment and into a subculture that had been little understood, stimulating further research and later the development of policy actions.

As we have seen, case studies could also be conceived as a collective – also referred to as multiple-case design. Selecting a multiple-case design follows **replication logic**, as I have mentioned above, and not sampling logic as is often understood (for further discussion, see Yin, 2014). In other words, the researcher might want to test a theory or finding by replicating the experiment, or altering one or more variables to see if the finding could still be duplicated. Applying this logic to multiple-case designs, each case must be carefully selected on the basis of similarity (literal replication), therefore predicting similar results; or of contrast drawing on theory (theoretical replication), with difference in findings or aspects of findings anticipated. If the latter, one could use **maximum variation** cases or three to four cases that are different on one dimension, say, location, size, etc. as a selection strategy (Flyvberg, 2006). As with grounded theory, if some of the cases do not turn out as predicted, the theory would need to be modified.

Multiple sources of evidence

As I have mentioned, the use of *multiple sources of evidence* are another defining feature of case studies. The purpose of using multiple sources of data is to gain in-depth understanding of the case, and, as Tellis (1997) notes, allows the researcher access to a range of perspectives and voices, including groups of actors and the interactions between them, characteristically giving 'a voice to the voiceless'. It is important to understand, however, that no one source has complete advantage over another, but using multiple methods has the advantage that the various methods could complement one another. What is of utmost importance in selecting sources of evidence for a case study, is that taken together the methods selected are the most appropriate to answer the research question.

The historical and epistemological association of case studies with qualitative methodologies has meant that research methods and techniques such as observation and informal and formal interviews (individual and/or small group) are more often used for data generation in conducting these studies. However, a wider range of data collection methods can be used as evidence, including documentary sources, archival records and physical artefacts. Indeed, documents have been a major data source in classic case studies. For example, in Lynd and Lynd's (1929) *Middletown: A Study of American Culture*, which looked at what is described as an average medium-sized American midwestern city during 1890–1925 – a period of major social change brought about by the Great Depression – a variety of contemporary documentary sources available from within the community were used. These included old newspapers, census data and school yearbooks (or annuals commemorating the previous school year), and statistical sources in the form of work records, which were seen to provide 'direct' access to the community and the period, and complemented empirical methods to provide nuanced understandings of basic forms of the town's social life. More recently, documents provided valuable evidence and insights for Graham Allison's study of governmental decision-making (Allison, 1971; Allison and Zelikow, 1999). Taking the case of the Cuban Missile Crisis referred to above (when the two superpowers 'paused at the nuclear precipice'), the authors drew, inter alia, on a broad array of documentary evidence, which included tens of thousands of pages of government documents. This was complemented by interviews with a large number of officials, with sharply focused research questions used to organise the data to be collected.

Whilst used to a lesser extent in case studies than qualitative methods, quantitative methods too may be used as sources of evidence, forming part of mixed method designs. In fact, surveys formed part of the empirical data generated in the Lynd and Lynd (1929) study that I mentioned above: the authors created schedules of questions which were sent out to local experts and members of clubs and associations they had contacted in Middletown, which complemented their qualitative data. A more recent example of a case study that included quantitative methods would be Crewe's (2001) study of an urban design project, which surveyed the views of a group of designers. Whilst in keeping with case study logic, the qualitative data would remain central, including quantitative data could provide considerable benefits if justified by the research question. To take an illustration from Yin (2014), in a case study about a school that seeks to explain student achievement, the collection of detailed quantitative data might be required, even though the main research questions are at a higher level that requires qualitative data: in other words, the quantitative data would support the overall analysis.

9.5 ANALYSING CASE STUDIES

Multiple sources of data allow for the development of converging lines of enquiry (Yin, 2014), a process of triangulation, which in analysis serves to clarify meanings and identify different ways in which the phenomenon is seen (Silverman, 1993). Multiple data sources are also often seen to support a case study's claims of validity.

In discussing case study analysis, I will be drawing mainly on the work of Robert Yin, who I believe, considers this aspect of case study research in most detail. Commenting that this aspect of case studies is one of the least developed, he notes (Yin, 2014: chapter 5) that analysing case data is particularly difficult because analytical techniques have not yet been well defined. He therefore advocates that researchers should develop an analytic strategy, which defines priorities for what to analyse and why. I have found three analytic strategies that he suggests to be particularly helpful, and these are listed in Box 9.6.

BOX 9.6

Three key analytical strategies

- Relying on theoretical propositions.
- Developing case descriptions.
- Examining plausible rival explanations.

Any of these could be used for most case studies, as I discuss below.

Relying on theoretical propositions

This is the preferred strategy of many researchers. It follows theoretical propositions developed through the literature review that lead to the case study and research questions, and have informed the research design and data collection. The propositions are therefore theoretically oriented and these can guide the analysis by helping focus attention on particular data and giving less attention to others. They can also help to organise the entire study and to identify other possible explanations for consideration, and guide the analysis in this way.

Developing case descriptions as a way of organising the study

A second strategy is to develop a descriptive framework for organising the data and supporting analysis. Sometimes the original purpose of the study might be descriptive, such as Lynd and Lynd's (1929) *Middletown*, mentioned above, which Yin uses as an example. There, the authors used descriptive categories relevant to community life in the early twentieth century to organise their data and their report. They are:

1 Getting a Living.
2 Making a Home.
3 Training the Young.
4 Using Leisure.
5 Engaging in Religious Practices.
6 Engaging in Community Activities.

As Yin (2014) notes, if you want to use a descriptive framework as your analytic strategy it would help if you had given it some thought prior to designing your research instruments.

Additionally, even if the original purpose of your case study might not have been descriptive a descriptive approach might help identify themes and links to be further analysed.

Testing rival explanations

This strategy could work together with both of the above. Taking the first strategy – relying on initial theoretical propositions – this might be disproved or proved insufficient through the analysis, leading to further propositions having to be developed and tested. Or, the original proposition might have included a rival explanation allowing both to be tested in the analysis and one or other to be disproved or both to be disproved and a different theory being suggested. Similarly, and taking the second strategy – developing a case description – contrasting perspectives of key informants or competing interest groups within the study may suggest rival conditions to be examined, resulting in alternative explanations needing to be tested.

A good example of the process of testing rival explanations in a case study is Allison's (1971) study of the Cuban Missile Crisis, which I referred to earlier. Allison advances three competing but complementary theories to explain the crisis and why a nuclear disaster did not ensue: that the USA and USSR performed as: '(a) rational actors, (b) complex bureaucracies, or (c) politically motivated groups of persons' (Yin, 2014: 7). Allison compares each theory's ability to explain the course of events and the respective actions and counteractions of the USA and the USSR, and why the USSR finally withdrew its missiles.

Overall, however, in analysing case studies, Yin's (ibid.) principles for producing an analysis of the highest quality contain excellent advice for researchers, as shown in Box 9.7.

■■ BOX 9.7 ■■■■■■■■■■■■■■■■■■■■■■■■■■■■■■■■■

Yin's principles of sound analysis

- Show that the analysis relied on all the evidence.
- Include all plausible rival interpretations in the analysis.
- Address the most significant aspect of the case study.
- Use the researcher's prior expert knowledge to further the analysis. (Ibid.)

9.6 ETHICAL ISSUES

As research involving human participants, case studies embody specific ethical issues common to all qualitative research, discussed in Chapter 5. In general, in embarking on case study research researchers need to be mindful that something of a contract, a moral obligation, exists between researcher and research participant – what Stake (2005: 459) describes as a 'disclosing and protective covenant'. For case studies, particular issues arise relating to the anonymity or otherwise of the case itself, and researchers have debated whether the case and participants should be identified, or the entire case and all participants anonymised. Yin, for example, argues that disclosure 'within the constraints of protecting human subjects' (2014: 81) will allow the reader to draw on information s/he already possesses in reading and interpreting the study; and that the absence of anonymised names will make the case easier to review. Whilst this makes the scientific case, I am not convinced that such disclosure is compatible with 'protecting human subjects' in most cases, and would argue that protecting research participants should take primacy. Even so, when focusing on specific organisations or institutions, providing pseudonyms might not in itself be sufficient to provide anonymity among participants who know one another. Research guidelines might prove helpful in considering ethical issues involved, but as Stake (2005: 459) suggests, case study researchers should seek to go beyond the rules, 'drawing in advisers and reviewers to extend the protective system'. However, as Swain discusses in Chapter 5, it is not always possible to assure complete confidentiality, and researchers will need to consider and weigh up ethical implications of their studies on an individual basis, consulting experts in the field to decide the most ethical path along which to proceed.

9.7 A 'CASE' IN POINT: 'EDUCATION AND SCHOOLING FOR ASYLUM-SEEKING AND REFUGEE STUDENTS IN SCOTLAND'

To illustrate some of the issues that I have discussed above, I shall use an example from my own research.

I have a long-standing interest in forced migration and issues around social inclusion and exclusion, which has led me together with colleagues to explore inter alia: asylum migration to the EU in 1995–96; the social lives of refugee children in 1996–98 and 1999–2000; and relations between asylum-seeking and 'host' students in secondary schools in 2005–06. Qualitative methods used in conducting these studies gave us unique insight into the worlds of children and adults seeking asylum and refuge in the West. The studies were conducted against a growing perception of 'asylum crisis' among income-rich Western nations including Britain, where the end of the Cold War, the outbreak of many ethnic and civil conflicts at the end of the twentieth century and unequal economic globalisation contributed to a rapid increase in the number of forced migrants (Gibney, 2004). A peak is said to have been reached in the mid-1990s with 18.2 million refugees worldwide; in the UK, asylum applications reached a peak in 2002 with 84,130 applications (excluding dependents). United Kingdom state responses to this 'crisis' saw a progressive reduction in financial and material supports to, and marginalisation of people seeking asylum from mainstream services, which was matched by their aggressive representation in the media (see Pinson et al., 2010).

A particularly significant policy response to the perceived crisis was the Asylum and Immigration Act 1999 which saw the compulsory dispersal of adults and families seeking asylum away from traditional areas of settlement in London and the South-East of England to predominantly White areas in England, to Scotland, Wales and Northern Ireland.

Dispersal was purportedly to avoid 'swamping' and possible related racial tensions, and to share the economic burden of supporting asylum-seekers. The reality was that asylum-seeking families were mostly located to areas where accommodation was available, in many cases in socially and economically deprived areas where they became targets for abuse (Bloch and Schuster, 2005). This policy also shaped schooling: in dispersal areas, many schools had little experience of multi-ethnic communities, and were ill-prepared for receiving children with English as an additional language and for diverse religious traditions.

Dispersal policy had particular importance for the context of the study. Whilst people had sought asylum in Scotland for many years, their numbers had been few until 1999 when just over 300 refugees from Kosovo arrived under the UK government's Humanitarian Evacuation Programme. That was the first experience of refugees in the Scottish city that received them. With the implementation of the 1999 Act in 2000, the numbers of people seeking asylum and refugees in Scotland rose dramatically, with their numbers now drawn from a range of sending countries including Africa, the Middle East, South and Central Asia and Turkey. In terms of schools and schooling, the receiving city then became one of only three UK cites outside of London with more than 2,000 asylum-seeking and refugee pupils in its school population (Multiverse, 2004).

It was against this background that 'Education and Schooling for Asylum-Seeking and Refugee Students in Scotland', a project which I designed and led, was funded by the Scottish Government in 2005, in order to obtain an overview of education provision for asylum-seeking and refugee children and to identify 'best practice' within the Scottish context for the integration of asylum-seeking/refugee pupils into school communities. In responding to the tender, I argued for a mixed methods study that would include a case study element, to which I now turn.

The case study: intrinsic, instrumental or collective?

Before I could approach a design-related question such as this, I needed to establish my research questions, for which I required deeper understandings than a broad contextual knowledge could give. A review of the literature on refugees and asylum (e.g., Rutter, 1994; Arshad et al., 1999), together with findings from my own research (Candappa and Egharevba, 2002), provided important contextual information, including that refugees are vulnerable and prone to Othering, often involving racist abuse in the country of refuge; whilst being categorised as an 'asylum-seeker' by definition involves facing economic hardship and dependence on state benefits. For children from asylum-seeking and refugee backgrounds, the school has a pivotal role in building their new lives, and language is crucial in the process, for social interaction and forming friendships as well as for educational achievement. However, the refugee experience could include overwhelmingly traumatic events, which could impact a child's emotional well-being and also their education.

The inclusive education discourse was also relevant to the study. That literature pointed to differences between concepts of 'integration' and 'inclusion': where 'integration' seeks to equip the student for the demands of the mainstream, 'inclusion' means including the student with his/her own culture and values in the school, within a culture that celebrates diversity (Corbett, 1999; Armstrong, 2008). This conceptual understanding of inclusive education is based on a belief that all members of a community have a right to participate in and have access to education on an equal basis, and is consonant with the Right to Education in the 1989 UN Convention on the Rights of the Child. In responding to the Call for Tenders, I therefore argued for identifying 'best practice' in relation to the *inclusion* of asylum-seeking and refugee students as successful learners within the school community, rather than their integration.

Informed by the above discourses and research aims, I devised the following 'How' and 'Why' research questions and sub-questions appropriate to case studies, to explore what could constitute 'good practice' for the education and schooling of asylum-seeking and refugee students in Scotland:

- In what ways, if any, have policies enacted by Education Authorities required change to meet the needs of asylum-seeking and refugee students in their school population, and how do they support schools to meet these students' needs?
- In what ways, if any, have schools' ethos, policies, pedagogies, and pastoral care required development to meet the needs of asylum-seeking and refugee students?

  o Have schools had to re-think their ethos and practice so as to be welcoming and inclusive towards students from asylum-seeking and refugee families, and in what ways?
  o In what ways if any has school policy and practice had to be developed to address the possible racist Othering of asylum-seeking and refugee students, and does this differ in contexts where there are relatively low numbers of asylum-seeking students and refugees, compared with where there are relatively high numbers?
  o Has pedagogy and classroom practice changed with the arrival of asylum-seeking and refugee students to take account of the needs of bilingual learners and their inclusion, and in what ways?
  o Have specific emotional needs related to forced migration been recognised by the school and has this led to the development of particular pastoral supports being provided to these students?
  o Have experiences of Othering in the wider community been recognised as impacting on asylum-seeking and refugee students' education and emotional well-being in providing pastoral supports?

- Have the ethos, pedagogical approaches and pastoral care provided by the school resulted in positive learning experiences and a sense of inclusion for asylum-seeking and refugee students?

It was clear that these research questions demanded I study at least two education authorities as well as a number of schools – therefore a collective (or 'multiple') case study with embedded units was required. The next design question was case selection: using theoretical replication logic and a version of maximum variation cases, I decided on two contrasting cases, one a 'dispersal city' with high numbers of people seeking asylum and refugees in its population (City A), and a second with fewer numbers but with a longer history of providing asylum and refuge (City B).

Each case included a sample of schools as embedded units or 'cases within the case' – as discussed above. The unit of analysis of each case was the relevant city's education authority; a sample of its schools would be embedded units within the larger case. The case boundaries for each case were drawn through the first research question, while the two subsequent research questions defined the boundaries for the embedded units. Each case included four embedded units: two primary and two secondary schools selected purposively[2] from schools identified by the education authorities as demonstrating inclusive practice.

The two cases held intrinsic interest for me because of their specific histories in relation to asylum and refuge, but they also held instrumental interest in terms of education policy and practice in relation to asylum-seeking and refugee students in Scotland, and more generally in the UK. I was conducting the study as a collective of cases; therefore this was at the same time an intrinsic, instrumental as well as collective case study.

Studying the case: sources of evidence

My research questions and resulting multiple-case design dictated my selection of best sources of evidence to achieve the research aims. For the two cases and research question 1 (on education policy and education authorities' support for schools), I proposed semi-structured interviews with key education authority officers and policy documents as my key sources, which would then be complemented by data from the cases-within-the-case (embedded units).

For each of the cases-within-the-case, I considered a wide range of sources was required to investigate the related research questions: unstructured observation; semi-structured interviews with the head/senior teacher, a purposive sample of asylum-seeking and refugee students and their parents; and documentary evidence. This range of sources allowed for in-depth exploration of the issues and questions identified and the possibility of multi-perspectival analysis. The focus of the study on a vulnerable and socially marginalised population meant that issues of voice (Hargreaves, 1996; Dona, 2007) assumed special importance; at a practical level this meant that bilingual researchers, proficient in a number of community languages were available to conduct interviews with students and parents, if preferred.

Strategy for analysis and dissemination of findings

In devising my analytic strategy, I considered that I would be writing for a policy audience and a key aim of the research was to identify and describe 'good practice'. I therefore decided

---

2 For more information, and a more detailed explanation about purposive sampling, see Chapter 7.

on developing a case description, which would serve as a framework for organising the study. Similar to the way in which Lynd and Lynd (1929) organised their *Middletown* study, I structured my analysis of embedded units around factors I had identified as of vital importance to school life in the rehabilitation and educational success of asylum-seeking and refugee students in the country of refuge (Box 9.8).

BOX 9.8

Key factors of importance to school life for refugees used in the analysis of the embedded units

- Ethos of school: response to diversity.
- Practice towards new arrivals: reception and settling in.
- Pastoral care: supporting emotional needs, fostering friendships.
- Pedagogical model for supporting bilingual learners.
- Curriculum issues, attainment, and encouraging achievement in all students.
- Othering: racism and bullying.
- Engagement with parents: home-school relations.

Each embedded unit was analysed separately prior to cross-case analysis along these themes across the embedded units of each case. A further analysis across the two parent cases identified issues that cross-cut the two cases, such as the relative merits of mainstreaming versus withdrawal as pedagogical models, and a need for a greater understanding of refugee experiences and their impact on a child's well-being and also their educational performance. Outstanding good practice was identified in some schools through this process, for example addressing the needs of the whole child (rather than just educational needs); as well as issues that needed further action, such as provision of specific and ongoing training for teachers around supporting the needs of asylum-seeking and refugee pupils, particularly in relation to behaviours and obstacles to learning resulting from past traumatic experiences.

A full report on the study geared to a policy audience, as well as a shorter summary covering key issues for a wider audience including practitioners and parents, was provided to the Scottish Government. In keeping with its commitment to the use of sound evidence in the development of policy and practice and to provide access to interested parties, both documents were published online for maximum impact. Hard copies of the summary were also provided to schools to assist in the development of good practice.

Reflections

Using a case study approach in this investigation allowed the research team to dig deep and generate rich data to fulfil the project's objectives; and using bilingual researchers in conducting fieldwork demonstrated a sensitivity towards participants and context that resulted in nuanced findings. However, identifying and accessing schools for case study could have proved a challenge within the seven-month period stipulated in the tender had the study not been backed by the Scottish Government, who requested the education authorities to support and facilitate the research, which they did. We ensured, though, that final selection of schools and how the study was conducted remained with us, to maintain research rigour. The decision to use a case study design meant of course that breadth was sacrificed in favour of depth, with implications for generalisability: in reporting, we therefore underlined the limits of generalisation, but pointed to key issues specific to the cases studied that could be useful to consider in developing policy and practice in similar or related areas.

9.8 CONCLUSION: A FINAL THOUGHT

In this chapter, I introduced key debates and principles around case study approaches to social investigation, exploring what a 'case' might be, defending the case study's knowledge claims, and outlining key aspects of conducting case study research. In concluding, I would like to introduce Simons's thoughts on what she calls 'the paradox of case study' and the contradiction between the study of the singular and the search for generalisation:

> Paradox for me is the point of case study. Living with paradox is crucial to understanding. The tension between the study of the unique and the need to generalise is necessary to reveal both the *unique* and the *universal* and the *unity* of that understanding. To live with ambiguity, to challenge certainty, to creatively encounter, is to arrive, eventually, at 'seeing' anew. (1996: 237–8)

▬▬ BOX 9.9 ▬▬▬▬▬▬▬▬▬▬▬▬▬▬▬▬▬▬▬▬▬▬▬▬▬▬▬▬▬▬▬▬▬▬

A summary of the key points

- There is little consensus on what actually constitutes a case study.
- The characteristic of 'boundedness' separates case studies from other form of qualitative enquiry.
- In terms of purpose, case studies can be exploratory, descriptive, explanatory or evaluative.
- Key types of case study are: intrinsic, instrumental and collective.
- Multiple sources of evidence and multi-perspectival analyses support a case study's claims of validity.

AREAS FOR DISCUSSION

- How would you know when to use case studies in your research and what reasons would you give for choosing this approach?
- How do you decide what to include and exclude in a case study when you are thinking about the boundaries of the case?

- Given the mass of data accumulated in a case study, how would you process this to provide a fair, balanced and credible report?
- What are some of the advantages and disadvantages of conducting case study research?
- Case study research is concerned with people's personal views and circumstances: how would you protect your participants from harm, including embarrassment and loss of self-esteem?

ANNOTATED BIBLIOGRAPHY

Flyvbjerg, B. (2006) 'Five misunderstandings about case-study research', *Qualitative Inquiry*, 12 (2): 219–44.

This article examines five common misunderstandings about case study research, to correct each in turn, and concludes by drawing on Kuhnian thought to posit that: 'a scientific discipline without a large number of thoroughly executed case studies is a discipline without systematic production of exemplars, and a discipline without exemplars is an ineffective one' (p. 219).

Simons, H. (1996) 'The paradox of case study', *Cambridge Journal of Education*, 26 (2): 225–40.

This article examines the case for case study as a form of research, and explores 'the paradox that is at the very heart of case study' – its uniqueness as against the search for universal understandings – and argues that through engaging holistically as well as in depth with complex phenomena, a case study can generate both unique and universal understandings.

Stake, R.E. (2005) 'Qualitative case studies', in N.K. Denzin and Y.S. Lincoln (eds), *The Sage Handbook of Qualitative Research*, 3rd edn. Thousand Oaks, CA: Sage.

This chapter explores case studies as a major strategy of social enquiry, exploring its history and uses in research, whilst at the same time embedding the discussion in social justice topics. Stake argues that case study can be a 'disciplined force in setting public policy and in reflecting on human experience' (p. 460), but the purpose of the case report is 'not to represent the world, but to represent the case' (ibid.).

Yin, R.K. (ed.) (2004) *The Case Study Anthology*. Thousand Oaks, CA: Sage.

This book provides readers with cases drawn from a variety of disciplines that illustrate different case study techniques (descriptive, explanatory, cross-case and methodological). Yin provides thoughtful insights and guidelines on the cases and the different approaches to doing case study research.

FURTHER READING

Eisenhardt, K.M. and Graebner, M.E. (2007) 'Theory building from cases: Opportunities and challenges', *Academy of Management Journal*, 50 (1): 25–32.

This article focuses on building theory from case studies, using one or more cases to create theoretical constructs and mid-range theory from case-based empirical evidence, and drawing on inductive logic. The article guides the reader through the process and its challenges, making it a valuable resource for the case study researcher.

George, A.L. and Bennett, A. (2005) *Case Studies and Theory Development in the Social Sciences*. **Cambridge, MA: MIT Press.**

This book offers a thorough analysis of research methods using case studies and examines the place of case studies in social science research. Of particular note is its emphasis on the importance of within-case analysis, discussion of process tracing, and development of the concept of typological theories.

Gomm, R., Hammersley, M. and Foster, P. (eds) (2000) *Case Study Method: Key Issues, Key Texts*. **London: Sage.**

This is a comprehensive guide to the uses and importance of case studies in social science research, which brings together key contributions from the field. In-depth review of the main arguments by the editors, and an annotated bibliography of the literature on case study research makes this an invaluable text for research students.

CHAPTER 10

MIXED METHODS IN EDUCATION RESEARCH

Olga Cara

10.1 INTRODUCTION

Mixed methods design is increasingly popular in the field of social sciences and a growing number of doctoral students and researchers make use of this methodological approach, that is, the use of both quantitative and qualitative methods within a single study. At the same time, surprisingly few details are known about how this combination of the methods should be used in practice. The overall aim of this chapter is to provide students with information, tools and guidance on using a mixed methods design in an informed and appropriate way.

The chapter will explain what mixed methods research is and discuss its advantages and challenges. The main body of the chapter will focus on practical issues that are involved in data collection, analysis and write-up when using some specific mixed methods design types. It will draw on examples of mixed methods studies from recent research produced at UCL/IOE.

10.2 WHAT IS MIXED METHODS RESEARCH? GETTING THE TERMINOLOGY RIGHT

Researchers have been conducting mixed methods research for several decades, and referring to it by an array of names. Early articles on the application of such designs have described them as 'multimethod', 'integrated', 'hybrid', 'combined' and 'mixed methodology' research and, more recently, 'mixed methods' research (Creswell and Plano Clark, 2007: 6).

Two of the first researchers to give a specific name to the use of several methods in one study were the psychologists Campbell and Fiske (1959) in their study of various personality traits. They called it 'multitrait' or 'mutlimethod' research but, because they only collected numerical data from different types of quantitative methods, their work would not be called mixed methods in contemporary understandings of the term (Bazeley, 2009). This is a very important distinction to make: multimethod research includes the use of more than one method from the same tradition in a research study and mixed methods research specifically includes the mixing of qualitative and quantitative data, methods, methodologies and/or paradigms.

A quarter of a century later, Fielding and Fielding (1986) use the phrase 'quantitative and qualitative methods' to simply acknowledge the research design's main focus of mixing the two methods. Other academics (e.g., Steckler et al., 1992; Creswell, 1994) use the terms 'integrated' or 'combined' research to describe how different forms of data collection and/ or analysis are blended or mixed together in one study. Tashakkori and Teddlie (1998) also use the term 'mixed methodology' and Morse (1991) uses 'methodological triangulation' to acknowledge that this type of research not only encompasses different methods but also often a specific philosophical worldview(s).

Currently, the most frequently used and widely recognised name is 'mixed methods' research, which is generally associated with the work of Tashakkori and Teddlie (2003b) and Creswell and Plano Clark (2007). Johnson et al., (2007) provide their definition of this approach by synthesising the perspectives from 31 leading researchers in the field (Box 10.2).

━━ BOX 10.2 ▬▬▬▬▬▬▬▬▬▬▬▬▬▬▬▬▬▬▬▬▬▬▬▬▬▬▬▬▬▬▬▬▬▬

A definition of mixed methods

Mixed methods research is the type of research in which a researcher or team of researchers combines elements of qualitative and quantitative research approaches (e.g., use of qualitative and quantitative viewpoints, data collection, analysis, inference techniques) for the broad purpose of breadth and depth of understanding and corroboration. (Johnson, 2007: 123)

Their definition is very similar to that given in the *Handbook of Mixed Methods Research* (Creswell and Plano Clark, 2007: 5). The central element of this definition is that mixed methods research involves the use of both quantitative and qualitative approaches on one or more of the levels of a research project, and this is the definition I am using in this chapter. For me, mixed methods research is a specific research design that includes rigorous, systematic and the planned use of different quantitative and qualitative methods for collecting and/or analysing data in the same study in order to understand a research problem.

It is important to define quantitative and qualitative in this context. The nature of quantitative data is in its power to summarise large amount of data in a succinct way. Quantitative data includes closed-ended information that is usually collected using precoded, structured instruments such as questionnaires, tests or observation schedules. Analysis involves working with all the information transferred into numbers. If used properly in a suitable context, it allows using statistical analysis to provide a concise, neat picture of a complex phenomenon. You can use quantitative analysis to describe, to compare groups, and relate them to a series of variables such as gender and/or ethnicity.

The nature of qualitative data is rich and very detailed. The data collection involves working with open-ended data, that is, texts, participants' views expressed in their own words, rich observational descriptions, and so on, and allows in-depth insights into a smaller number of cases. The analysis often involves, in generic terms, aggregating textual data into categories of information or themes and presenting the diversity of ideas gathered (Creswell and Plano Clark, 2007). Qualitative analysis can be used for 'thick' description, the development of themes and exploring the relationships between the themes.

Thus, quantitative and qualitative approaches can be described based on the type of data (numerical or textual), the technique of data collection (large survey or in-depth interviews), the method of analysis (statistical or interpretive) or, going even further, to consider underlying paradigm(s) or epistemologies (e.g., positivist/post-positivist or constructionist/interpretivist). As a result, the mixed methods research can use not only quantitative and qualitative approaches in its narrowest form of numerical and textual data, but can also use quantitative and qualitative data collection techniques, apply quantitative and qualitative analysis and mix different epistemologies within one study.

Therefore, the actual mixing, or integration, of the methods can take place at different stages and can involve merging/blending, nesting/embedding, or connecting (see Figure 10.1 on p. 201). Furthermore, there are examples when the mixing is just the side-by-side or sequential use of different quantitative and qualitative methods with very minimal or full integration in a single analysis (Greene and Caracelli, 1997). Yet, as a minimum, all mixed methods research has to involve integrating the results from the various strands of the study into the conclusion.

Mixed methods research is not merely the use of the qualitative and quantitative approaches in one study, as these approaches have to produce something more than two separate single studies (a qualitative and a quantitative one) to come to a better understanding of a research problem under investigation. Drawing on Bryman's work (2007), Wooley (2009) defines integration within the mixed methods context as shown in Box 10.3.

━━ BOX 10.3 ━━━

A definition of integration within mixed methods

Quantitative and qualitative components can be considered 'integrated' to the extent that these components are explicitly related to each other within a single study and in such a way as to be mutually illuminating, thereby producing findings that are greater than the sum of the parts. (Wooley, 2009: 7)

According to Denzin (1978), there are three outcomes to the triangulation, which in our case means the triangulation or mixing of methods: convergence/agreement, inconsistency and contradiction of the findings from different types of data and their analysis. Based on Denzin's writings, all of these outcomes can provide researchers with a superior or value-added explanation of the observed social phenomena and justify the use of the mixed methods research design in appropriate research contexts.

10.3 HISTORICAL AND THEORETICAL UNDERPINNINGS

The first use of mixed methods in social research can already be seen in the early twentieth century (Creswell, 1999: 458; Johnson et al., 2007: 113). However, although sociologists and anthropologists in the first 60 years of the twentieth century blended quantitative and qualitative methods together relatively successfully (e.g., Lynd and Lynd, 1929; Jahoda et al., 1931; Hollingshead, 1949), there was no wider intellectual debate within the academy about this practice including its advantages and disadvantages.

As I have already stated, Campbell and Fiske (1959) are generally regarded as being the first researchers who explicitly discussed the use of multiple (rather than mixed) methods for validation purposes. They wrote about 'multiple operationalism' when more than one method is used to ensure that the findings are not the product of a particular method (e.g., qualitative or quantitative), but are, indeed, the result of the underlying phenomenon, behaviour or attitude under investigation. Subsequently, their work encouraged other academics to mix not only different quantitative methods, but also quantitative and qualitative methods such as interviews and surveys in one study (e.g., Sieber, 1973).

The ideas of multiple operationalisation by Webb et al. (1966) that further extended the ideas of multiple operationalisation are credited with being the first to develop and use the term triangulation. As they suggested:

> Once a proposition has been confirmed by two or more independent measurement processes, the uncertainty of its interpretation is greatly reduced. The most persuasive evidence comes through a triangulation of measurement processes. (Ibid.: 3)

Following them, Denzin (1970) took the idea of triangulation further by distinguishing between four forms of triangulation, as listed in Box 10.4.

━━ BOX 10.4 ━━

Four forms of triangulation (based on Denzin, 1970)

1 Data triangulation, which involves collecting data from several different samples, so that sets of data reflect different times and social situations, as well as a variety of people.
2 Investigator triangulation, which requires the work of more than one researcher to gather and interpret the same data.
3 Theoretical triangulation, which refers to the use of more than one theoretical approach during data interpretation.
4 Methodological triangulation, which refers to the use of more than one method for gathering data.

When Denzin (1970, 1978) explained methodological triangulation, he distinguished between within-method (or multimethod) and between-methods triangulation (mixed methods). Denzin suggested that the within-method approach is weaker because it does not solve any inherent weaknesses of the particular method(s) used. So, he recommended the use of between-methods triangulation, the result of which would be 'a convergence upon the truth about some social phenomenon' (1978: 14).

The recognition of the limitations of different methods helped not only to develop the idea of the validation of data (Campbell and Fiske, 1959), but also the understanding that mixing methods can reduce or even cancel out weaknesses and biases of different methods. As Jick (1979, 1983) suggests, triangulation not only allows researchers to be more confident in their findings and provide richer data, it also stimulates innovative ways of data collection and analysis and can even lead to the creation of new theories by integrating or contradicting existing ones.

Despite a certain existing rationale for the use of mixed methods research and its advantages, some researchers began to question whether the combination of qualitative and quantitative methods is possible at all since they are linked to inherently different paradigms (Cook and Reichardt, 1979; Smith, 1983, 1986; Guba and Lincoln, 1988). These paradigms address issues intrinsic to the philosophical foundations of social inquiry that we have seen discussed in Chapter 4, such as: *epistemology* (beliefs about the nature of knowledge, including those related to the objectivity/subjectivity dualism); *ontology* (beliefs about the nature of reality); *axiology* (beliefs about the role of values or ethics in conducting research); and others (e.g., the possibility of generalisations, the nature of causality, etc.).

These debates were not new; they have existed for decades within the social and behavioural sciences as a 'schism' that separates the qualitative and quantitative research traditions (Tashakkori and Teddlie, 2003a; Teddlie and Tashakkori, 2003), and hence issues of the epistemological foundations have been central to mixed methods research since its inception and continue to be so.

In this chapter, I do not intend to go into too much discussion about the philosophical foundation of mixed methods research since my main aim is to introduce the more practical side of this approach and there is a lot of academic articles dealing specifically with this question (e.g., Greene and Caracelli, 1997; Onwuegbuzie, 2002; Bryman, 2007; Morgan, 2007; Denscombe, 2008; Greene, 2008; Denzin, 2010; Feilzer, 2010). Nevertheless, I will provide a short summary below of the arguments about the use of different paradigms in the mixed methods research.

A 'purist' stance (Lincoln and Guba, 1985) advocates the 'incompatibility' thesis, arguing that paradigms cannot be mixed because their underlying assumptions are incommensurable – hence, mixed methods is an invalid approach. However, the rapid development of mixed methods research was seen in itself by some in the academy as heralding the end of the incompatibility thesis as it had demonstrated that paradigms could be combined within a single study.

Consequently, some researchers (e.g., Greene and Carcelli, 1997; Maxwell and Loomis, 2003; Greene, 2007) suggest a 'dialectic' approach that allows the use of multiple paradigms in the same research, but implies that they need to be made explicit and honoured. In this way, mixed methods research can lead to new philosophical and theoretical insights. Other proponents (e.g., Creswell and Plano Clark, 2007) propose that multiple paradigms can be used, but they can relate to different design and stages in the research. A third way of approaching the link between paradigms and mixed methods research advocates the creation of a new paradigm that would embrace mixed methods. As the traditional paradigms already had well-developed epistemologies, and there was often no place for mixed methods, some theorists felt it necessary to find a separate philosophical foundation to support and differentiate the concept (Tashakkori and Teddlie 2003a). There are three main 'new' paradigms that are often mentioned in this context: *pragmatism, transformative research* and *mixed methods*.

Some theorists (e.g., Tashakkori and Teddlie, 2003a; Johnson and Onwuegbuzie, 2004; Creswell and Plano Clark, 2007; Denscombe, 2008; Feilzer, 2010) see pragmatism as being a research paradigm that can comfortably accommodate mixed methods research because of its main focus is on the research question(s) rather than either the methods used or the worldview that underlies it.

Similarly to pragmatists, others (e.g., Mertens, 2003; Teddlie and Tashakkori, 2003) see the transformative perspective as appropriate for the mixed methods research. A transformative view is a problem- or issue-oriented approach striving to bring change by transforming the lives of underrepresented, marginalised groups and is collaborative by its nature with a large toolkit. A combination of quantitative and qualitative approaches can be used in these type of studies without contradicting each other.

Finally, for some researchers, mixed methods is in itself 'the third methodological movement' (Tashakkori and Teddlie 2003b) that sits alongside quantitative and qualitative traditions, and was recently claimed to be a 'third paradigm' (Johnson and Onwuegbuzie 2004; Johnson et al., 2007) in a trinity of otherwise incommensurable approaches.

Alongside discussions about a more philosophical nature of the mixed methods approach, there has been an increasing interest in, and advocacy for, mixed methods studies coupled with an evolving understanding of what mixed methods research is and the practicalities involved in carrying it out. There has also been a lot of work on the development of mixed methods research designs and innovative techniques. In 1989, Greene, Caracelli and Graham wrote a classic article that set out a series of typologies of mixed methods, which laid foundations for mixed methods research designs (which I will describe and discuss in the next section). The core ideas and practices have been further developed in the works of: Creswell (1994, 1998, 1999, 2002, 2003, 2007, 2008, 2012; Creswell and Plano Clark, 2007); Greene (Greene and McClintock, 1985; Caracelli and Greene, 1993; Greene and Caracelli, 1997); Onwuegbuzie (2002; Onwuegbuzie and Leech, 2004, 2005; Onwuegbuzie et al., 2004; Johnson and Onwuegbuzie, 2004; Onwuegbuzie and Johnson, 2004, 2006); Tashakkori and Teddlie (1998, 2003a, 2003b; Teddlie and Tashakkori, 2003); Bryman (1988, 2006, 2007); and many others.

In the next section, I will discuss in more detail a more structured framework for the use of mixed methods research by looking at different types of the mixed methods designs and analyses exemplified with real life research studies.

10.4 HOW TO DO IT: MIXED METHODS RESEARCH DESIGN TYPES, DATA COLLECTION, ANALYSIS AND WRITING UP STRATEGIES (WITH EXAMPLES)

An important point to make is that mixing methods does not necessarily lead to better research outcomes than using a single method or more than one method from the same tradition. The choice of mixed methods and a specific mixed methods design type will always be dependent on the aim(s) of the research and the research question(s). So, before you start thinking about using mixed methods research design you have to focus on the purpose of your study. When you feel confident that you have identified your research problem and have constructed your research question(s) you can start planning your methodology. At this point, you can decide whether or not you are going to use mixed methods and would have to justify why this would be an appropriate approach for you. Thinking from the research methods perspective, you will need to consider: why you plan on working with both qualitative and quantitative data and what research objective it will accomplish. In your justification for the use of mixed methods, you will need to link the methods to your research question(s), taking into account the main differences between the qualitative and quantitative data and forms of analysis you intend to employ.

You will have to provide a statement about the purpose of your study and what you hope it will achieve in addition to your research questions and a more detailed description of the methodology. According to Creswell and Plano Clark (2007: 98), it needs to include: (a) the overall content aim; (b) the type of mixed method design; (c) the forms of data collection that will be used (very general); (d) the data collection site(s); and (e) the reason for collecting both forms of data.

Greene et al. (1989) propose five broad rationales for the use of mixed methods approach (see Box 10.5):

━━ BOX 10.5 ━━━

Five rationales for using mixed methods
(adapted from Greene et al., 1989)

- *Triangulation*: this was one of the first rationales for using mixed methods research (Denzin, 1970). It is used to test the consistency of findings from using different approaches.
- *Complementarity*: this clarifies and illustrates results from one method with the use of another method.
- *Development*: the results of analysis using one method shapes subsequent methods or steps in the research process.
- *Initiation*: this stimulates new research questions or challenges results obtained through one method.
- *Expansion*: this provides richness and detail by building on the findings of either qualitative or quantitative methods.

There are also more pragmatic reasons why researchers might decide to employ a mixed methods design. Some may argue that the use of either quantitative or qualitative methods on their own are insufficient to answer their research question(s), or that quantitative and qualitative approaches provide different 'pictures' that are able to gather more evidence. Others argue that mixed methods may be the preferred approach within a specific scholarly community or that this approach more accurately mirrors 'real life', where you rarely see or use numerical or textual data and/or approaches on their own.

Typologies of mixed method designs

Up to now, I have been talking about a mixed methods approach in general but, as Greene (2008) noticed, there are many different typologies of mixed methods design. Most of the work in this area has been done by: Jennifer C. Greene (Greene et al., 1989; Greene, 2008), Abbas Tashakkori and Charles Teddlie (1998, 2006, 2010), along with John Creswell (2008). For this next section, I will rely mainly on the work of the methodologist Creswell (2008, 2012; Creswell and Plano Clark, 2007) to describe the different mixed methods research types. In their work on producing a systematic framework for approaching mixed methods research (Creswell et al., 2003), they present three central decisions (see Figure 10.1) that need to inform the design of a mixed methods study (see also the work of Greene, 2008). These three areas of consideration are the *sequence* of the quantitative and qualitative data collection; the relative *priority* or **weighting** given to the quantitative and qualitative data collection and collection; and the *integration*, or the way that the quantitative and qualitative data can be mixed together at different stages of research.

By the early 1970s, Sieber (1973) had already described how qualitative and quantitative methods could be mixed at different stages of the research to achieve different purpose, such as in the design, data collection and data analysis. In some ways, he was actually outlining different mixed methods designs without actually naming them. In his view, methods could be mixed at the research design stage where quantitative data can help to identify a specific sample for the qualitative data collection. Similarly, qualitative data at the design stage can help with the conceptual development of instruments for the subsequent quantitative field-work. At the data collection stage, quantitative data can provide the necessary sampling framework to minimise a selection bias in the qualitative sample, while qualitative data collected at the same stage of data collection can help facilitate quantitative data collection. Finally, analysis of quantitative data can assist with the assessment of reliability and gener-alisability of the qualitative data, while qualitative data can play an essential role in clarifying, validating and interpreting the quantitative findings.

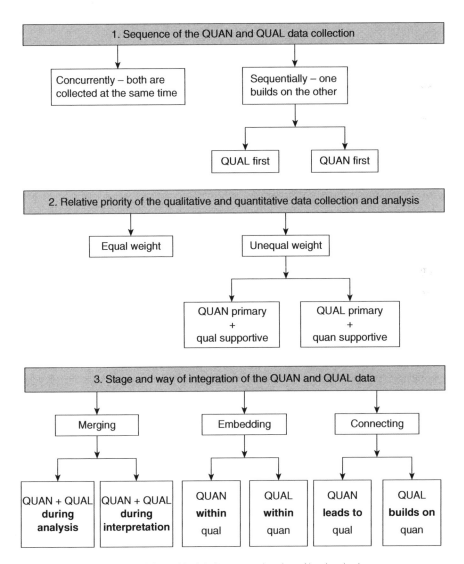

Figure 10.1 The three decisions that inform a mixed methods study

Source: Adapted from Creswell and Plano Clark (2007).

Sampling

One way of integrating two different types of data is through the sampling. Before you start your data collection and any subsequent analysis within the framework of this mixed methods design, you will need to decide on the strategies you are going to use for your qualitative and quantitative samples and site(s) for data collection. You can use four different sampling strategies as identified by Onwuegbuzie and Collins in their 'Two-Dimensional Mixed Methods Sampling Model' (2007) – see Box 10.6.

▬▬▬ BOX 10.6 ▬▬▬▬▬▬▬▬▬▬▬▬▬▬▬▬▬▬▬▬▬▬▬▬▬▬▬▬▬▬▬▬▬▬

Mixed methods design sampling types
(based on Onwuegbuzie and Collins, 2007)

- *Identical sampling*: collecting data exactly from the same respondents in both qualitative and quantitative phase of the study.
- *Parallel*: two different samples for each method that come from the same sampling frame or population of interest.
- *Nested*: qualitative sample can be a smaller subset of the quantitative.
- *Multilevel*: two samples can be completely separate representing different populations.

The choice will depend on your research questions and a sequence of the qualitative and quantitative data collection. There could be issues with different sample sizes and sampling strategies (e.g., random vs purposive) for the quantitative and qualitative data that makes comparison or convergence of findings difficult. For example, it is difficult to compare responses from 1,000 randomly selected individuals representing all London students with answers given by only 10 London students purposively selected based on their gender and ethnicity. There are three different options of how you could try to ease this problem (Creswell and Plano Clark, 2007). You could increase the qualitative sample and sacrifice a degree of depth and detail of information you are collecting. Alternatively, you could weight the qualitative data to compare it with a similar number of quantitative cases. Finally, you can simply define it as a limitation of your study and state that the comparison and convergence of the data is restricted because of discrepancy in sample size and sampling strategies.

Data analysis

Another way of the data integration within the mixed methods research is the use of different data analysis strategies. The four most frequently used data analysis techniques are *data transformation, data comparison, data consolidation* and *typology development*, although these analysis strategies often overlap and you can also use more than one in a single study.

A *data transformation technique* involves the conversion of one type of data into the other so that both can be analysed together or the results can be compared (e.g., Caracelli and Greene, 1993;

Tashakkori and Teddlie, 1998; Onwuegbuzie and Teddlie, 2003; Onwuegbuzie and Dickinson, 2008). One of the most common data transformation techniques is to convert qualitative data into quantitative, by what is called 'quantitising' (Tashakkori and Teddlie, 1998; Onwuegbuzie and Dickinson, 2008). In quantitising, qualitative themes are numerically represented in scores, scales, indices, counts or clusters in order to describe and/or interpret a target phenomenon (Sandelowski, 2001: 231). One example of this process would be to create codes and themes qualitatively and count the number of times they occur in the text data; then carry out a **factor analysis** of the quantitative data to create factors or themes and their occurrence in the quantitative dataset then compare quantitative factors with the counts of the themes from the qualitative database. Although quantitising of qualitative data helps a qualitative analysis by allowing a reliability check and allows further statistical analysis of data, information is always lost when converting qualitative/textual data to quantitative/numerical form.

Another option is to qualitise quantitative data (Tashakkori and Teddlie, 1998; Onwuegbuzie and Dickinson, 2008). This can be done through narrative profile formation from the quantitative data. For example, one can use quantitatively obtained questionnaire data in a qualitative description of a subject. For instance, one can obtain survey data on teachers' career pathways. In this case, the analysis can use factor analysis to create themes (different types of attitudes towards career) or **cluster analysis** to create groups of individuals (teachers with different sociodemographic characteristics) and then describe their characteristics and career pathways in a narrative way and compare with the qualitative data findings from the in-depth biographical interviews.

Another data analysis technique that is often used, particularly in a triangulation design, is *data comparison through matrices or a discussion* (Creswell and Plano Clark, 2007). Comparison through matrices involves combining quantitative and qualitative data in a table/matrix with row and columns representing different types of data. For example, you can have four main leadership types with percentages from the survey in rows and main leadership qualities in columns that come from interviews. In the cells you have quotations from the interviews, and by looking at cells across columns you can see how different types of leaders perceive main leadership qualities. Yet another practical example of the data comparison through matrices can be found in Kate R. Fitzpatrick's book (2008) *A Mixed Methods Portrait of Urban Instrumental Music Teaching*. The matrices can be produced manually or by using specialist software, such as **NVivo** or **MAXQDA**.

Rather than using matrices you can also compare your results in a discussion section. The most common strategy is to report statistical findings and then provide some quotations, or your can discuss a theme from the qualitative approach that confirms or contradicts a quantitative finding. There are other strategies for data comparison, such as warranted assertion analysis – carefully reviewing all the data for purposes of generating of meta inferences (Smith, 1997); pattern matching (Marquart, 1990) – pattern comparison using matrices.

Some methodologists also talk about *data consolidation or merging* (Louis, 1982) as another separate data analysis strategy. Caracelli and Greene (1993: 200) define this as a sophisticated use of both data types to create new or consolidated variables or data sets. These new variables can be expressed in a qualitative or in a quantitative form. The difference here from the data transformation is that this strategy is not only the addition of transformed and original data into one new dataset, but variables are created through the merging of the information contained in the quantitative and qualitative data.

Finally, *typology development* (ibid.) is a similar to data transformation strategy that can be used in concurrent and sequential design. In this case, the analysis of one data set is used to create typologies and those then are used as a framework for the analysis of the other type of data. For the quantitative data, you can use factor and cluster analysis to create factors (groups of variables) or clusters (groups of cases) and then use those as a base structure for the analysis of the qualitative data. Alternatively, you can yield typologies from the qualitative data and use those as a framework for the descriptive or inferential quantitative analysis.

In mixed methods research, during the analysis stage, analytical software such as NVivo may be of a great help since it not only will count specific themes and codes in your textual data, but will also allow you to merge quantitative and qualitative data through the use Excel add-on data files.

Main types of design

As it was mentioned above (see Figure 10.1), there are three main considerations in the process of choosing an appropriate mixed methods design. The first is the data collection and analysis sequence. Based on these criteria, Creswell et al. (2003) have classified mixed methods designs into two major categories: *concurrent and sequential. Concurrent designs* are characterised by the collection of both types of data during the same stage; in contrast, in *sequential designs*, either the qualitative or quantitative data are collected at an initial stage, followed by the collection of the other data type during a second stage. Within each of these two categories, there are specific designs based on the other two criteria: the weight given to the qualitative and quantitative data (equal or unequal) and also the process used to analyse and integrate the data (ibid.).

In accordance with the recent typology (Creswell and Plano Clark, 2007), there are two main types of *concurrent* mixed methods designs: concurrent triangulation and concurrent embedded, and two types of *sequential* mixed methods designs: sequential exploratory and sequential explanatory. There are also different subtypes for these designs. Figure 10.2 illustrates the most popular mixed methods design types.

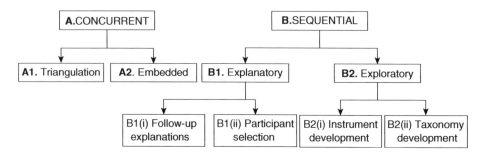

Figure 10.2 Main types of mixed methods designs

I will go through each main design separately, explaining what is the most appropriate context for its use as well as discussing advantages and challenges associated with each. I will also provide some examples from my work at ULC/IOE in the last 10 years.

A. Concurrent designs

A1. Concurrent triangulation

A concurrent triangulation design is probably the most well-known and used a mixed methods approach, even if people do not use this term to describe their research. In this design, usually qualitative and quantitative data are collected at the same time and are merged at the analysis or conclusion stage to better understand a specific research problem (Creswell and Plano Clark, 2007). Usually, both types of data are given equal weight. Typically, this type of design is used when one form of data is insufficient by itself and there is a need to bring together the strengths of both quantitative and qualitative approaches to answer the same broad research question. This design is often framed within the pragmatism or transformative research paradigms, but a dialectical approach (Greene and Caracelli, 1997) can also be used successfully.

This is a basic design (see Figure 10.3) that often serves as a framework and a base for mixed methods research. It is quite efficient since in this one phase design the data can be collected and analysed separately, but within the same timeframe. One can use this research when there are one or more broader research questions that both types of data can help to answer. On the flip side, a lot of effort, resources and expertise is required to carry out this mixed methods design effectively and get the best results out of it. There are also some challenges that are related to this type of design. A lot of thought needs to be put into the data analysis techniques, such as whether to use data transformation, data comparison or data consolidation, and it still can be problematic to come up with the explanations when qualitative and quantitative findings disagree.

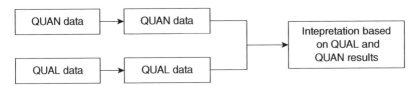

Figure 10.3 Concurrent triangulation design

Source: Adapted from Creswell and Plano Clark (2007).

As regards to the presentation of the findings of a concurrent triangulation study, the quantitative and qualitative data collection may be presented in the report in separate sections, although usually the analysis and interpretation combines the two forms of data to seek convergence among the results. The structure of this type of mixed methods study does not clearly make a distinction between the quantitative and qualitative phases.

An example of this design comes from a study that I worked on with Jon Swain between 2009 and 2012 (see Box 10.7).

━━ BOX 10.7 ━━━

An example of a triangulation model

The Armed Forces Basic Skills Longitudinal Study

Research questions:

1 What is the nature and what are the characteristics of Basic Skills (BS) provision and support in each Service?
2 What are the connections between BS interventions, military training and operational effectiveness? What are the links between learning and using literacy and numeracy skills in each Service?
3 How do Service personnel experience BS provision? How do personnel perceive and value BS learning in relation to their professional identity, job performance and career progression?

The study was a three-year longitudinal investigation into literacy and numeracy provision in the Army, Royal Navy and Royal Air Force. We used a mixed methods triangulation model to investigate the relationship between the acquisition of literacy and numeracy through basic skills provision and individuals' operational effectiveness in each Service. There were two strands of complementary concurrent research: a qualitative exploration undertaken for each of the three Services, and an additional quantitative study undertaken amongst Army recruits. Each strand was conducted in three stages: (1) at the start of recruits' Phase 1 (basic) training; (2) during and soon after their Phase 2 (specialist trade) training; and (3) during their first appointments in the field.

The quantitative study in the Army assessed the literacy and numeracy skills levels and reviewed the literacy and numeracy needs and learning of around 1600 Army recruits during their first two-and-a-half years of training and service. The analysis of this representative sample of recruits with low literacy and/or numeracy skills was used to support and complement the qualitative evidence, which, in turn, was used to inform the quantitative evidence.

The in-depth qualitative study focused on a sample of individual case studies (between 22 and 29 recruits from each Service) and we used nested sampling strategy for the Army. The evidence from these groups was supplemented by testimony from the recruits' line managers, trainers and senior officers from their chain of command, as well as from education staff and literacy and numeracy practitioners.

We used various analytical strategies in this study, such as data comparison through matrices and data transformation for the comparison. For example, we transformed qualitative data into numerical data by, first, thematically coding it, and then specific codes within certain themes (such as the concept of 'operational effectiveness') were counted and analysed using descriptive statistics and compared with the results from the survey analysis.

The full report can be downloaded at WEBLINK 1

WEBLINK 1

Armed forces basic skills longitudinal study

A2. Concurrent embedded

When you need one type of data to support the other type of data, you can use an embedded mixed methods research design (Creswell and Plano Clark, 2007). The data priority is unequal in this design; the second type of data collected plays a secondary role within a design that is primarily build based on the first type of data (see Figure 10.4). Although the study can be framed within the primary approach methodology and paradigm, there is still just a single data collection phase where both data types are collected simultaneously, which means that this design is similar to the triangulation approach and is also concurrent. The data is collected separately and then is often mixed later during data analysis. Since, in most cases, there will be primary and secondary questions addressing different data types, the analysis of each data set can also be kept separate and it is possible to integrate the results when writing up the conclusions. The integration of the data as the name of the design states is through embedding.

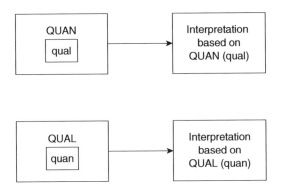

Figure 10.4   Embedded design

Source: Adapted from Creswell and Plano Clark (2007).

To distinguish between this and a triangulation design, you have to judge whether the supportive data are useful and meaningful outside the current study and if not embedded within a primary data type (Creswell and Plano Clark, 2007: 69). Within the triangulation design, the supportive data could be used as a small study on their own.

This design is often used when the supportive data type is able to address a different but specific research question and can expand on findings from the other type of data or add additional knowledge. This design can also be used when you have less time and fewer resources to use the two types of data in an equal way. It is frequently used when researchers need to embed a qualitative element into a quantitative experimental or survey **cross-sectional analysis** (correlational) design. There are fewer examples of a primarily qualitative study with an embedded quantitative element. It could, for example, be an ethnographic study with a small element of survey data analysis around the same problematic.

With regards to the sampling strategies with this design, you are more likely to use concurrent nested sampling (Onwuegbuzie and Collins, 2007) when the qualitative data is collected from a subset of the quantitative sample. However, parallel and multilevel sampling can also be used (see section on concurrent triangulation design on pp. 205–6 for more information).

There are also a couple of challenges associated with this design. Certain decisions need to be made with regards to the timing of the qualitative and quantitative data collection and sampling procedures. First, you have to decide exactly when the qualitative data collection will take place: is it before, during or after the quantitative experiment or a larger survey? This decision has to be based on the purpose of the chosen design. Nevertheless, since in this design participants of one data collection are often also considered as a sample for the other type of data collection, it is important to think about a potential bias that might be introduced into the study. For example, in some experiments you might introduce a bias if you interview your participants between pre- and post-tests and it is possible that your questions could influence an outcome.

If your design includes qualitative interviews or observations that are scheduled to take place after the main quantitative data (e.g., from an experiment or survey) has been collected, then decisions will need to be made about how to sample the qualitative study participants and what criteria to use. Here, you can use different sampling strategies in order to select you qualitative sample using a preconceived criteria and choosing average/typical cases or extreme/**outlier cases** or you can use intensity sampling (choosing atypical, but not extreme cases). This will depend on your research aim and questions. For example, you can sample from only those who received a treatment and got a negative or a positive treatment outcome. Similarly, you can choose individuals for the follow-up that fit a specific profile based on their responses in the survey.

Similarly to triangulation design (see previous section), data can be analysed by data transformation, consolidation or merging, comparison and in some cases through typology development.

The report for the concurrent embedded design is typically organised into separate sections for the procedures of quantitative and qualitative data collection, followed by analysis section where the types of data are combined. Alternatively, depending on the analysis type, you can have separate sections for the analysis of the quantitative and qualitative data followed by conclusions or interpretation phase of the study where you discuss how the qualitative findings helped to elaborate on, explain or deepen, the main quantitative results. An example of an embedded mixed methods design can be seen in a study of family literacy (FL) programmes (Swain et al., 2015).

■■■ BOX 10.8 ■■

An example of a concurrent embedded model

The impact of family literacy programmes on children's literacy skills and the home literacy environment

Research questions:

1 What impact does participation in family literacy programmes have on children's progress in reading and writing?
2 To what extent does parental participation in family literacy programmes change family literacy practices, attitudes and beliefs outside the classroom?
3 How do parents translate and implement what they learn from family literacy programmes into the home setting?

Family literacy provision is where parents attend classes (usually) in schools and work alongside their children, learning how they are taught to read and write. We used this design to embed a qualitative element into a quantitative quasi-experimental design. The quantitative element answered a main question about the impact FL programmes have on young children's emergent literacy skills (in terms of attainment), and on literacy practices and attitudes to literacy in the home setting. The qualitative data played a supportive role provide an in-depth understanding of how parents translate messages from FL programmes outside the formal classroom including the home setting.

The data collection was concurrent with a combined nested multilevel sample. Defined by our sampling strategies for our qualitative work, we selected a subset of families who participated in the main quantitative data collection. Then we used different family members for two types of data collection. We used questionnaires and cognitive tests to collect quantitative data from the children and a survey of their parents, prior and post the FL course. In addition we used observations of a subset of the FL programmes and pre and post interviews with the parents in the qualitative fieldwork.

This approach brought together the strengths of both quantitative and qualitative methods. However, we slightly expanded the embedded design and in our study, and the qualitative data was used not only to explain and substantiate the quantitative findings, but also to explore separate aspects, such as how parents use what they are taught in the FL programmes at home, which it is unsuitable to investigate with statistical methods only.

In the report, we had separate sections to describe sampling and data collection procedures for the quantitative and qualitative data, and then thematically organised sections that combined both types results form the data analysis.

The full report can be downloaded at WEBLINK 2.

WEBLINK 2

A report on family literacy provision

Further examples of research studies using concurrent triangulation and embedded designs can be found in WEBLINK 3.

WEBLINK 3

Studies using concurrent triangulation & embedded designs

B Sequential designs

The second major category of mixed methods designs is the sequential design and, once again, this is divided into two: B1 *sequential explanatory*; and B2 *sequential exploratory*. Each of the designs has two subtypes that I will explain in the subsequent sections.

B1 Sequential explanatory

The sequential explanatory design (see Figure 10.5), consists of two distinct phases of data collection and analysis (Ivankova et al., 2006). First, you collect and analyse one type of data, and then a second phase builds on the first one. This means that the two types of data are integrated through connecting in the intermediate stage. There are two subtypes of the sequential explanatory design: B1(i) *a follow-up model*; and B1(ii) *a participant selection model*.

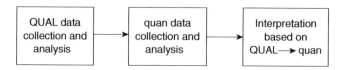

Figure 10.5 Sequential explanatory design

Source: Adapted from Creswell and Plano Clark (2007).

B1(i) In the *follow-up model*, quantitative data is collected and analysed first, which is then followed by the collection and analysis of the qualitative data (see Figure 10.6). In this design, quantitative results by themselves are found to be inadequate to answer research questions and so qualitative data are needed to explain or illuminate quantitative findings (Tashakkori and Tedlie, 1998; Creswell et al., 2003; Creswell and Plano Clark, 2007). The data priority in this design is unequal with the quantitative approach playing the primary role and the qualitative data being secondary in a supportive position. The main mixing happens between the two phases through the identification of questions or themes for the follow-up. For example, one can carry out a survey and after the analysis of the data identify some questions to follow up in the qualitative study by exploring participants' views in depth. An example of this model is an American study (Ivankova et al., 2006) of students' persistence in an online learning programme. In the first, quantitative phase of this study, a survey of students was carried out and after the analysis of the data four specific themes were chosen that were then followed up in a second qualitative phase using in-depth interviews with a sub sample of the same group of students (see Figure 10.6).

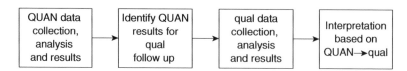

Figure 10.6 Sequential explanatory design: follow-up model

Source: Adapted from Creswell and Plano Clark (2007).

B1(ii): In the *participant selection model* (Creswell and Plano Clark, 2007), quantitative data is again collected and analysed first, followed by qualitative data collection, but in this design the quantitative stage plays a supportive role (see Figure 10.7). This, again, is unequal data weight design; the main qualitative phase builds on the quantitative data and their analysis. The main purpose of the quantitative stage is to provide information for the selection of the participants for the in-depth qualitative study. The main link or 'mixing' here is the selection of participants for the qualitative study based on the information from the quantitative findings. This model can be exemplified by an American study of a state-wide education policy initiative (Sharp et al., 2012), where a four-stage sequential explanatory design was used to select eight sites in order to capture not only a broader context of the study, but also any contextual nuances that shape policy implementation.

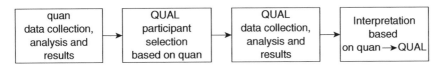

Figure 10.7 Explanatory design: participant selection model

Source: Adapted from Creswell and Plano Clark (2007).

Sampling is quite important here and takes a central role for the participant selection model of the sequential explanatory design. The sampling for the qualitative phase is usually based on preconceived criteria. One can choose average/typical cases, extreme/outlier cases or intense/saturated, but not extreme cases.

Even if the framework for the sampling is purposeful, it is still possible to combine it with a random sampling to make it more robust and reliable, and open more opportunities for generalisation. You can randomly choose from a probability sample a smaller number of cases for in-depth study or you can also use stratified purposeful sampling to select particular cases based on preselected parameters. The procedure involves choosing a couple of criteria and putting them into a crosstab and sampling from cells, choosing one or two cases from each that exemplify the kinds and degree of variation relevant to understanding a target phenomenon. This will not give you a statistically representative sample, but it will be informationally representative that is important in this mixed methods design.

Finally, you need to think about the sampling strategies within the sequential explanatory design, and decide what the relationship is between the quantitative and qualitative phases. Within the participant selection model, the usual strategy is nested sequential sampling (Onwuegbuzie and Collins, 2007), whereas within the follow-up model, both nested and parallel sampling strategy can be used.

On the positive side, the two-phase structure of this design is clear, easy to implement and write up in a final report although it can still be very time consuming. The additional challenge is the fact that the final number of the qualitative phase participants cannot be specified at the start and so the methodology has to be flexible enough to adapt and change after the first stage.

The report for this type of sequential analysis is typically divided into quantitative data collection and analysis followed by qualitative data collection and analysis. In this structure, the writer usually will present the project as two distinct phases, with separate headings of each. The section with the supportive data description and its analysis is usually shorter and is followed by the much longer and more in-depth primary data analysis. Then, in the conclusions, or interpretative phase of the study, the researcher comments on how the qualitative findings helped to elaborate on or extend the quantitative results. Alternatively, you can also discuss how the sampling procedure was based on the supportive quantitative data.

B2 Sequential exploratory

Another mixed methods design is sequential exploratory (see Figure 10.8). Similarly to the explanatory mixed methods approach, this is a two-phase design where the findings from the first type of method help to inform the use and analysis of the second type of data (e.g., Greene et al., 1989; Creswell and Plano Clark, 2007). The integration of the data as with the previous design happens through the connecting of the two types of data. There are two subtypes of the sequential explanatory design: B2(i) an *instrument development model*; and B2(ii) a *taxonomy development model*.

Usually, the qualitative data collection and analysis phase is followed by the quantitative data collection and analysis. The main purpose of this design, as stated in its name, is to prepare for the quantitative data collection and analysis by exploring the qualitative data. This is necessary when measures or instruments are not readily available and/or there is no guiding theory to conceptualise variables. This design allows for both creating new theories and testing aspects of these emerging theories or classifications (Morgan, 1998).

Figure 10.8 Sequential exploratory design

Source: Adapted from Creswell and Plano Clark (2007).

In this design, researchers generally first gather qualitative data and analyse it to come up with some themes, categories or specific statements. In the next phase, these statements are used as specific items and the themes to create a survey instrument that is grounded in the views of the participants. A third, and final, phase is either to validate the instrument with a large sample representative of a population or to investigate the prevalence of these views or categories in a specific group. The design is most suitable for two main subtypes of research that I explain below.

B2(i): An *instrument development model* allows using qualitative data to identify variables and constructs as well as to develop items and scales to go into a quantitative instrument to be used and validated in a quantitative stage (see Figure 10.9). Here, unequal weight is given to two different types of data; the quantitative approach is usually central and the qualitative plays a supportive role. A study by Crede and Borrego (2013) used this design to examine American graduate student retention. The researchers started from nine months of ethnographic observations and interviews that were analysed to come up with several themes, which in the next phase of the study were configured into constructs and survey questions to be piloted and used in a quantitative survey.

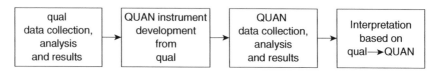

Figure 10.9 Sequential exploratory design: instrument development model

Source: Adapted from Creswell and Plano Clark (2007).

B2(ii): A *taxonomy development model* allows you to generalise the findings from the qualitative phase in the form of items, scales and taxonomies to different groups by the use of a quantitative approach, drawing on its advantages (Morse, 1991), such as its larger numbers and probability sampling that are associated with greater generalisability (Figure 10.10). The design not only helps test aspects of emerging theory or classification (Morgan, 1998), but also to explore a particular phenomenon in a more depth and then measuring its prevalence. This subtype again gives unequal weight to qualitative and quantitative approaches. It starts from the qualitative data collection and analysis, which in this design usually plays a primary role, and is followed by the quantitative stage that plays a secondary role. Using this design, Goldenberg et al. (2005) in the first phase of their study using qualitative methods identified family literacy practices. In the second phase of the same study, they then tested these identified practices by using quantitative path analysis.

Figure 10.10 Sequential exploratory design: taxonomy development model

Source: Adapted from Creswell and Plano Clark (2007).

One of the advantages of this sequential exploratory mixed methods approach is that it is uncomplicated two-phase design. This makes it relatively straightforward to implement and analyse. The quantitative data and their analysis in this design bring greater possibilities for validation and generalisation to a quite extensive qualitative data. On the flip side, it is quite time consuming. It is also quite challenging to provide a very detailed description of the quantitative data collection strategy with specific numbers for the sample and sampling framework. A lot of time is needed on the identifying qualitative findings to be used in the quantitative phase. In additions, decisions need to be made whether to use nested (where qualitative data is a subsample from the quantitative) or parallel (where there are different samples for the qualitative and quantitative, but they come from the same sampling framework) sampling strategies to connect the two datasets.

The report for this design will be typically organised into a section about procedures for quantitative and qualitative data collection followed by two separate sections for qualitative and quantitative data analysis. Then, in the conclusions or interpretation phase of the study, the researcher comments on how the quantitative findings helped to generalise the quantitative results or how qualitative findings helped to develop a quantitative instrument. Alternatively, the qualitative data collection and analysis can come first followed by the quantitative data collection and analysis. In either structure, the two approaches will be presented as two quite distinct phases.

An example of a sequential explanatory and exploratory mixed method design can be seen in the Skills for Life (SfL) Teachers study (Cara et al., 2010) (Box 10.9).

═══ BOX 10.9 ═══

An example of a sequential explanatory and exploratory design

The Teacher Study: the impact of the skills for life strategy on teachers

Research questions:

1 What is the general profile of teachers delivering to learners within the SfL agenda?
2 To what extent are teachers exposed to the new SfL learning infrastructure?
3 What are the attitudes of teachers to the SfL national strategy?
4 How do teachers perceive their profession and their professional identity/role definition?
5 How does the organisational environment in which teachers work affect their attitudes, perceptions and behaviour?

In this study, the quantitative strand was given priority vis-à-vis the study's overall objectives. The primary purpose of this study was to use quantitative longitudinal panel survey data at three time points or phases to provide SfL teachers' profile and build statistical models to explain their professional behaviour and attitudes. Qualitative data was collected on just over 1,000 teachers to better understand the mechanisms influencing teachers' behaviour and attitudes, and to describe how teachers make their professional choices (explanatory). In addition, qualitative data was used to re-evaluate the quantitative survey (exploratory).

We used both follow-up and participant selection models of the explanatory design in this study. The explanatory aspect of the study involved the quantitative results being used to help inform the development of the qualitative strand of the study: identifying questions for the follow-up for creating the interview schedule and also to create a sample for the qualitative fieldwork. It was important to complement quantitative findings by the data from the in-depth interviews to increase the interpretability and meaningfulness of a quantitative study.

Because of the longitudinal nature and multiple phases of the study, in the second phase, the qualitative findings were applied to help to re-evaluate and redesign the quantitative questionnaire for the third phase. Because of the lack of established items for the survey in the field of the SfL teachers, we needed help from practitioners to validate the items for the survey and to provide us with the recent developments in the field that we might have missed.

The design used a nested sampling strategy when we selected a subset of about 60 teachers from the survey to participate in the qualitative interviews. For the analysis, we used data consolidation and typology development. For example, through the use of NVivo, we could link all quantitative information to the interview texts for the teachers who participated in the qualitative strand. Using this new consolidated data set, we created typologies for the career of the SfL teachers and investigated sociodemographic characteristics of different career types and career trajectories.

The full report can be downloaded from WEBLINK 4.

WEBLINK 4

The Teacher Study

WEBLINK 5

Studies using sequential exploratory & explanatory mixed methods designs

Other examples of research studies using sequential exploratory and explanatory mixed methods designs can be found in WEBLINK 5.

BOX 10.10

A summary of the key points

- Mixed methods research is a specific research design that includes rigorous, systematic and the planned use of different quantitative and qualitative methods for collecting and/or analysing data in the same study in order to understand a research problem.
- Although mixed methods design has developed rapidly in recent decades, and there has been a lot of work on the evolving understanding of what mixed methods research is, and how it can be carried out, the actual first use of mixed methods in social research was first seen early in the twentieth century.
- Mixing methods does not necessarily lead to better research outcomes than using a single method or more than one method from the same tradition. The choice of mixed methods and a specific mixed methods design type will always be dependent on the aim(s) of the research and the research question(s).
- You can use mixed methods research for various purposes, such as triangulation, complementarity, development, initiation and expansion.
- There are two main types of concurrent mixed methods designs: *concurrent triangulation* and *concurrent embedded*; and two types of sequential mixed methods designs: *sequential exploratory* and *sequential explanatory*. There are also different subtypes for these designs.
- There are various sampling strategies that are associated with different mixed methods designs. These are: identical, nested, parallel and multilevel.
- The main analysis techniques that can be used to integrate qualitative and quantitative data are data transformation, data comparison through matrices or a discussion, data consolidation or merging and typology development.

AREAS FOR DISCUSSION

1 How would you justify using mixed methods research in the context of competing worldviews or paradigms?

2 Proponents of mixed methods argue that it increases validity of research findings. It this always the case?

3 What are some of the main advantages of using mixed methods?

4 What are some of the theoretical and practical challenges associated with the carrying out a mixed methods study and how would you deal with these?

5 Think about research contexts that are appropriate for a mixed methods design and say why these are particularly appropriate for this approach?

ANNOTATED BIBLIOGRAPHY

Caracelli, V.J. and Greene, J.C. (1993) 'Data analysis strategies for mixed-method evaluation designs', *Educational Evaluation and Policy Analysis*, 15 (2): 195–207.

The article provides a good overview, with some practical examples of the four main data analysis strategies used in mixed methods research.

Creswell, J.W. and Plano Clark, V.L. (2010) *Designing and Conducting Mixed Methods Research*, **2nd edn. Thousand Oaks, CA: Sage.**
The book is one of the few that not only discusses the more abstract side of the mixed methods research, such as epistemology and other more philosophical aspects, but also provides practical advice on how actually to design and carry out mixed methods studies.

Johnson, R.B., Onwuegbuzie, A.J. and Turner, L.A. (2007) 'Toward a definition of mixed methods research', *Journal of Mixed Methods Research*, **1 (2): 112–33.**
The authors examine definitions of mixed methods research as well as providing a brief history of the field and a discussion of areas for further advancement.

Onwuegbuzie, A.J. and Collins, K.M.T. (2007) 'A typology of mixed methods sampling designs in social science research', *Qualitative Report*, **12 (2): 281–316.**
A very good description and explanation of different sampling strategies used in mixed methods studies.

FURTHER READING

Bazeley, P. (2009) 'Integrating data analyses in mixed methods research', *Journal of Mixed Methods Research*, **3 (3): 203–7.**
The author challenges the idea that mixed methods research ensures greater validity of research results by providing an overview of sampling, analysis and reporting issues involved.

Greene, J.C. (2008) 'Is mixed methods social inquiry a distinctive methodology?', *Journal of Mixed Methods Research*, **2 (1): 7–22.**
The author discusses whether mixed methods can be seen as a distinctive methodology by providing a critical summary of philosophical foundations, methodological issues, practicalities and sociopolitical commitments of mixed methods research.

Morgan, D.L. (2007) 'Paradigms lost and pragmatism regained: Methodological implications of combining qualitative and quantitative methods', *Journal of Mixed Methods Research*, **1 (1): 48–76.**
The article is an overview of methodological issues in mixed methods research using Kuhn's concept of 'paradigm shift' to explain changes from metaphysical to methodological concerns in social research.

CHAPTER 11

SUMMARY AND CONCLUSIONS

Jon Swain

11.1 INTRODUCTION: THE BOOK'S MAIN OBJECTIVES

In this final chapter, I want to pursue further some of the themes and issues that have been presented and discussed in the preceding ten chapters, including some additional thoughts about the thesis.

To repeat the statement that I wrote at the very beginning of the introductory chapter: the overarching theme of this book has been about conceptualising and designing an empirical research project at doctoral level within a coherent conceptual framework. In addition to examining four different research designs (as well designs using mixed methods), the main objectives have been to discuss the processes involved in constructing a research design, including some of the main challenges such as developing researchable questions; to raise awareness about the nature of knowledge and being in research (and introduce some of the key language and ideas that underpin these debates); to increase students' understanding of terms such as 'deductive' and 'inductive', 'methodology', 'conceptual framework' and the 'principles of selection'; to discuss the role and use of theory in doctoral research; to highlight the main ethical considerations involved; to set the designs in their social, political and historical contexts; and give students an opportunity to reflect on and discuss with their supervisors, fellow academics and their peers, a range of issues in the context of their own work.

11.2 MAIN THEMES AND ISSUES RAISED

One of the constant refrains that runs throughout the book is that carrying out doctoral research is seldom easy and presents many challenges. We have also seen how constructing a well thought out research design is ongoing process and is a vital and necessary constituent of an effective study and, ultimately, successful thesis. A sound research design is part of a well-articulated and coherent conceptual framework, which should provide your work with a systematic way of articulating what you are doing, or what you have done, and the reasons behind the decisions you are making or have made.

Gaining a doctorate is generally going to take over your life for a few years, and so it is crucial that you are enthusiastic about, and committed to, your research project, otherwise you are going to find it very difficult to finish. Chapter 1 includes a discussion of some of the decisions affecting a research design, including practical and emotional considerations, which are sometimes neglected in some of the other literature about gaining a doctoral thesis. In Chapter 1, I also discuss these and other issues that arose during my own PhD research.

As I wrote above, doing research is rarely straightforward; it is often frustrating, messy and generally needs a lot of thinking about. It is better to take time at the beginning of the process to think about your ideas for the design, identify and read as much of the surrounding literature as possible, and to make a judgement as to whether the study is achievable (both in the time frame and the resources you have at your disposable), and with the design you have constructed, or are constructing, to answer your original problem/questions. It is exasperating to have conducted your fieldwork and then realise you have missed out some vital questions, or to recognise that it would have been better to use another method to gain your data, say, for example, in-depth interviews rather than structured questionnaires.

Although you are ultimately responsible for your research, none of these decisions needs to be made alone. Research is a dialogue, not only with other theories/theorists and other similar research studies found in your readings, but also in face-to-face discussions with other academics/researchers and your peers, and of course with the most important person of all, your supervisor. Key figures in the research process, including the relationship with, and the role of, a student's supervisor(s) are discussed in Chapter 2. Some supervisors like their students to work in the same way as themselves: if they used interviews in their doctorate, they may want their students to use the same method and this may not always be appropriate to their own design. Students need to be able to think for themselves and, although they will generally be highly influenced by their supervisors, they should not let themselves be coerced into doing everything the supervisor suggests.

Chapter 2 introduces readers to eight doctoral students whom I have worked with closely and are used as a medium to consider issues about designing and managing a doctoral research project in the early years of study, including some of the challenges that these students have actually faced. One of the hardest parts of a doctoral study is making sure that your research questions are well thought out and can be answered using the design you have constructed. First ideas and research questions often start big and need to be narrowed down to a manageable and doable study.

Students begin their doctoral studies with a range of backgrounds, interests and experiences of working in different research traditions, but the great majority begin as novices and the journey they take over the next few years (usually between three and seven) is a kind of apprenticeship into learning about the principles and rules, and carrying out the practices of research. They need to be able to come up with a researchable problem and construct a series of questions to answer it; they need to identify theoretical and empirical fields in which their research is to be positioned or situated (see below) and this involves learning how to critically interrogate the surrounding literature and theories, and (often) negotiating access to a empirical setting; they need to learn about different methods and methodologies and ways the data they collect or generate can be analysed, written up and presented.

I argue in Chapter 2 that studying for a doctorate can transform students' identity: they become different people and see the world in a different way. They will also need a highly developed set of interpersonal skills as well as the attributes such as patience, resilience and humour when things don't go to plan. They also need independence (alluded to above), imagination and creativity of thought, and I see this as being a major difference between carrying out research at doctoral and master's level. Students also need to have, or develop, a 'personal objectivity', which is like an instinctive antennae that begins to ring warning bells when, for example, their research problem is becoming too wide and unmanageable by using too many theories or too many empirical contexts, and the area needs to be narrowed down and have a sharper focus.

Chapter 3 looks at two major designs and contrasting approaches to research: deductive and inductive. It also draws on the work of Dowling and Brown (2010) and introduces us to two arenas within which the research process occurs as it begins to specialise and localise: these are the *empirical field* and the *theoretical field*. This chapter also interrogates terms such as 'conceptual framework', 'methodology' and 'theory' and discusses the concept of the 'principles of selection'.

Some of the themes in the book, particularly in Chapter 4, about theories of knowledge and being (or existence) are complex, and however accessible Will Gibson has made them, they may need rereading and discussing before they start to make complete sense. Don't worry if you are like me and understanding develops and gradually falls into place over time as other pieces of the jigsaw begin to fit together. These debates about epistemology and ontology are very much live issues in the social 'sciences', and although there is no universally agreed upon solution to the problems these issues raise, Will maintains that it is useful for students (and researchers) to have a sense of the general arguments as they will frequently come across these terms in the literature. However, Will also maintains that the problems raised by the debates should not get in the way of your ultimate aim in carrying out empirical research, which is to produce knowledge.

Interest in ethical issues is a growing and important area of research and is discussed in Chapter 5. These issues are also often complex and rarely straightforward, and it is important for students (and researchers in general) to have debates about them as part of their research community. Writing an ethical review is a research activity in itself; it is also an ongoing, continuous process as many ethical issues are dynamic and rooted within a particular localised context, and this means researchers often need to be both reflective and reflexive. There has recently been a move away from the authority of the researcher, and a number of key principles have evolved that are enshrined within a number of guidelines and frameworks, which researchers are expected to be familiar with and adhere to: these include explanations about what the research is about; informed consent; voluntary participation; rights to privacy; avoidance of harm; and data protection (including stewardship and security).

Each of the four main research designs, or approaches, in this book have different sets of ethical principles and priorities, but, in general, qualitative researchers using inductive approaches generally face more challenging issues that those using more quantitative and deductive approaches, as many decisions have to be made in situ within a particular localised context.

Each of the chapters on specific research designs (Chapters 6–10) contain examples of research carried out by each author, which show the possibilities of using each design, and set the research in the real world. The five researchers are working from different positions and their own epistemological and ontological perspectives mean that they see the world through different lenses. They also have different interests, focuses and practices, and points of disagreement. However, there is a greater commonality between the epistemological assumptions of experiments and surveys and between ethnography and case studies. The first two (particularly experiments) use quantitative methods and deductive designs (top-down), while the latter two tend to employ more qualitative methods and inductive designs (bottom-up).

In Chapter 6, Jane Hurry also maintains that researches using experimental designs researchers need a lot of prior knowledge about the field/area they are investigating as hypotheses should draw on theory and evidence, where possible from correlational and longitudinal studies; while, in Chapter 7, Charlie Owen contends that survey researchers need to devote a lot of time and effort examining their methods and refining their research questions in order to try and achieve a high internal, external and face validity. In contrast, in Chapter 8, Rebecca O'Connell argues that ethnographic research is an iterative process, where initial theories, ideas and research questions are modified in the light of new information generated during the fieldwork, and this process is also reiterated in Chapter 9 by Mano Candappa on case studies.

The type of design and approach will also have an effect on how generalisable the findings are beyond the specific setting in which the research was carried out. In order for research

Table 11.1 Similarities and differences between the four research designs

Design	Quant or Qual approaches	Deductive	Inductive	Findings are often generalisable	Use of interviews	Use of questionnaires	Use of observations
Experiment	Quan	Yes	No	Yes	Rare	Yes	Yes (structured)
Survey	(Mainly) Quan	Yes	No	Yes	Rare	Yes	Rare
Ethnography	Qual	No	Yes	No	Yes	Rare	Yes (participant observation)
Case study	(Mainly) Qual	No	Yes	No	Yes	Yes	Yes

to be generalisable the sample needs to be representative of the wider population and so this will generally be more applicable to experiments and surveys. Ethnographies, and most case studies, do not usually attempt to generalise their findings analytically.

Some of the similarities and differences (in terms of approach and methodology) between the four designs can be seen in Table 11.1, although this should be taken as a rough, simplistic guide.

Different designs each have their own advantages, disadvantages, strengths and weaknesses, but, as Olga Cara writes in Chapter 10, when arguing for the case of using mixed methods, mixing methods will not necessarily lead to better research outcomes than using a single method or more than one method from the same tradition. The choice of mixed methods and of any design will always be dependent on the aim(s) of the research, the research question(s) and the methodology employed. Each research design is trying to do different things.

11.3 THE THESIS

The outcome of your doctoral research is the thesis, which you will be required to defend at a viva voce.[1] You will need to produce a consistent and articulate argument, be able to explain and defend your design and conceptual framework, and illustrate how you have made an original contribution to the field in which your research is located. As I wrote in Chapter 3, it is a good idea to think of the thesis as a pedagogic text, where you are leading the examiner by the hand through the research process, showing them the selections and organisation principles you have enacted, and justifying the decisions you have made. Make sure that the research process is made as visible and transparent as possible so that a judgement can be made of how you reached your conclusions.

Remember that a thesis is above all an artefact or a construction, which is prepared and created by you. Examiners and other readers in general do not need to always know about the things that may have gone wrong: for instance, if you find that a research question cannot be answered (possibly because you did not have the right sample of people and/or you have insufficient data), you do not have to write about this – the research question can disappear when the final version is completed.

In respect of presenting a well-articulated argument, it is important to realise that one can ever achieve full coherence as this is a valued judgement and different individuals will inevitably disagree. Any activity, such as researching, will mean that there is going to be a range of practices and a range of positions, that offer themselves to a series of different interpretations. This is not to say that the evaluations of the examiners about the merits of a thesis will often be marked by differences; they may sometimes be but in my experience most examiners will agree on most of the points and conclusions presented. The examiners will generally have knowledge and expertise in the field in which your work is situated, and in many countries students and supervisors can choose the individuals they wish to examine

---

1 I am aware that these events vary considerably between countries, and that some are more public than others.

their thesis. It is therefore generally a good idea to try and make sure that examiners are not only cited in your research, but that their work is mentioned in a positive light. I would caution against derogating the work of a person who I had chosen to examine my own.

Based, once again, on my experience, two of the 'classic' mistakes that some students make in their thesis concern the research questions and use of theory. First, make sure that you return to the research questions at the end of the thesis to show how they have been addressed; second, I have read a number of theses where in the early part of the report the student sets out the theory or theories they are drawing on only for them to disappear when they present their finding. One of purposes of having theories is that they inform the findings and therefore they need to be integrated into the data as it is presented. In this way, your analysis should move on from the level of description to one of critical engagement and analysis.

As I wrote in Chapter 3, remember that, although writing an 80,000-word PhD thesis or a 40–45,000-word EdD thesis can seem daunting, once you have written the introduction, a literature review (if you have one), chapters on the methodology and process of analysis and a conclusion (and including in the case of an EdD thesis, a section on professional implications of the research), you are left with fewer words than you may think to present and interrogate your findings. However, make sure that the findings section is the bulk of the work, about 35 to 40 per cent of the final word count.

I often think it is harder for EdD than PhD students to write a thesis as they have to try and fit in all the sections that a PhD student will include (plus the section on professional implications of the research) in about half the number of words. It is usually harder to be concise than verbose, and so perhaps the EdD student needs to be even more certain that every sentence counts, although all doctoral writing in general needs to be sharp and succinct. Sometimes, an EdD student can be asked at their viva why they did not write more about a particular area of a topic (e.g., ethical considerations, or the process of the analysis), but hard choices have to be made and justified regarding the word count and you cannot write about all the areas in as much detail as you may have wanted to. As long as you can defend your choices, you should be OK.

As long as a doctoral thesis in education/social science is able to make a contribution in terms of adding knowledge to the field, it does not necessarily have to help or inform people such as practitioners and can be an end in itself. However, I would argue that, ultimately, the aim of educational/social research is to produce some knowledge and understanding of the world. For many researchers, there is also a desire to use that knowledge to make the world a better place; i.e., not just to create some abstract academic understanding, but to do so in a way that has impact outside of academia. In education, some people think the conclusions should inform educational policy or teachers' practice, and this may often be the case, particularly for EdD students, As a caveat, Dowling and Brown (2010) remind us that it is important that doctoral students who are also educational practitioners make sure that they move outside of their daily educational practice and into the activity of educational and academic research, which we must remember should be regarded as a distinct field of activity in its own right.

11.4 CONCLUSION: THE FINAL WORD

I want to thank the contributing authors for applying their knowledge and for their hard work, and the eight students who willingly gave up their time to share their experiences with me about studying for a doctorate.

I hope that this book has provided the reader with a range of different designs that are exemplified and set in the real world of research, and which can act as resources to familiarise themselves with and use for their own projects.

I also hope that, although readers will see that designing a doctoral study is usually complex and it takes time to learn the skills, the codes and practices of research, they will be infected with an enthusiasm for producing a sound research design and regard it as a creative, imaginative, stimulating and exciting process. And remember: you will be a different person at the end of it.

▬ BOX 11.2 ▬▬▬▬▬▬▬▬▬▬▬▬▬▬▬▬▬▬▬▬

A summary of the key points

- The main theme of the book is about conceptualising and designing empirical research for doctoral students and their tutors/lecturers/researchers.
- Conducting doctoral research is complex and can be difficult and it is crucial to have a sound research design.
- Research should involve a dialogue with theories and other research studies, but this also involves conversations with people including your supervisor, who will be expected to play a key role.
- The processes involved in the research need to be justified and made visible.
- The choice of the design to be used will always be dependent on the aim(s) of the research, the research question(s) and the methodology employed.
- The thesis should present an argument that can be defended, and the research needs to make a distinct contribution to the field.
- The main part of the thesis should be the presentation of the findings.

GLOSSARY

The following definitions are to be treated with care as they are very brief and the debates they refer to are often complicated. It is important to use these definitions as a way into the debates and not as a fixed characterisation of them.

A priori reason: Relating to reasoning or knowledge, which derives from theoretical deduction rather than from observation or experience.

Agency: Often a controversial term, agency can be viewed as the capacity to take decisions and act, albeit within surrounding structures and structural contexts. It is not about voluntarism of rational choice and is influenced by past, present and future considerations.

Analysis of Variance: A statistical test to measure group differences (three groups or more) on a given dependent variable.

Auto-ethnography: A contested research approach in which texts claim to be research but the topic/focus of the research is really the author herself or himself.

Bias: This is a form of systematic error that is considered primarily a function of the research process (i.e., design and methods). There are many different causes to the bias. These can be related to the sampling, the method of data collection or the measurement strategies, as well as to the attitudes or preferences of a researcher and the lack of control of all contextual factors that may distort the observed associations. Bias can lead to errors both in the findings and to an incorrect interpretation of the uncovered relationships.

Biased sample: This is where the sample is not simply unrepresentative, but systematically inclined to favour a particular group.

Boundedness: This relates to the boundaries of a study and is a feature of case study as a research strategy. In case studies, the boundaries between case and context is not always clear; however, the conceptual boundaries of the case always have to be drawn through the research question.

Census: A count or survey of a complete population.

Cluster analysis: This is a statistical analysis type that helps to identify groups of individuals or objects that are similar to each other but different from individuals in other groups.

Cluster sampling: See under sampling.

Conceptual framework: A systematic way of organising, articulating all the elements of the research process from beginning to end as well as the reasons behind the decisions that you are making or have made. They should be regarded as organic, malleable and ongoing, which evolve over time as connections and relationships become more apparent.

Conceptualising: The process whereby underlying concepts are developed and clarified.

Confounding variable: A variable which explains the relationship between two other variables, previously and wrongly interpreted to be cause and effect. The confounding variable is the true cause.

Constructionism: The view that our understanding of the world is constituted in human constructs, particularly through language.

Convenience sampling: See under sampling.

Covertly: Or secretly. In covert research, the participants are unaware that the researcher is observing them and that they are part of a research study.

Critical realism: The theoretical schema associated particularly with the work of Roy Bhaskar that attempts to define a position between relativism and realism.

Cross-sectional analysis (also known as a cross-sectional study): This is a type of observational study often based on the survey results of a population or its representative subset at one specific time point. This differs from longitudinal analysis that traces individuals or objects over time.

Deductive research: A research design that begins with the process of deducing a hypothesis from theory and then testing out the hypothesis to see whether or not it is confirmed.

Demand characteristics: Denotes a situation where the results of an experiment are biased because the researchers' expectations create an implicit *demand* for participants to provide them with the responses they are looking for.

Dependent variable: The variable you are seeking to explain, typically the outcome variable in experimental designs. An example would be if a researcher were investigating the effect of phonological awareness on children's reading. The amount of phonics teaching is the independent variable (see below) and the children's reading scores are the dependent variable.

Descriptive statistics: These are a set of brief descriptive coefficients that summarises a particular data set.

Desistance theory: A criminological theory, which seeks to explain the reasons why a criminal stops committing crimes.

Distal effects: See under proximal effects.

Effect size: A standardised measure of the magnitude of the effect of an intervention. The effect sizes referred to here are Cohen's d and Hedges g, both of which express effect sizes as standard deviation units of progress (an effect size of 1 = 1 standard deviation unit of progress).

Emic: An emic approach (sometimes referred to as 'insider', 'inductive' or 'bottom-up') takes as its starting point the perspectives of research participants from inside the research setting.

Empirical research: Research to gain knowledge that is based on direct or indirect experience of observable information, or interaction with, the world.

Empirical and theoretical fields: The empirical field is a broad range of practices, experiences and locations. The theoretical field refers to the theories, debates and other empirical findings and this includes the community of academics/researchers, professionals and/or practitioners who comprise the authorities on the particular area that you are researching.

Empiricism: The idea that we can come to understand the world through our experiences of it, gathering information through our senses.

Episteme: Is another word for knowledge, but also has a more technical meaning in the work of Michel Foucault, where it refers to systems of knowledge and their relationship to historical processes.

Epistemological assumptions: These are assumptions about the grounds of knowledge – about how we understand the world and communicate this as knowledge to fellow human beings. These assumptions entail ideas, for example about what forms of knowledge can be and how they can be obtained.

Epistemology: A branch of philosophy and a set of debates that are concerned with how and what we can know about the world.

Etic: An etic approach (sometimes referred to as 'outsider', 'deductive', or 'top-down') uses as its starting point perspectives of the observer from outside of the research setting.

External validity: See under validity.

Face validity: See under validity.

Factor analysis: This is a statistical data reduction or structure detection technique. The basic idea is to reduce a large set of variables to a smaller number of variables called factors. Factors in this case represent underlying concepts that often cannot be measured directly (e.g., happiness, life-satisfaction).

Gatekeepers: A term used to refer to persons (e.g., head teachers) who are able to arbitrate access to a setting, structure or organisation.

Generalisability: This is concerned with whether research findings can be generalised beyond the specific setting in which the research was carried out. A study may be valid in one setting but not in another and so are not generalisable. Whether or not generalisation is possible depends on the type of study, the research context, the specific characteristics of the study and the sampling methodology.

Hawthorne effect: The tendency for people to improve an aspect of their behaviour in response to their awareness of being observed, or as a result of taking part in a research study.

Hypothesis testing: This is the process by which the researcher tests a statistical hypothesis, with the aim of either accepting or rejecting it.

Independent variable: The explanatory variable. In experimental design, the proposed cause is an independent variable, as are other variables expected to have an effect on the dependent variable. For example, baseline scores on the outcome variable, or key demographic variables relating to age, gender, social class or ethnicity (see the example used with dependent variable).

Inductive research: A research design that begins with the generation of data from a specific research context in order to formulate a hypothesis by identifying patterns in the data.

Inferences: Conclusions reached on the basis of evidence and reasoning.

Insider ethnographies: This is when the researcher belongs to, or is part of, the community he or she is researching.

Internal validity: See under validity.

Interpretivism: A set of debates relating to the ways in which people make meaning in their participation in the world.

Interpretivist framework: See under interpretivism.

InVivo: This is a computer software package that is used for organising data and for analysis mainly in qualitative and mixed methods research.

Logical positivism: A philosophical movement that attempted to specify the relation between philosophy and science, and to develop a logical language through which scientific work could be conducted.

Longitudinal research: This is research in which data is gathered for the same subjects repeatedly over a period of time. In some cases this may be years.

Maximum variation: Usually associated with purposive sampling in qualitative research and with case study selection when using multiple cases following theoretical replication logic (see replication logic below). Here, cases selected will be as different from each other as possible to disclose the range of variation and differentiation in a field.

Member checking: This involves showing the transcript to a participant, with the promise that they can remove any section that they feel to be controversial.

Methodology: A framework that offers principles of reasoning, which are informed by particular theoretical positions. Some writers also refer to methodology as a strategy, or the plan of action, linking the chosen methods to particular conceptual assumptions, and showing how a research design is able to offer answers to the research questions.

Methods: The tools or techniques used to collect, or generate, and analyse data.

Morpheme: A meaningful morphological unit of a language that cannot be further divided (e.g., *in, come, -ing*, forming *incoming*).

Multiple regression models: A multivariate statistical analysis which can compare group differences whilst controlling for a number of other variables. It is particularly useful for looking at mediation and moderation.

Necessary conditions: A state of affairs that must prevail if another is to occur, a prerequisite. However, it does not mean that there will be such an occurrence.

Non-probability sampling: This is a technique where selected samples are based on the subjective judgement of the researcher, rather than random selection used in probability sampling.

Normative statements: These are statements that are value judgments about whether a situation is subjectively desirable or undesirable. It looks at the world as it 'should' be.

NVivo and MAXQDA: Two software programs that are used most often for computer-assisted qualitative and mixed methods data analysis.

Ontology: A branch of philosophy and a set of debates related to discussing the nature of being and the contents of the world.

Outliers or extreme cases: These are observations that are drastically different from average cases in the dataset. There are some statistical techniques for how to detect them, but in most cases in quantitative and qualitative datasets it is up to a researcher to define what is normal and abnormal in a particular study.

Overtly or openly: In overt research, the participants know that the researcher is observing them and that they are part of the research.

Participant observation: This method is where the researcher joins in or participates with the group that she or he is studying so they can understand the meaning behind the behaviour of the group they observing and/or working with.

Population: The target group under investigation.

Positivism: The view that we should produce knowledge that is verifiable through empirical methods, that we should use the scientific method to do such verification, and in a manner that is objective, free from bias, and leading to generalisations.

Post-positivism: A set of critiques and amendments to 'classic' positivism, which attempt to maintain the aim of producing rigorous generalisable knowledge of the world.

Postmodernism: A theoretical movement with an interest in deconstructing the apparent stability of meaning, particularly as a reaction against modernism.

Power calculations: The power is the ability of a test to detect an effect, if the effect actually exists. Power analysis can be used to calculate the minimum sample size required so that researchers can be reasonably likely to detect an effect of a given size.

Principles of selection: The choices that all researchers have to make and justify throughout the entire research process from research questions, empirical and theoretical fields, sampling, methods of data collection and analysis, and so on.

Probability sampling: See under sampling.

Proximal and distal effects: Proximal effects are those most closely related to an intervention. Distal effects are further removed. The proximal effect of drinking a cup of tea would be a quenching of thirst, a distal effect might be a more positive attitude to work.

Purposive sampling: See under sampling.

Purposively: Connected to purposive sampling – see under sampling.

Quota sampling: See under sampling.

Random sampling: See under sampling.

Reading Recovery Programme: A daily, one-to-one reading intervention for children who are experiencing reading difficulties after their first year of school, typically lasting for one or two terms.

Realism: The view that we can accurately come to understand the objective features of the world.

Reflexive: Where the researcher reflects on the research (including their interpretations), and is aware of the effect of their presence on the setting and research process from beginning to end.

Regression analysis: This is a statistical type of analysis for investigating the relationships among variables. It includes many techniques for looking at several variables, when the focus is on the relationship between a dependent variable and one or more independent variables. This analysis predicts a value of a dependent variable based on values of independent variables. For example, regression analysis will allow you to predict the success of university entry based on a cognitive test score, gender, ethnicity and social class of an individual.

Relativism: A set of views relating to the relative character of meaning, and the impossibility of creating stable, context independent or generalisable meanings.

Reliability analysis: There are two definitions of this term. The first relates to measures of the overall consistency of the items that are used to define a scale. As a result, we are given sample size, number of items and reliability coefficients in this analysis. The second meaning refers to the degree of agreement between sets of data collected independently from the same individual or object by two different researchers or by the same researcher at different time points. Reliable data collected by different researchers, or at different times, should only rarely disagree. Reliability analysis is used to train new researchers in coding schemes and data collection – for example, by testing their data against a reference data set, both collected from the same observations.

Replication: This refers to the process used in experimental designs, where a finding from a single experiment is sought to be replicated by conducting more experiments, some attempting to duplicate the conditions of the original experiment, some by altering one or two unimportant conditions to test if the results could be replicated.

Replication logic: This is the basis of multiple case study designs, and is opposed to sampling logic, and analogous to the logic underlying multiple experiments. Using replication logic cases are selected on the basis of similarity (literal replication), predicting similar results, or of contrast drawing on theory (theoretical replication), anticipating difference in findings or aspects of findings.

Sample: A subset of a population selected for measurement, observation or questioning, to provide statistical information.

Sampling

- **Cluster sampling:** This is part of probability sampling and used where the population is already grouped together in clusters such as schools, hospitals or local authorities.
- **Convenience sampling:** Sometimes also called 'opportunistic' sampling, it is one of the main types of non-probability sampling methods, and is made up of people who are available and easy to reach, often so that data can be gathered quickly. It is frequently used to trial a particular method with a relatively small number of participants.
- **Probability sampling:** A sampling technique that involved random selection and gives all the individuals in the population an equal chance of being selected.
- **Purposive sampling:** Is part of non-probability sampling, where the researcher choses the participants based on the knowledge of a population and the purpose of the study. The subjects are selected because of a particular characteristic. As the sample is unrepresentative, this makes statistical generalisations impossible.
- **Quota sampling:** This is where the sample attempts to gain representatives of known characteristics of the total population in the proportions that they occur. The main difference between quota and stratified sampling is that the sample is not randomly selected.
- **Random sampling:** This is the basic sampling technique where a group of subjects is selected for research from a larger population. Each individual is chosen entirely by chance and each member of the population has an equal chance of being included.
- **Snowball sampling:** Or 'chain-referral' sampling, is a non-probability sampling technique where participants who have particular characteristics are used as informants to help researchers recruit more participants from among their acquaintances.
- **Stratified sampling:** This is a probability sampling technique where the population is divided into homogeneous groups (called strata) with similar characteristics, and then randomly sampled within the strata.
- **Systematic sampling:** This is a type of probability sampling method in which sample members are selected from a list at fixed intervals (e.g., every tenth person) with a random starting point.

Sampling frame: A complete list of the items or people that/whom researchers want to study, so forming a population from which a sample can be taken.

Snowball sampling: See under sampling.

Stratified sampling: See under sampling.

Structural functionalism: This theoretical approach attempts to explain how society functions as a whole by focusing on the relationships between the social institutions that make up society such as religion, law, government and kinship.

Sufficient conditions: A state of affairs that will invariably lead to a specified outcome. Smashing a thin pane of glass with a hammer is a sufficient action to cause the pane to shatter. It is not a necessary condition – the pane of glass could shatter because it was dropped, for example.

Systematic sampling: See under sampling.

T-tests: A statistical test to measure differences between two groups on a given dependent variable.

The literary turn: Sometimes referred to as the linguistic turn, in anthropology this began in the late 1980s and involved attention to the processes of anthropological inscription, including how ethnographies are written.

Theory: An integrated set of statements from a particular paradigm and the analytical frameworks, which provide insights that help us explain what is going on. They move the research beyond description and by abstracting ideas from your data they move to deeper explanation.

Thick description: The term was introduced by the twentieth-century philosopher Gilbert Ryle, and later developed by anthropologist Clifford Geertz. It is commonly used to mean rich or detailed descriptions that explain not just participants' behaviour, but also its context so that it becomes more meaningful.

Triangulation: An approach that uses more than one method or analysis so that the accuracy of data can be compared and checked to see if they produce the same finding(s).

Validity: The degree to which a study accurately reflects or assesses the specific concept that the researcher is attempting to measure.

- **External validity:** The extent to which the results of a study are generalisable or transferable.
- **Face validity:** How a measure or procedure appears.
- **Internal validity:** (1) The rigour with which the study is designed and, if the study is exploring causal relationships, (2) the extent to which the designers of a study have taken into account alternative explanations for any causal relationships they find.

Weighting or weighted data: This process is where data collected from a sample are adjusted to represent the population from which the subset was drawn. The weighting process involves computing and assigning a weight to each case in a sample. The weight indicates the number of cases in the population the response in the sample represents. Information about demographic characteristics – such as gender, age, ethnicity, social class – are used to develop the weights. The weight does not change a respondent's answer; rather, it gives an appropriate relative importance to it.

REFERENCES

Adler, P.A. and Adler, P. (1998) 'Observational techniques', in N.K. Denzin and Y.S. Lincoln (eds), *Collecting and Interpreting Qualitative Materials*. Thousand Oaks, CA: Sage.

Agar, M.H. (1994) *Language Shock: Understanding the Culture of Communication*. New York: William Morrow.

Aggleton, P. (1987) *Rebels Without a Cause? Middle Class Youth and the Transition from School to Work*. London: The Falmer Press.

Alderson, P. and Morrow, V. (2004) *Ethics, Social Research and Consulting with Children and Young People*. Barkingside: Barnardo's.

Alegria, J., Pignot, E. and Morais, J. (1982) 'Phonetic analysis of speech and memory codes in beginning readers', *Memory & Cognition*, 10: 451–6.

Allison, G.T. (1971) *Essence of Decision: Explaining the Cuban Missile Crisis*. Boston, MA: Little, Brown.

Allison, G.T. and Zelikow, P. (1999) *Essence of Decision: Explaining the Cuban Missile Crisis*, 2nd edn. New York: Addison Wesley Longman.

American Association for Public Opinion Research (2013) *Response Rates: An Overview*. Available at: www.aapor.org/Response_Rates_An_Overview1/3720.htm (accessed 7 July 2016).

American Educational Research Association (AERA) (2011) 'Code of ethics', *Educational Researcher*, 40 (3): 145–56.

Anderson, G. L. and Jones, F. (2000) 'Knowledge generation in educational administration from the inside out: the promise and perils of site-based, administrator research', *Educational Administration Quarterly*, 36 (3): 428–464.

Anderson, K. and Overy, K. (2010) 'Engaging Scottish young offenders in education through music and art', *International Journal of Community Music*, 3: 47–64.

Armstrong, F. (2008) 'Inclusive education', in G. Richards and F. Armstrong (eds), *Key Issues for Teaching Assistants: Working in Diverse and Inclusive Classrooms*. Abingdon and New York: Routledge.

Arshad, R., Closs, A. and Stead, J. (1999) *Doing our Best: Scottish School Education, Refugee Pupils and Parents – A Strategy for Social Inclusion*. Edinburgh: Centre for Education for Racial Equality in Scotland (CERES).

Association of Internet Researchers (AoIR) (2012) *Ethics*. Available at: http://aoir.org/ethics/ (accessed 7 July 2016).

Association of Social Anthropologists (ASA) (2011) http://www.theasa.org/ (accessed 22 July 2016).

REFERENCES

Australian Code for the Responsible Conduct of Research (ARC): Australian Government, National Health and Medical Research Council, Australia (NHMRC) (2007) Available at: www.nhmrc.gov.au/guidelines-publications/r39 (accessed 14 July 2016).

Avramidis, E., Bayliss, P. and Burden, R. (2000) 'A survey into mainstream teachers' attitudes towards the inclusion of children with special educational needs in the ordinary school in one local education authority', *Educational Psychology*, 20 (2): 191–211.

Baker, S. and Edwards, R. (2012) 'How many qualitative interviews is enough? Expert voices and early career reflections on sampling and cases in qualitative research', National Centre for Research Methods (NCRM) Review Paper. Available at: http://eprints.brighton.ac.uk/11632/ (accessed 29 March 2016).

Ball, S. J. (1981) *Beachside Comprehensive : A Case Study of Secondary Schooling.* Cambridge and New York: Cambridge University Press.

Baron, R.M. and Kenny, D.A. (1986) 'The moderator–mediator variable distinction in social psychological research: Conceptual, strategic and statistical considerations', *Journal of Personality and Social Psychology*, 51: 1173–82.

Bassey, M. (1999) *Case Study Research in Educational Settings.* Buckingham: Open University Press.

Bazeley, P. (2009) 'Integrating data analyses in mixed methods research', *Journal of Mixed Methods Research*, 3 (3): 203–7.

Becker, H.S. (1992) 'Cases, causes, conjunctures, stories and imagery', in C.C. Ragin and H.S. Becker (eds), *What is a Case? Exploring the Foundations of Social Inquiry.* Cambridge: Cambridge University Press.

Becker, H.S., Geer, B., Hughes, E.C. and Strauss, A. (1961) *Boys in White: Student Culture in Medical School.* Chicago, IL: University of Chicago Press.

Benton, T. and Craib, I. (2001) *Philosophy of Social Science: The Philosophical Foundations of Social Thought.* Basingstoke: Palgrave.

Bernard, H.R. (2006) *Research Methods in Anthropology: Qualitative and Quantitative Approaches*, 4th edn. Oxford: AltaMira Press.

Betts, P. and Lound, C. (2010) 'The application of alternative modes of data collection in UK government social surveys', *Survey Methodology Bulletin*, 67: 1–13.

Bhaskar, R. (1978) *A Realist Theory of Science.* Hemel Hempstead: Harvester.

Bhaskar, R. (1998) 'Philosophy and scientific realism', in M. Archer and R. Bhaskar (eds), *Critical Realism: Essential Readings.* London: Routledge.

Blaikie, N. (2007) *Approaches to Social Enquiry: Advancing Knowledge*, 2nd edn. Cambridge: Polity.

Blaikie, N. (2010) *Designing Social Research*, 2nd edn. Cambridge: Polity.

Blatchford, P., Russell, A. and Webster, R. (2012) *Reassessing the Impact of Teaching Assistants: How Research Challenges Practice and Policy.* Abingdon: Routledge.

Bleach, K. (ed.) (1998) *Raising Boys' Achievements in Schools.* Stoke-on-Trent: Trentham Books.

Bloch, A. and Schuster, L. (2005) 'At the extremes of exclusion: Deportation, detention and dispersal', *Ethnic and Racial Studies*, 28 (3): 491–512.

Blommaert, J. and Jie, D. (2010). *Ethnographic Fieldwork: A Beginner's Guide.* Bristol: Multilingual Matters.

Blumer, H. (1954) 'What is wrong with social theory?', *American Sociological Review*, 19: 3–10.

Boddy, J., Jennings, S., Morrow, V., Alderson, P., Neumann, T., Rees, R. and Gibson, W. (2010) *The Research Ethics Guidebook: A Resource for Social Scientists.* Available at: www.ethicsguidebook.ac.uk (accessed 7 July 2016).

Bonell, C., Fletcher, A., Morton, M., Lorenc, T. and Moore, L. (2012) 'Realist randomised controlled trials: A new approach to evaluating complex public health interventions', *Social Science and Medicine*, 75: 2299–2306.

Borgatti, S. (1993/1994) 'Cultural domain analysis', *Journal of Quantitative Anthropology*, 4: 261–78.

Boswell, G., Wedge, P. and Price, A. (2004) *The Impact of Fathers Inside: An OLSU and Safe Ground Parenting Course for Male Prisoners at HMP Ashwell.* Leicester: De Montefort University. Available at: www.safeground.org.uk/wp-content/uploads/FathersInsideEvaluationReport.pdf (accessed 25 August 2015).

Botvin, G.J. and Griffin, K.W. (2014) 'Life skills training: Preventing substance misuse by enhancing individual and social competence', *New Directions for Youth Development*, 141: 57–65.

Bourdieu, P. (1977) *Outline of a Theory of Practice.* Cambridge and New York: Cambridge University Press.

BPS (2013) *Ethics Guidelines for Internet-Mediated Research 2013.* Available at: www.bps.org.uk/system/files/Public%20files/inf206-guidelines-for-internet-mediated-research.pdf (accessed 14 July 2016).

Bradford, W. (1997) *Raising Boys' Achievement.* Kirklees: Kirklees Education Advisory Service.

Bradley, L., and Bryant, P. (1985) *Rhyme and Reason in Reading and Spelling.* Ann Arbor: University of Michigan Press.

Brannen, J. (2005) 'Mixed methods research: A discussion paper', Economic and Social Research Council (ESRC) National Centre for Research Methods (NCRM) Review Papers NCRM/005. Available at: http://eprints.ncrm.ac.uk/89/1/MethodsReviewPaperNCRM-005.pdf (accessed 7 July 2016).

Brannen, J. and O'Connell, R. (2015) 'Data Analysis I: Overview of data analysis strategies', in S. Hesse-Biber and R. Burke Johnson (eds), *Oxford Handbook of Mixed and Multimethod Research.* Oxford: Oxford University Press.

Brettell, C. (1998) 'Fieldwork in the archives: Methods and sources in historical anthropology', in H. Russell Bernard (ed.), *Handbook of Methods in Cultural Anthropology.* Walnut Creek, CA: AltaMira Press.

Bridges, D. (2009) 'Four issues for ethical code makers'. Paper presented at the British Educational Research Association Annual Conference, 2–5 September, Manchester.

British Educational Research Association (BERA) (2011) *Ethical Guidelines for Educational Research.* Available at: www.bera.ac.uk/files/2011/08/BERA-Ethical-Guidelines-2011.pdf (accessed 7 July 2016).

British Psychological Society (BPS) (2010) *British Psychological Society Code of Human Research Ethics*, updated 2010. Available at: www.bps.org.uk/sites/default/files/documents/code_of_human_research_ethics.pdf (accessed 14 July 2016).

British Sociological Association (BSA) (2002) *British Sociological Association Statement of Ethical Practice*, updated 2004. Available at: www.britsoc.co.uk/the-bsa/equality/statement-of-ethical-practice.aspx (accessed 14 July 2016).

Brockmann, M. (2011) 'Problematising short-term participant observation and multi-method ethnographic studies', *Ethnography and Education*, 6 (2): 229–43.

Brooks, R., te Riele, K. and Maguire, M. (2014) *Ethics and Education Research*. London: Sage.

Brown, A. and Dowling, P. (1998) *Doing Research/Reading Research: A Mode of Investigation for Education*. London: Falmer Press.

Bryant, A. (1985) *Positivism in Social Theory and Research*. London: Macmillan.

Bryant, P. and Bradley, L. (1985) *Children's Reading Problems*. Oxford: Blackwell.

Bryman, A. (1988) *Quantity and Quality in Social Research*. London: Unwin Hyman.

Bryman, A. (2004) *Social Research Methods*, 2nd edn. Oxford: Oxford University Press.

Bryman, A. (2006) 'Integrating quantitative and qualitative research: How is it done?', *Qualitative Research*, 6 (1): 97–113.

Bryman, A. (2007) Barriers to integrating quantitative and qualitative research', *Journal of Mixed Methods Research*, 1 (1): 8–22.

Bryman, A. (2012) *Social Research Methods*, 4th edn. Oxford: Oxford University Press.

Burgess, R.G. (1988) 'Conversations with a purpose: the ethnographic interview in educational research', in R.G. Burgess (ed.), *Studies in Qualitative Methodology: A Research Annual*, Vol. 1, pp. 137–155. London: JAI Press Ltd.

Burgess, R.G. (ed.) (1989) *The Ethics of Educational Research*. Lewis: Falmer Press.

Burrowes, N., Disley, E., Liddle, M., Maguire, M., Rubin, J., Taylor, J. and Wright, S. (2013) *Intermediate Outcomes of Arts Projects: A Rapid Evidence Assessment*. London: National Offender Management Service (NOMS). Available at: www.gov.uk/government/uploads/system/uploads/attachment_data/file/254450/Intermediate-outcomes-of-arts-projects.pdf (accessed 2 September 2015).

Callegaro, M., Baker, R., Bethlehem, J., Goritz, A.S., Krosnick, J.A. and Lavrakas, P.J. (eds) (2014) *Online Panel Research: A Data Quality Perspective*. Chichester: Wiley.

Calvey, D. (2008) 'The art and politics of covert research: Doing "situated ethics" in the field', *Sociology*, 42 (5): 905–18.

Cameron, C., Owen, C. and Moss, P. (2001) *Entry, Retention and Loss: A Study of Childcare Students and Workers*, Department for Education and Skills (DfES) Research Report 275. London: DfES.

Campbell, D.T., and Fiske, D.W. (1959) 'Convergent and discriminant validation by the multitrait-multimethod matrix', *Psychological Bulletin*, 56 (2): 81–105.

Candappa, M. and Egharevba, I. (2002) 'Negotiating boundaries: Tensions within home and school life for refugee children', in R. Edwards (ed.), *Children, Home and School*. London: RoutledgeFalmer.

Cara, O., Litster, J., Swain, J. and Vorhaus, J. (2010) *The Teacher Study: The Impact of the Skills for Life Strategy on Teachers*. London: National Research and Development Centre for Adult Literacy and Numeracy.

Caracelli, V.J. and Greene, J.C. (1993) 'Data analysis strategies for mixed-method evaluation designs', *Educational Evaluation and Policy Analysis*, 15 (2): 195–207.

Carspecken, P. F. (1991) *Community Schooling and the Nature of Power: The Battle for Croxteth Comprehensive*. London: Taylor and Francis.

Chalmers, I. (2001) 'Invalid health information is potentially lethal', *British Medical Journal*, 322 (7292): 998.vc. Available at: www.ncbi.nlm.nih.gov/pmc/articles/PMC1120156/ (accessed 14 July 2016).

Chambers, R. (1994) 'The origins and practice of participatory rural appraisal', *World Development*, 22 (7): 953–64.

Charsley, S. (1987) 'Interpretation and custom: The case of the wedding cake', *Man*, New Series, 22 (1): 93–110.

Clark, A., Flewitt, R., Hammersley, M. and Robb, M. (2013) *Understanding Research with Children and Young People*. London; Sage.

Clark, A. and Moss, P. (2001) *Listening to Young Children: The Mosaic Approach*. London: National Children"s Bureau Enterprises Ltd.

Clark, M.C. and Sharf, B.F. (2007) 'The dark side of truth(s): Ethical dilemmas in researching the personal', *Qualitative Inquiry*, 13 (3): 319–416.

Clifford, J. and Marcus, G. (eds) (1986) *Writing Culture: The Poetics and Politics of Ethnography*. Berkeley, CA: University of California Press.

Cohen, J. (1988) *Statistical Power Analysis for the Behavioral Sciences*, 2nd edn. Mahwah, NJ: Lawrence Erlbaum.

Cohen, L., Manion, L. and Morrison, K. (2011) *Research Methods in Education*, 7th edn. New York: Routledge.

Cohen, M. (2009) 'Choral singing and prison inmates: Influences of performing in a prison choir', *Journal of Correctional Education*, 60: 52–65.

Connolly, A. and Parkes, J. (2011) 'Innovation, ethics and the psycho-social? A qualitative study with "hard to reach" young people'. Unpublished paper for the British Sociology Association Conference, 6–8 April, London School of Economics.

Cook, B., Buysse, V., Klinger, J., Landrum, T., McWilliam, R., Tankersley, M. and Test, D. (2015) 'CEC's standards for classifying the evidence base of practices in Special Education', *Remedial and Special Education*, 36 (4): 220–34.

Cook, C., Heath, F. and Thompson, R.L. (2000) 'A meta-analysis of response rates in web- or internet-based surveys', *Educational and Psychological Measurement*, 60 (6): 821–36.

Cook, T.D. and Campbell, D.T. (1979) *Quasi-Experimentation: Design and Analysis Issues for Field Settings*. Boston, MA: Houghton Mifflin.

Cook, T.D. and Reichardt, C.S. (eds) (1979) *Qualitative and Quantitative Methods in Evaluation Research*. Beverly Hills, CA: Sage.

Converse, J.M. and Presser, S. (1986) *Survey Questions: Handcrafting the Standardized Questionnaire*. London: Sage.

Corbett, J. (1999) 'Inclusive education and school culture', *International Journal of Inclusive Education*, 3, (1): 53–61.

Crabtree, A (2012) 'Research ethics and the moral enterprise of ethnography: Conjunctions and contradictions', *Ethics and Social Welfare*, 7 (4): 359–78.

Crede, E. and Borrego, M. (2013) 'From ethnography to items: A mixed methods approach to developing a survey to examine graduate engineering student retention', *Journal of Mixed Methods Research*, 7 (1): 62–80.

Creswell, J.W. (1994) *Research Design: Qualitative and Quantitative Approaches*. Thousand Oaks, CA: Sage.

Creswell, J.W. (1998) *Qualitative Inquiry and Research Design: Choosing among Five Traditions*. Thousand Oaks, CA: Sage.

Creswell, J.W. (1999) 'Mixed-method research: Introduction and application', in C. Ciznek (ed.), *Handbook of Educational Policy*. San Diego, CA: Academic Press.

Creswell, J.W. (2002) *Educational Research: Planning, Conducting, and Evaluating Quantitative and Qualitative Research*. Upper Saddle River, NJ: Pearson Education.

Creswell, J.W. (2007) *Qualitative Inquiry and Research Method: Choosing among Five Approaches*, 2nd edn. Thousand Oaks, CA: Sage.

Creswell, J.W. (2008) *Research Design: Qualitative, Quantitative, and Mixed Methods Approaches*, 3rd edn. Thousand Oaks, CA: Sage.

Creswell, J.W. (2012) *Educational Research: Planning, Conducting, and Evaluating Quantitative and Qualitative Research*, 4th edn.Upper Saddle River, NJ: Pearson Education.

Creswell, J. (2013) *Qualitative Inquiry and Research Design: Choosing among Five Approaches*, 3rd edn. London: Sage.

Creswell, J.W. and Plano Clark, V.L. (2007) *Designing and Conducting Mixed Methods Research*. Thousand Oaks, CA: Sage.

Creswell, J.W. and Plano Clark, V.L. (2010) *Designing and Conducting Mixed Methods Research*, 2nd edn. Thousand Oaks, CA: Sage.

Creswell, J.W., Plano Clark, V.L., Gutmann, M. and Hanson, W. (2003) 'Advanced mixed methods research designs', in A. Tashakkori and C. Teddlie (eds), *Handbook of Mixed Methods in Social and Behavioral Research*. Thousand Oaks, CA: Sage.

Crewe, K. (2001) 'The quality of participatory design: The effects of citizen input on the design of the Boston Southwest Corridor', *APA Journal*, 67: 437–55.

Crossley, M., and Vulliamy, G. (1984) 'Case study research methods and comparative education', *Comparative Education*, 20 (2): 193–207.

Crotty, M. (1998) *The Foundations of Social Research*. London: Sage.

Crotty, M. (2009) *The Foundations of Social Research*. St Leonards, NSW, Australia: Allen & Unwin.

Cumming, R.G. (1990) 'Is probability sampling always better? A comparison of results from a quota and a probability sample survey', *Community Health Studies*, 14 (2): 132–7.

Curtice, J. (2016) *The Benefits of Random Sampling*. London: NatCen Social Research.

Data Protection Act (DPA) (1998) *Data Protection Act*. Available at: www.legislation.gov.uk/ukpga/1998/29/contents (accessed 14 July 2016).

de Boer, H., Donker, A.S. and van der Werf, M.P.C. (2014) 'Effects of the attributes of educational interventions on students' academic performance: A meta-analysis', *Review of Educational Research*, 84 (4): 509–45.

de Leeuw, E.D., Hox, J.J. and Dillman, D.A. (eds) (2008) *International Handbook of Survey Methodology*. New York and London: Lawrence Erlbaum.

de Vaus, D.A. (2013) *Surveys in Social Research*, 6th edn. London: Routledge.

Delamont, S. (2007) 'Arguments against auto-ethnography', *Qualitative Researcher*, 4: 2–4.

Denscombe, M. (2008) 'Communities of practice: A research paradigm for the mixed methods approach?', *Journal of Mixed Methods Research*, 2 (3): 270–83.

Denzin, N.K. (1970) *The Research Act in Sociology*. Chicago, IL: Aldine.

Denzin, N.K. (1978) 'Strategies of multiple triangulation', in N.K. Denzin (ed.), *The Research Act in Sociology: A Theoretical Introduction to Sociological Method*. New York. McGraw-Hill.

Denzin, N.K. (1989) *The Research Act: A Theoretical Introduction to Sociological Methods*. London: Aldine.

Denzin, N.K. (2010) 'Moments, mixed methods, and paradigm dialogs', *Qualitative Inquiry*, 16 (6): 419–27.

Denzin, N.K. and Lincoln, Y.S. (eds) (2011) *The Sage Handbook of Qualitative Research*, 4th edn. Thousand Oaks, CA: Sage.

Department of Business, Innovation and Skills (2014) *The Allocation of Science and Research Funding 2015/16*. Available at: www.gov.uk/government/uploads/system/uploads/attachment_data/file/332767/bis-14-750-science-research-funding-allocations-2015-2016-corrected.pdf (accessed 25 August 2015).

Department of Health Education and Welfare (DHEW) (1979) *The Belmont Report: Ethical Principles and Guidelines of the Protection of Human Subjects of Research*. Washington, DC: Department of Health, Education and Welfare, National Commission for the Protection of Biomedical and Behavioral Research. Available at: http://videocast.nih.gov/pdf/ohrp_appendix_belmont_report_vol_2.pdf (accessed 14 July 2016).

Derrida, J. (1978) *Writing and Difference*, trans. Alan Bass. Chicago: University of Chicago Press.

Domínguez, D., Beaulieu, A., Estalella, A., Gómez, E., Schnettler, B. and Read, R. (2007) *Virtual Ethnography*. Forum Qualitative Sozialforschung / Forum: *Qualitative Social Research*, 8(3) Available at: http://nbn-resolving.de/urn:nbn:de:0114-fqs0703E19 (accessed: 22 July, 2016).

Dona, G. (2007) 'The microphysics of participation in refugee research', *Journal of Refugee Studies*, 20 (2): 210–29.

Doncaster, K. and Thorne, L. (2000) 'Reflection and planning: Essential elements of professional doctorates', *Reflective Practice*, 1 (3): 391–9.

Dowling, P. and Brown, A. (2010) *Doing Research/Reading Research*. London: Routledge.

Durkheim, E. (1897) *Suicide: A Study in Sociology*. New York: Free Press.

Economic and Social Research Council (ESRC) (2015) *ESRC Framework for Research Ethics*, updated 2015. Available at: www.esrc.ac.uk/files/funding/guidance-for-applicants/esrc-framework-for-research-ethics-2015/ (accessed 14 July 2016).

Eisenhardt, K.M. and Graebner, M.E. (2007) 'Theory building from cases: Opportunities and challenges', *Academy of Management Journal*, 50 (1): 25–32.

Eisner, E.W. (1985) *The Art of Educational Evaluation*. London and Philadelphia, PA: Falmer Press.

REFERENCES

Eisner, E.W. (1991) *The Enlightened Eye: Qualitative Inquiry and the Enhancement of Educational Practice*. New York: Macmillan.

Elliot, J. (2001) 'Making evidence-based practice educational', *British Journal of Educational Research*, 27 (5): 555–74.

Emerson, R.M., Fretz, R.L. and Shaw, L.L. (1995) *Writing Ethnographic Fieldnotes*. Chicago, IL: University of Chicago Press.

Engel, U., Jann, B., Lynn, P., Scherpenzeel, A. and Sturgis, P. (eds) (2014) *Improving Survey Methods: Lessons from Recent Research*. London: Routledge.

Epstein, D., Elwood, J. Hey, V. and Maw, J. (eds) (1998) *Failing Boys? Issues in Gender and Achievement*. Buckingham: Open University Press.

Evans-Pritchard, E.E. (1940) *The Nuer: A Description of the Modes of Livelihood and Political Institutions of a Nilotic People*. Oxford: Clarendon Press.

Fan, W. and Yan, Z. (2010) 'Factors affecting response rates of the web survey: A systematic review', *Computers in Human Behavior*, 26 (2): 132–9.

Farrugia, D. (2013) 'The possibility of symbolic violence in interviews with young people experiencing homelessness', in K. te Riele and R. Brooks (eds), *Negotiating Ethical Challenges in Youth Research*. New York: Routledge.

Feagin, J.R., Orum, A.M. and Sjoberg, G. (eds) (1991) *A Case for the Case Study*. Chapel Hill, NC: University of North Carolina Press.

Feilzer. M.Y. (2010) 'Doing mixed methods research pragmatically: Implications for the rediscovery of pragmatism as a research paradigm?', *Journal of Mixed Methods Research*, 4 (10): 6–16.

Feyerabend, P. (2011) *The Tyranny of Science*. Cambridge and Malden, MA: Polity Press.

Fielding, N. (1981) *The National Front*. London: Routledge & Kegan Paul.

Fielding, N. and Fielding, J. (1986) *Linking Data: The Articulation of Qualitative and Quantitative Methods in Social Research*. Beverly Hills, CA: Sage.

Fisher, R.A. (1925) *Statistical Methods for Research Workers*. Edinburgh: Oliver and Boyd.

Fitzpatrick, K.R. (2008) *A Mixed Methods Portrait of Urban Instrumental Music Teaching*. Chicago, IL: Proquest.

Flyvbjerg, B. (2006) 'Five misunderstandings about case-study research', *Qualitative Inquiry*, 12 (2): 219–44.

Flyvbjerg, B. (2011) 'Case studies', in N.K. Denzin and Y.S. Lincoln (eds), *The Sage Handbook of Qualitative Research*. Thousand Oaks, CA: Sage.

Foddy, W. (1993) *Constructing Questions for Interviews and Questionnaires*. Cambridge: Cambridge University Press.

Foster, K. (1996) 'A comparison of the census characteristics of respondents and non-respondents to the 1991 Family Expenditure Survey (FES)', *Survey Methodology Bulletin*, 38: 9–17.

Geertz, C. (1973) 'Thick description: toward an interpretive theory in culture', in C. Geertz (ed.), *The Interpretation of Cultures: Selected Essays*. New York: Basic Books.

George, A.L. and Bennett, A. (2005) *Case Studies and Theory Development in the Social Sciences*. Cambridge, MA: MIT Press.

Gibney, M. (2004) *The Ethics and Politics of Asylum: Liberal Democracy and the Response to Refugees*. Cambridge: Cambridge University Press.

Giddens, A. (1974) 'Introduction', in A. Giddens (ed.), *Positivism and Sociology*. London: Heinemann Educational.

Gilbert, R., Salanti, G., Harden, M. and See, S. (2005) 'Infant sleeping position and the sudden infant death syndrome: Systematic review of observational studies and historical review of recommendations from 1940 to 2002', *International Journal of Epidemiology*, 34 (4): 874–87.

Gillham, B. (2008) *Small-Scale Social Survey Methods*. London: Continuum.

Gillies, V. and Robinson, Y. (2012) 'Developing creative research methods with challenging pupils', *Creative Methods with Young People*, Special Issue, *International Journal of Social Research Methodology*, 15 (2): 161–73.

Glaser, B. and Strauss, A. (1967) *The Discovery of Grounded Theory: Strategies for Qualitative Research*. Chicago, IL: Aldine.

Goffman, E. (2007/1959) 'The presentation of self in everyday life', in C. Calhoun, J. Gerteis, J. Moody, S. Pfaff and I. Virk (eds), *Contemporary Sociological Theory*, 2nd edn. . Oxford: Blackwell.

Goldenberg, C., Gallimore, R. and Reese, I. (2005) 'Using mixed methods to explore Latino's children literacy development', in T.S. Weisner (ed.), *Discovering Successful Pathways in Children's Development: Mixed Methods in the Study of Childhood and Family Life*. Chicago, IL: University of Chicago Press.

Gomm, R., Hammersley, M. and Foster, P. (eds) (2000) *Case Study Method: Key Issues, Key Texts*. London: Sage.

Gordon, T., Holland, J. and Lahelma, E. (2001) 'Ethnographic research in educational settings', in P. Atkinson, A. Coffey, S. Delamont, J. Lofland and L. Lofland (eds), *Handbook of Ethnography*. London: Sage.

Gray, J. (1992) *Men are from Mars, Women are from Venus*. London: HarperElement.

Greene, J.C. (2007) *Mixed Methods in Social Inquiry*. San Francisco, CA: Jossey-Bass.

Greene, J.C. (2008) 'Is mixed methods social inquiry a distinctive methodology?', *Journal of Mixed Methods Research*, 2 (1): 7–22.

Greene, J.C. and McClintock, C. (1985) 'Triangulation in evaluation: Design and analysis issues', *Evaluation Review*, 9: 523–45.

Greene, J.C., Caracelli, V.J. and Graham, W.F. (1989) 'Toward a conceptual framework for mixed-method evaluation designs', *Educational Evaluation and Policy Analysis*, 11 (3): 255–74.

Greene, J.C. and Caracelli, V.J. (eds) (1997) *Advances in Mixed-Method Evaluation: The Challenges and Benefits of Integrating Diverse Paradigms*: *New Directions for Evaluation*, No. 74. San Francisco, CA: Jossey-Bass.

Greene, J. C. and Caracelli, V. J. (1997) 'Defining and describing the paradigm issues in mixed-method evaluation', in J. C. Greene and V. J. Caracelli (eds), *Advances in Mixed-Method Evaluation: The Challenges and Benefits of Integrating Diverse Paradigms* (pp. 5–18). San Francisco, CA: Jossey-Bass.

Groves, R.M. (2006) 'Nonresponse rates and nonresponse bias in household surveys', *Public Opinion Quarterly*, 70 (5): 646–75.

Groves, R.M., Dillman, D.A., Eltinge, J.L. and Little, R.J.A. (eds) (2002) *Survey Nonresponse*. New York: Wiley.

Guba, E.G. and Lincoln, Y.S. (1988) 'Do inquiry paradigms imply inquiry methodologies?', in D.M. Fetterman (ed.), *Qualitative Approaches in Evaluation in Education*. New York: Praeger.

Gunzler, D., Chen, T., Wu, P. and Zhang, H. (2013) 'Introduction to mediation analysis with structural equation modelling', *Shanghai Archives of Psychiatry*, 25: 390–4.

Hacking, I. (1983) *Representing and Intervening*. Cambridge: Cambridge University Press.

Hammersley, M. (1992) *What's Wrong with Ethnography: Methodological Explorations*. London: Routledge.

Hammersley, M. (1995) *The Politics of Social Research*. London: Sage.

Hammersley, M. (2000) 'The relevance of qualitative research', *Oxford Review of Education*, 26 (3): 393–405.

Hammersley, M. (2001) 'On Michael Bassey's concept of the fuzzy generalisation', *Oxford Review of Education*, 27 (2): 219–25.

Hammersley, M. (2002) *Educational Research, Policymaking and Practice*. London: Paul Chapman.

Hammersley, M. (2006) 'Are ethics committees ethical?', *Qualitative Researcher*, 2, ESRC National Centre for Research Methods. Available at: www.cardiff.ac.uk/socsi/qualiti/QualitativeResearcher/QR_Issue2_06.pdf (accessed 27 September 2016).

Hammersley, M. and Atkinson, P. (1995) *Ethnography: Principles in Practice*. London and New York: Routledge.

Hammersley, M. and Atkinson, P. (2007) *Ethnography: Principles in Practice*, 3rd edn. Trowbridge: Tavistock.

Hammersley, M. and Traianou, A. (2012) *Ethics and Educational Research*. Available at: www.bera.ac.uk/wp-content/uploads/2014/02/Ethics-and-Educational-Research.pdf (accessed 14 July 2016).

Hargreaves, A. (1996) 'Revisiting voice', *Educational Researcher*, 25 (1): 12–19.

Hargreaves, D. (1967). *Social Relations in Secondary School*. London: Routledge and Kegan Paul.

Hargreaves, D. (1997) 'In defence of research for evidence-based teaching: A rejoinder to Martyn Hammersley', *British Educational Research Journal*, 23 (4): 405–19.

Hattie, J. (2002) 'What are the attributes of excellent teachers?', in B. Webber (ed.), *Teachers Make a Difference: What is the Research Evidence?*. Wellington: New Zealand Council for Educational Research (NZCER).

Hattie, J. (2009) *Visible Learning: A Synthesis of over 800 Meta-Analyses Relating to Achievement*. London: Routledge.

Herring, S.C. (1996) 'Linguistic and critical research on computer-mediated communication: Some ethical and scholarly considerations', *Information Society*, 12 (2): 153–68.

Hitchcock, G. and Hughes, D. (1995) *Research and the Teacher: A Qualitative Introduction to School-Based Research*. London: Taylor and Francis.

Hochschild, A.R. (1989) *The Second Shift*. New York: Viking.

Hockey, J. (1986) *Squaddies: Portrait of a Subculture*. Exeter: Exeter University Press.

Hodkinson, P. (2005) 'Insider research in the study of youth cultures', *Journal of Youth Studies*, 8 (2): 131–49.

Holliday, A. (2007) *Doing and Writing Qualitative Research*, 2nd edn. London: Sage.

Hollingshead, A.B. (1949) *Elmtown's Youth*. New York: John Wiley.

Holloway, I. (1997) *Basic Concepts for Qualitative Research*. London: Blackwell Science.

Howell, D. (2009) *Statistical Methods for Psychology*, 7th edn. Belmont, CA: Wadsworth.

Hróbjartsson, A. and Gøtzsche, P.C., (2010) 'Placebo interventions for all clinical conditions', *Cochrane Database Systematic Reviews*, 106 (1): CD003974.

Humphreys, L. (1970) *Tearoom Trade: A Study of Homosexual Encounters in Public Places*. New York: Aldine de Gruyter.

Hurry, J. and Sylva, K. (2007) 'Long-term outcomes of early reading intervention', *Journal of Reading Research*, 30: 227–48.

Hurry, J., Nunes, T., Bryant, P., Pretzlik, U., Parker, M., Curno, T. and Midgley, L. (2005) 'Transforming research on morphology into teacher practice', *Research Papers in Education*, 20 (1): 187–206.

Ivankova, N.V., Creswell. J.W. and Stick, S.L. (2006) 'Using mixed-methods sequential explanatory design: From theory to practice', *Field Methods*, 18 (1): 3–20.

Jacobson, M. (2012) Personal communication with Professor Michael Jacobson, London, June.

Jackson, J.E. (1990) '"I am a fieldnote": Fieldnotes as a symbol of professional identity', in R. Sanjek (ed.), *Fieldnotes: The Making of Anthropology*. Ithaca, NY: Cornell University Press.

Jackson, P. (2000) 'Writing up qualitative data', in D. Burton (ed.), *Research Training for Social Scientists*. London: Sage.

Jahoda, M., Lazarsfeld, P.F. and Zeisei, H. (1931) *Marienthal: The Sociography of an Unemployed Community*. New Brunswick, NJ: Transaction Publishers.

Jeffrey, B. and Troman, G. (2010) 'Time for ethnography', *British Educational Research Journal*, 30 (4): 535–48.

Jenkins, R. (2002) *Pierre Bourdieu*, revd edn. London: Routledge.

Jick, T.D. (1979) 'Mixing qualitative and quantitative methods: Triangulation in action', *Administrative Science Quarterly*, 24: 602–11.

Jick, T.D. (1983) 'Mixing qualitative and quantitative methods: Triangulation in action', in J. Van Maanen (ed.), *Qualitative Methodology*. Beverly Hills, CA: Sage.

Johnson, R.B. and Onwuegbuzie, A.J. (2004) 'Mixed methods research: A research paradigm whose time has come', *Educational Researcher*, 33 (7): 14–26.

Johnson, R.B., Onwuegbuzie, A.J. and Turner, L.A. (2007) 'Toward a definition of mixed methods research', *Journal of Mixed Methods Research*, 1 (2): 112–33.

Jowell, R., Hedges, B., Lynn, P., Farrant, G. and Heath, A. (1993) 'The 1992 British election: The failure of the polls', *Public Opinion Quarterly*, 57 (2): 238–63.

Kahneman, D. (2011) *Thinking Fast and Slow*. New York: Macmillan.

Kemmis, S. (1980) 'The imagination of the case and the invention of the study', in
H. Simons (ed.), *Towards a Science of the Singular*. Norwich: Centre for Applied Research
in Education, University of East Anglia.

King, S.A. (1996) 'Researching Internet communities: Proposed ethical guidelines for the
reporting of results', *Information Society*, 12, (2): 119–28.

Kolakowski, L. (1972) *Positivist Philosophy: From Hume to the Vienna Circle*, trans. by
N. Guterman, 1st English edn. Harmondsworth: Penguin.

Kraemer, H., Stice, E., Kazdin, A., Offord, D. and Kupler, D. (2013) 'How do risk factors
work together? Mediators, moderators, and independent, overlapping, and proxy risk
factors', *American Journal of Psychiatry*, 158: 848–56.

Krosnick, J.A. (2002) 'The causes of no-opinion responses to attitude measures in surveys:
They are rarely what they appear to be', in R.M. Groves, D.A. Dillman, J.L. Eltinge and
R.J.A. Little (eds), *Survey Nonresponse*. New York: Wiley.

Kuhn, T.S. (1962) *The Structure of Scientific Revolutions*. Chicago, IL: University of Chicago Press.

Kusenbach, M. (2003) 'Street phenomenology: The go-along as ethnographic research tool',
Ethnography, 4: 455–85.

Kvale, S. (1996) *InterViews: An Introduction to Qualitative Research Interviewing*. Thousand
Oaks, CA, New York and London: Sage.

Lacey, C. (1970). *Hightown Grammar*. Manchester: Manchester University Press.

Lahaut, V.M.H.C.J., Jansen, H.A.M., van de Mheen, D. and Garretsen, H.F.L. (2002)
'Non-response bias in a sample survey on alcohol consumption', *Alcohol and Alcoholism*,
37 (3): 256–60.

Langer, G. (2003) 'About response rates: Some unresolved questions', *Public Perspective*,
14 (3): 16–18. Available at: www.ropercenter.uconn.edu/public-perspective/
ppscan/143/143016.pdf (accessed 14 July 2016).

Lincoln, Y.S. and Guba, E.G. (1985) *Naturalistic Inquiry*. Beverly Hills, CA: Sage.

Loftland, J. (1976) *Doing Social Life: The Qualitative Study of Human Interaction in Natural
Settings*. New York: Wiley.

Lohr, S.L. (2010) *Sampling: Design and Analysis*, 2nd edn. Boston, MA: Brooks/Cole.

Louis, K.S. (1982) 'Sociologist as sleuth: Integrating methods in the RDU study', *American
Behavioral Scientist*, 26 (1): 101–20.

Lynd, R.S. and Lynd, H.M. (1929) *Middletown: A Study in Modern American Culture*. New
York: Harcourt Brace Jovanovich.

Lynn, P., Clarke, P., Martin, J. and Sturgis, P. (2002) 'The effects of extended interviewer
efforts on nonresponse bias', in R.M. Groves, D.A. Dillman, J.L. Eltinge and R.J.A Little
(eds), *Survey Nonresponse*. New York: Wiley.

Mackie, J.L. (1974) *The Cement of the Universe*. Oxford: Oxford University Press.

Malinowski, B. (1922) *The Argonauts of the Western Pacific*. London: Routledge and Kegan Paul.

Malone, S. (2003) '"Ethics at home": Informed consent in your own back yard', *Qualitative
Studies in Education*, 16 (6): 797–815.

Marcus, G.E. and Fischer, M.J. (1986) *Anthropology as Cultural Critique: An Experimental
Moment in the Human Sciences*. Chicago, IL: University of Chicago Press.

Markham, A. and Baym, N. (eds) (2009) *Internet Inquiry: Conversations about Method.* London: Sage.

Marquart, J.M. (1990) 'A pattern-matching approach to link program theory and evaluation data', In L. Bickman (ed.), *Advances in Program Theory*, New Directions for Evaluation, No. 47 . San Francisco, CA: Jossey-Bass.

Maslen, G. (2013) 'The changing PhD: Turning out millions of doctorates', *University World News*, 266. Available at: www.universityworldnews.com/article.php?story= 20130403121244660 (accessed 12 January 2016).

Massey, A. and Walford, G. (1998) 'Children learning: Ethnographers learning', in G. Walford and A. Massey (eds), *Children Learning in Context.* New York: Jai Press.

Mattingly, C. (2005) 'Towards a vulnerable ethics of research practice', *Health: An Interdisciplinary Journal of the Social Study of Health, Illness and Medicine*, 9 (4): 453–71.

Maxwell, J.A. and Loomis, D.M. (2003) 'Mixed methods design: An alternative approach', in A. Tashakkori and C. Teddlie (eds), *Handbook of Mixed Methods in Social and Behavioral Research.* Thousand Oaks, CA: Sage.

May, T. (2001) *Social Research: Issues, Methods and Processes.* Buckingham: Open University Press.

McConney, A., Rudd, A. and Ayres, R. (2002) 'Getting to the bottom line: A method for synthesising findings within mixed-methods programme evaluations', *American Journal of Evaluation*, 23 (2): 121–40.

McKee, H.A. and Porter, J.E. (2009) *The Ethics of Internet Research: A Rhetorical Case-Based Process.* New York: Peter Lang.

McNeill, F. (2006) 'A desistance paradigm for offender management', *Criminology and Criminal Justice*, 6 (1): 39–62.

McWhorter, J.H. (2014) *The Language Hoax: Why the World Looks the Same in any Language.* New York: Oxford University Press.

Mead, M. (1928) *Coming of Age in Samoa: A Psychological Study of Primitive Youth for Western Civilisation.* New York: Morrow.

Mellon, J. and Prosser, C. (2015) *Investigating the Great British Polling Miss: Evidence from the British Election Study.* Available at: http://ssrn.com/abstract=2631165 (accessed 7 July 2016).

Menning, N. (2010) 'Singing with conviction: New Zealand prisons and Maori populations', *International Journal of Community Music*, 3: 111–20.

Mercer, J. (2007) 'The challenges of insider research in educational institutions: Wielding a double-edged sword and resolving delicate dilemmas', *Oxford Review of Education*, 33 (1): 1–17.

Merriam, S.B. (1988/1991) *Case Study Research in Education: A Qualitative Approach.* San Francisco, CA: Jossey-Bass.

Mertens, D. M. (2003) 'Mixed methods and the politics of human research: The transformative emancipatory perspective', in A. Tashakkori & C. Teddlie (eds), *Handbook of Mixed Methods in Social and Behavioral Research* (pp. 135–164). Thousand Oaks, CA: Sage.

Miles, M. and Huberman, A.M. (1994) *Qualitative Data Analysis: A Sourcebook of New Methods.* London: Sage.

Miles, M. and Huberman, A.M. (2013) *Qualitative Data Analysis: A Methods Sourcebook*. London: Sage.

Milgram, S. (1974) *Obedience to Authority: An Experimental View*. HarperCollins.

Mitchell, J. Clyde (1983) 'Case and situation analysis', *Sociological Review*, 31 (2): 187–211.

Mitchell, J. Clyde (1987) 'Case studies', in R.F. Ellen (ed.), *Ethnographic Research: A Guide to General Conduct*. London: Academic Press.

Morgan, D. L. (1998) 'Practical strategies for combining qualitative and quantitative methods: Applications to health research', *Qualitative Health Research*, 8 (3): 362–376.

Morgan, D.L. (2007) 'Paradigms lost and pragmatism regained: Methodological implications of combining qualitative and quantitative method', *Journal of Mixed Methods Research*, 1 (1): 48–76.

Morse, J.M. (1991) 'Approaches to qualitative–quantitative methodological triangulation', *Nursing Research*, 40: 120–3.

Moss, P., (1994) 'Defining quality: values, stakeholders and processes', in P. Moss and P. Pence (eds), *Valuing Quality in Early Childhood Services: New Approaches to Defining Quality*. London: Paul Chapman: 1–19.

Multiverse (2004) *Statistics on Asylum-Seeking & Refugee Children in School 2003*. Available at: www.multiverse.ac.uk/viewArticle.aspx (accessed).

Murphy, E. and Dingwall, R. (2007) 'Informed consent, anticipatory regulation and ethnographic practice', *Social Science & Medicine*, 65 (11): 2223–34.

Murray, R. (2006) *How to Write a Thesis*. Maidenhead: Open University Press.

Murray, R. (2011) *How to Write a Thesis*, 3rd edn. Maidenhead: Open University Press.

National Offender Management Service (NOMS) (2012) *NOMS Commissioning Intentions for 2013–14: Negotiation Document*. Available at: www.gov.uk/government/uploads/system/uploads/attachment_data/file/280922/commissioning-intentions-2014.pdf (accessed 14 July 2016).

National Reading Panel (2000) *Teaching Children to Read* www.nichd.nih.gov/publications/pubs/nrp/documents/report.pdf (accessed 7 July 2016).

Nisbet, J. (1999) 'How it all began: Educational research 1880–1930', *Scottish Educational Review*, 31 (1): 3–9.

O'Connell, R., (2008) The Meaning of Home-based Childcare in an Era of Quality: Childminding in an inner London borough and the encounter with professionalization, PhD Thesis, UCL.

O'Connell, R. (2010) 'How is childminding family like? Family day care, food and the reproduction of identity at the public/private interface', *Sociological Review*, 58 (4): 563–86.

O'Connell, R. (2011) 'Paperwork, posters, words and rotas: An anthropological account of some inner London childminders' encounters with professionalization', *Sociological Review*, 59 (4): 779–802.

O'Connell, R. and Brannen, J. (2016) *Food, Families and Work*. London: Bloomsbury.

O'Leary, Z. (2014) *The Essential Guide to Doing your Research Project*, 2nd edn. London: Sage.

O'Reilly, K. (2009) *Key Concepts in Ethnography*. London: Sage.

Oakley, A., Fullerton, D., Holland, J., Arnold, S., France-Dawson, M., Kelley, P. and McGrellis, S. (1995) 'Sexual health interventions for young people: A methodological review', *British Medical Journal*, 310: 158–62.

Onwuegbuzie, A.J. (2002) 'Positivists, post-positivists, post-structuralists, and post-modernists: Why can't we all get along? Towards a framework for unifying research paradigms', *Education*, 122: 518–30.

Onwuegbuzie, A.J. and Collins, K.M.T. (2007) 'A typology of mixed methods sampling designs in social science research', *Qualitative Report*, 12 (2): 281–316.

Onwuegbuzie, A.J. and Dickinson, W.B. (2008) 'Mixed methods analysis and information visualization: Graphical display for effective communication of research results', *Qualitative Report*, 13 (2): 204–25.

Onwuegbuzie, A.J. and Johnson, R.B. (2004) 'Mixed method and mixed model research', in R.B. Johnson and L.B. Christensen (eds), *Educational Research: Quantitative, Qualitative, and Mixed Approaches*. Needham Heights, MA: Allyn and Bacon.

Onwuegbuzie, A.J. and Johnson, R.B. (2006) 'The validity issue in mixed research', *Research in the Schools*, 13 (1): 48–63.

Onwuegbuzie, A.J. and Leech, N.L. (2004) 'Enhancing the interpretation of "significant" findings: The role of mixed methods research', *Qualitative Report*, 9 (4): 770–92.

Onwuegbuzie, A.J. and Leech, N.L. (2005) 'Taking the "Q" out of research: Teaching research methodology courses without the divide between quantitative and qualitative paradigms', *Quality and Quantity: International Journal of Methodology*, 3: 267–96.

Onwuegbuzie, A.J. and Teddlie, C. (2003) 'A framework for analyzing data in mixed methods research', in A. Tashakkori and C. Teddlie (eds), *Handbook of Mixed Methods in Social and Behavioral Research*. Thousand Oaks, CA: Sage.

Onwuegbuzie, A.J., Jiao, Q.G. and Bostick, S.L. (2004) *Library Anxiety: Theory, Research, and Applications*. Lanham, MD: Scarecrow Press.

Open Science Collaboration (2015) 'Estimating the reproducibility of psychological', *Science*. Available at: http://science.sciencemag.org/content/349/6251/aac4716 (accessed 7 July 2016).

Oppenheim, A.N. (1992) *Questionnaire Design, Interviewing and Attitude Measurement*, 2nd edn. London: Pinter.

Orne, M.T. (1962) 'On the social psychology of the psychological experiment: With particular reference to demand characteristics and their implications', *American Psychologist*, 17 (11): 776–83.

Ozga, J. and Gerwitz, S. (1994) 'Sex, lies and audiotape: Interviewing the education policy elite', in D. Halpin and B. Troyna (eds) *Research Education Policy: Ethical and Methodological Issues*. London: The Falmer Press. pp. 121–136.

Ozga, J. and Walker, L. (1999) 'In the company of men', in S. Whitehead and R. Moodley (eds), *Transforming Managers*. London and New York: Routledge.

Parkes, J. (2010) 'Research on/as violence: Reflections on injurious moments in research and friendship groups', *International Journal of Qualitative Studies in Education*, 23 (3): 347–61.

Patton, M.Q. (1990) *Qualitative Evaluation and Research Methods*. Newbury Park, CA: Sage.

Pawson, R. and Tilley, N. (1997) *Realistic Evaluation*. London: Sage.

Pelto, P.J. and Pelto, G.H. (1993) *Anthropological Research: The Structure of Inquiry*. New York: Cambridge University Press.

Peytchev, A., Peytcheva, E. and Groves, R.M. (2010) 'Measurement error, unit nonresponse, and self-reports of abortion experiences', *Public Opinion Quarterly*, 78 (2): 319–27.

Phillips, E. and Pugh, D. (2006) *How to Get a PhD: A Handbook for Students and their Supervisors*, 4th edn. Maidenhead: Open University Press.

Phillips, E. and Pugh, D. (2010) *How to Get a PhD: A Handbook for Students and their Supervisors*, 5th edn. Maidenhead: Open University Press.

Pink, S. (2001) *Doing Visual Ethnography*. London: Sage.

Pinson, H., Arnot, M. and Candappa, M. (2010) *Education, Asylum and the 'Non-Citizen' Child: The Politics of Compassion and Belonging*. London: Palgrave Macmillan.

Plummer, K. (2001) *Documents of Life 2: An Invitation to a Critical Humanism*. London: Sage.

Popper, K. (1979) *Objective Knowledge: An Evolutionary Approach*. Oxford: Oxford University Press.

Popper, K. (2002/1934) *The Logic of Scientific Discovery*, 2nd edn. London: Routledge.

Porporino, F.J. and Robinson, D. (1992) *Can Educating Adult Offenders Counteract Recidivism?* Correctional Service of Canada: Research Branch. Available at: www.csc-scc.gc.ca/005/008/092/r22e_e.pdf (accessed 7 July 2016).

Pring, R. (2000) *Philosophy of Educational Research*. London: Continuum.

Public Opinion Quarterly (2006) *Nonresponse Bias in Household Surveys*, Special Issue. Available at: http://poq.oxfordjournals.org/content/vol70/issue5/#ARTICLES (accessed 14 July 2016).

Punch, K. (2016) *Developing Effective Research*, London: Sage.

Punch, K. and Oancea, A. (2014) *Introduction to Research Methods in Education*. London: Sage.

Radley, A. and Taylor, D. (2003) 'Images of recovery: A photo-elicitation study on the hospital ward', *Qualitative Health Research*, 13 (1): 77–99.

Ravitch, S. and Riggan, M. (2012) *Reason & Rigor: How Conceptual Frameworks Guide Research*. London: Sage.

Rich, M. and Chalfen, R. (1999) 'Showing and telling asthma: Children teaching physicians with visual narrative', *Visual Sociology*, 14: 51–71.

Rivers, D. and Wells, A. (2015) *Polling Error in the 2015 UK General Election: An Analysis of YouGov's Pre- and Post-Election Polls*. London: YouGov. Available at: https://d25d2506sfb94s.cloudfront.net/cumulus_uploads/document/x4ae830iac/YouGov%20%E2%80%93%20GE2015%20Post%20Mortem.pdf (accessed 14 July 2016).

Robson, C. (2011) *Real World Research: A Resource for Social Scientists and Practitioner Researchers*, 3rd edn. Oxford: Blackwell.

Robson, C. and McCartan, K. (2016) *Real World Research*, 4th edn. Chichester: John Wiley & Sons.

Rosenshine, B., Chapman, S. and Meister, C. (1996) 'Teaching students to generate questions: a review of the intervention studies', *Review of Educational Research*, 66, 181–221.

Rosenthal, R. and Rosnow, R.L. (1975) *The Volunteer Subject*. New York and London: Wiley-Interscience.

Ruane, J.M. (2005) *Essentials of Research Methods: A Guide to Social Science Research*. Malden, MA: Blackwell.

Rutter, J. (1994) *Refugee Children in the Classroom*. Stoke-on-Trent: Trentham Books.

Sandelowski, M. (2001) 'Real qualitative researchers don't count: The use of numbers in qualitative research', *Research in Nursing & Health*, 24: 230–40.

Savage, R., Abrami, P., Piquette-Tomei, N., Wood, E., Delevauux, G., Sanghera-Sidhu, S. and Burgos, G. (2013) 'A pan-Canadian cluster randomized control effectiveness trial of the ABRACADABRA web-based literacy program', *Journal of Educational Psychology*, 105: 310–28.

Schrag, Z. (2011) 'The case against ethics review in social sciences', *Research Ethics*, 7 (4): 120–31.

Schutz, A. (1944) '"The Stranger": An essay in social psychology', *American Journal of Sociology*, 49 (6): 499–507.

Schwandt, T.A. (1993) 'Theory for the moral sciences: Crisis of identity and purpose', in D.J. Mills and G.E. Flinders (eds), *Theory and Concepts in Qualitative Research*. New York: Teachers College Press.

Searle, J. (1995) *The Construction of Social Reality*. London: Penguin.

Seethaler, P. M. and Fuchs, L. S. (2005) 'A drop in the bucket: Randomized contact trials testing reading and math interventions', *Learning Disabilities Research and Practice*, 20: 98–102.

Shadish, W.R., Cook, T.D. and Campbell, D.T. (2002) *Experimental and Quasi-Experimental Designs for Generalized Causal Inferences*. Boston, MA: Houghton Mifflin. Available at: http://impact.cgiar.org/experimental-and-quasi-experimental-designs-generalized-causal-inference (accessed 10 January 2016).

Sharp, J.L., Mobley, C., Hammond, C., Withington, C., Drew, S., Stringfield, S. and Stipanovic, N. (2012) 'A mixed methods sampling methodology for a multisite case study', *Journal of Mixed Methods Research*, 6 (1): 34–54.

Sherman, L.W., Gottfredson, D.C., MacKenzie, D.L., Eck, J., Reuter, P. and Bushway, S.D. (1998) *Preventing Crime: What Works, What Doesn't, What's Promising*, Research Brief. College Park, MD: National Institute of Justice; Department of Criminology and Criminal Justice, University of Maryland at College Park. Available at: www.ncjrs.gov/pdffiles/171676.PDF (accessed 25 August 2015).

Shih, T.H. and Xitao, F. (2008) 'Comparing response rates from web and mail surveys: A meta-analysis', *Field Methods*, 20 (3): 249–71.

Shorthouse, R. (2015) *Reducing Poverty by Promoting more Diverse Social Networks for Disadvantaged People from Ethnic Minority Groups*. York: Joseph Rowntree Foundation.

Shweder, R. (2004) *Tuskergee Re-examined*. Available at: www.spiked-online.com/newsite/article/14972 (accessed 8 August 2014).

Sieber, S.D. (1973) 'The integration of fieldwork and survey methods', *American Journal of Sociology*, 73: 1335–59.

Silber, L. (2005) 'Bars behind bars: the impact of a women's prison choir on social harmony', *Music Education Research*. 7 (2): 251–271.

Silverman, D. (1993) *Interpreting Qualitative Data*. London: Sage.

Simons, H. (1996) 'The paradox of case study', *Cambridge Journal of Education*, 26 (2): 225–40.

Simons, H. (2009) *Case Study Research in Practice*. London: Sage.

Simons, H. and Usher, R. (eds) (2000) *Situated Ethics in Educational Research*. London and New York: RoutledgeFalmer.

Skeggs, B. (1997) *Formations of Class and Gender*. London: Sage.

Smart, C. (2010) 'Disciplined writing: On the problem of writing sociologically', *Realities Working Paper*, No. 13. Morgan Centre, University of Manchester Realities. Available at: http://hummedia.manchester.ac.uk/schools/soss/morgancentre/research/wps/13-2010-01-realities-disciplined-writing.pdf (accessed 14 July 2016).

Smith, J.K. (1983) 'Quantitative versus qualitative research: An attempt to clarify the issue', *Educational Researcher*, 12 (3): 6–13.

Smith, M.L. (1986) 'The whole is greater: Combining qualitative and quantitative approaches in evaluation studies', in D.D. Williams (eds), *Naturalistic Evaluation*. San Francisco, CA: Jossey-Bass.

Smith, M.L. (1997) 'Mixing and matching: Methods and models', in J.C. Greene and V.J. Caracelli (eds), *Advances in Mixed-Method Evaluation: The Challenges and Benefits of Integrating Diverse Paradigms: New Directions for Evaluation*. San Francisco, CA: Jossey-Bass.

Somekh, B. and Lewin, C. (eds) (2011) *Theory and Methods in Social Research*, 2nd edn. London: Sage.

Spicker, P. (2011) 'Ethical covert research', *Sociology*, 45 (1): 118–33.

Spock, B. (1958) *The Common Sense Book of Baby and Child Care*. New York: Duell, Sloan and Pearce.

Spradley, J. (1979) *The Ethnographic Interview*. New York: Holt, Rinehart & Winston.

Spradley, J. (1980) *Participant Observation*. Belmont, CA: Wadsworth Cengage Learning.

Squire, P. (1988) 'Why the 1936 Literary Digest poll failed', *Public Opinion Quarterly*, 52 (1): 125–33.

Stake, R.E. (1978) 'The case study method in social inquiry', *Educational Researcher*, 7 (2): 5–8.

Stake, R.E. (2003) 'Case studies', in N.K. Denzin and Y. Lincoln (eds), *Strategies of Qualitative Inquiry*. Thousand Oaks, CA: Sage.

Stake, R.E. (2005) 'Qualitative case studies', in N.K. Denzin and Y. Lincoln (eds), *The Sage Handbook of Qualitative Research*, 3rd edn. Thousand Oaks, CA: Sage.

Steckler, A., McLeroy, K.R., Goodman, R.M., Bird, S.T. and McCormick, I. (1992) 'Towards integrating qualitative and quantitative methods: An introduction', *Health Education Quarterly*, 19 (1): 1–8.

Stolberg, H.O., Norman, G. and Trop, I. (2004) 'Randomized controlled trials', *American Journal of Roentgenology*, 183 (6): 1539–44.

Sturgis, P. (2016) *The Inquiry into the Failure of the 2015 Pre-election Polls: Findings and Preliminary Conclusions*. Available at: www.ncrm.ac.uk/training/show.php?article=6062 (accessed 7 July 2016).

Swain, J. (2000) '"The money's good, the fame's good, the girls are good": The role of playground football in the construction of young boys' masculinity in a junior school', *British Journal of Sociology of Education*, 21: 91–109.

Swain, J. (2001) 'An ethnographic study into the construction of masculinity of 10–11-year-old boys in three junior schools', PhD thesis. Institute of Education, London.

Swain, J. (2002) 'The right stuff: Fashioning an identity through clothing in a junior school', *Gender and Education*, 14 (1): 53–69.

Swain, J. (2006) 'Reflections on patterns of masculinity in school settings', *Men and Masculinities*, 8: 331–49.

Swain, J., Cara, O., Vorhaus, J. and Litster, J. (2015) *The Impact of Family Literacy Programmes on Children's Literacy Skills and the Home Literacy Environment,* Research Report. London: Nuffield Foundation and National Research and Development Centre for adult literacy and numeracy. Available at: www.nuffieldfoundation.org/sites/default/files/files/Nuffield-Family-Literacy-Report.pdf (accessed 14 July 2016).

Szanton, P. (1981) *Not Well Advised.* New York: Russell Sage Foundation and Ford Foundation.

Tashakkori, A. and Teddlie, C. (1998) *Mixed Methodology: Combining Qualitative and Quantitative Approaches.* Thousand Oaks, CA: Sage.

Tashakkori, A. and Teddlie, C. (2003a) 'The past and future of mixed methods research: From data triangulation to mixed model designs', in A. Tashakkori and C. Teddlie (eds), *Handbook of Mixed Methods in Social and Behavioral Research.* Thousand Oaks, CA: Sage.

Tashakkori, A. and Teddlie, C. (eds) (2003b) *Handbook of Mixed Methods in Social and Behavioral Research.* Thousand Oaks, CA: Sage.

Tashakkori, A. and Teddlie, C. (eds) (2010) *Sage Handbook of Mixed Methods in Social and Behavioral Research.* Thousand Oaks, CA: Sage.

Teddlie, C. and Tashakkori, A. (2003) 'Major issues and controversies in the use of mixed methods in the social and behavioral sciences', in A. Tashakkori and C. Teddlie (eds), *Handbook of Mixed Methods in social and Behavioral Research.* Thousand Oaks, CA: Sage.

Teddlie, C. and Tashakkori, A. (2006) 'A general typology of research designs featuring mixed methods', *Research in the Schools*, 13 (1): 12–28.

Teddlie, C. and Yu, F. (2007) 'Mixed methods sampling: A typology with examples', *Journal of Mixed Methods Research*, 1: 77–100.

Tellis, W. (1997) 'Introduction to case study', *The Qualitative Report*, 3 (2): July. Available at: www.nova.edu/ssss/QR/QR3-2/tellis1.html (accessed 7 July 2016).

Tett, L., Anderson, K., McNeill, F., Overy, K. and Sparks, R. (2012) 'Learning, rehabilitation and the arts in prisons: A Scottish case study', *Studies in the Education of Adults*, 44 (2): 171–85. Available at: http://www2.law.ed.ac.uk/file_download/publications/0_1829_learningrehabilitationandtheartsinprison.pdf (accessed 14 July 2016).

Thomas, G. (2013) *How to Do your Research Project: A Guide for Students in Education and Applied Social Sciences.* London: Sage.

Thomson, R. (2007) 'The qualitative longitudinal case history: Practical, methodological and ethical reflections', *Social Policy and Society*, 6 (4): 571–82.

Thomson, R. and Holland, J. (2003) 'Hindsight, foresight and insight: The challenges of longitudinal qualitative research', *International Journal of Social Research Methodology*, 6 (3): 233–44.

Thorne, B. (1980) '"You still takin' notes?" Fieldwork and problems of informed consent', *Social Problems*, 27 (3): 284–97.

Tooley, J. and Darby, D. (1998) *Educational Research: A Critique*. London: Office for Standards in Education, Children' (Ofsted).

Tooley, J., Dixon, P. and Gomathi, S.V. (2007) 'Private schools and the millennium development goal of universal primary education: A census and comparative survey in Hyderabad, India', *Oxford Review of Education*, 33 (5): 539–60.

Trochim, W.M.K (2006) Research Methods Knowledge Base. Available at: www. socialresearchmethods.net/kb/strucres.php (accessed 7 July 2016).

Troia, G. (1999) 'Phonological awareness intervention research: A critical review of the methodology of experimental methodology', *Reading Research Quarterly*, 34: 28–52.

Van Maanen, (1988) *Tales of the Field*. Chicago, IL: University of Chicago Press.

Waite, E.R.T. (2003) 'The impact of socialist rule on a Muslim minority in China: Islam amongst the Uyghurs of Kashgar', PhD thesis. Cambridge University.

Waite, E. (2006a) 'From holy man to national villain: Popular historical narratives about Apaq Khoja amongst Uyghurs in contemporary Xinjiang', *Inner Asia*, 8 (1): 5–28.

Waite, E. (2006b) 'The Impact of the state on Islam amongst the Uyghurs: Religious knowledge and authority in the Kashgar Oasis', *Central Asian Survey*, 25 (3): 251–65.

Waite, E. (2007) 'The emergence of Muslim reformism in contemporary Xinjiang Province: Implications for the Uyghurs' positioning between a Central Asian and Chinese context', in I. Bellér-Hann, C. Cesàro, R. Harris and J. Smith (eds), *Situating The Uyghurs between China and Central Asia*. Ashgate: Aldershot.

Walford, G. (2004) 'Finding the limits: Auto-ethnography and being an Oxford University proctor', *Qualitative Research*, 4 (3): 403–17.

Wallman, S. (1984) *Eight London Households*. London: Tavistock.

Webb, E.J., Campbell, D.T., Schwartz, R.D. and Sechrest, L. (1966) *Unobtrusive Measures: Non-Reactive Research in the Social Sciences*. Chicago, IL: Rand McNally.

Wells, A. (2015) 'The Polling Inquiry public meeting', *UKPollingReport*. Available at: http:// ukpollingreport.co.uk/blog/archives/9447 (accessed 14 July 2016).

Whiteman, N. (2010) 'Control and contingency: Maintaining ethical stances in research', *International Journal of Internet Research Ethics*, 3 (12): 6–22.

Whiteman, N. (2012) *Undoing Ethics: Rethinking Practice in Online Research*. London: Springer.

Whorf, B.L. (1956) 'An American Indian model of the universe', in J.B. Carroll (ed.), *Language, Thought and Reality: Selected Writings of Benjamin Lee Whorf*. Cambridge, MA: MIT Press.

Whyte, W. Foote (1955/1943) *Street Corner Society: The Social Structure of an Italian Slum*. Chicago, IL: University of Chicago Press.

Wiles, R., Crow, G., Charles, V. and Heath, S. (2004) *Informed Consent in Social Research: A Literature Review*. Swindon: Economic and Social Research Council, National Centre for Research Methods.

Wiles, R., Heath, S., Crow, G. and Charles, V. (2007) 'Informed consent and the research process: Following rules or striking balances?', *Sociological Research Online*, 12 (2). Available at: www.socresonline.org.uk/12/2/wiles.html (accessed 14 July 2016).

Williams, K., Bethell, E., Lawton, J., Parfitt-Brown, C., Richardson, M. and Rowe, V. (2010) *Planning your PhD*, Pocket Study Skills. Basingstoke: Palgrave Macmillan.

Williams, K., Bethell, E., Lawton, J., Parfitt-Brown, C., Richardson, M. and Rowe, V. (2011) *Completing your PhD*, Pocket Study Skills. Basingstoke: Palgrave Macmillan.

Williams, M. (2003) *Making Sense of Social Research*. London: Sage.

Willis, P. (1977) *Learning to Labour: How Working Class Kids Get Working Class Jobs*. Farnborough: Saxon House.

Wilson, I., Huttly, S.R.A. and Fenn, B. (2006) 'A case study of sample design for longitudinal research: Young lives', *International Journal of Social Research Methodology*, 9 (5): 351–65.

Winch, P. (1964) 'Understanding a primitive society', *American Philosophical Quarterly*, 1 (4): 307–24.

Wolcott, H. (1994) *Transforming Qualitative Data: Description, Analysis, and Interpretation*. Thousand Oaks, CA: Sage.

Wolcott, H. (1995) *The Art of Fieldwork*, 2nd edn. Walnut Creek, CA: AltaMira.

Wolcott, H. (2001) *Writing up Qualitative Research*, 2nd edn. Thousand Oaks, CA: Sage.

Wolcott, H. (2008) *Ethnography: A Way of Seeing*. Lanham, MD: Altamira Press.

Wolcott, H. (2009). *Writing Up Qualitative Research*. 3rd edn. Thousand Oaks, CA: Sage.

Wolf, E. (1982) *Europe and the People without History*. Berkeley, CA: University of California Press.

Woods, P. (1979) *The Divided School*. London: Routledge and Kegan Paul.

Woods, P. (1996) *Researching the Art of Teaching: Ethnography for Educational Use*. London: Routledge.

Wooley, C.M. (2009) 'Meeting the mixed methods challenge of integration in a sociological study of structure and agency', *Journal of Mixed Methods Research*, 3 (1): 7–25.

Yin, R.K. (1989) 'The case study as a serious research strategy', *Knowledge: Creation, Diffusion, Utilisation*, 3: 97–114.

Yin, R.K. (2012) *Applications of Case Study Research*, 3rd edn. Thousand Oaks, CA: Sage.

Yin, R.K. (2014) *Case Study Research Design and Methods*, 5th edn. Thousand Oaks, CA: Sage.

Zimmer, M. (2009) '"But the data is already public!": On the ethics of research in Facebook', in *Open Conference Systems, Internet Research 10.0*. Available at: http://link.springer.com/article/10.1007%2Fs10676-010-9227-5#page-1 (accessed 19 November 2014).

INDEX